The Art of Retail Buying

An Insider's Guide to the Best Practices from the Industry

The Art of Retail Buying

An Insider's Guide to the Best Practices from the Industry

Marie-Louise Jacobsen

WILEY

John Wiley & Sons (Asia) Pte. Ltd.

Published in 2009 by John Wiley & Sons (Asia) Pte. Ltd.
2 Clementi Loop, #02-01, Singapore 129809

Photos from © Getty Images and Leng Peng® Fashion Book Centre

Other Wiley Editorial Offices

John Wiley & Sons, Inc., 111 River Street, Hoboken, NJ 07030, USA
John Wiley & Sons Ltd., The Atrium Southern Gate, Chichester P019 8SQ, England
John Wiley & Sons (Canada) Ltd., 5353 Dundas Street West, Suite 400, Toronto, Ontario, M9B 6HB, Canada
John Wiley & Sons Australia, Ltd., 42 McDougall Street, Milton, Queensland 4064, Australia
Wiley-VCH, Boschstrasse 12, D-69469 Weinheim, Germany

Library of Congress Cataloging-in-Publication Data
ISBN: 978-0-470-82322-4

Typeset in 11 points, Rotis Serif by Hot Fusion
Printed in Singapore by Markono Print Media Pte Ltd
10 9 8 7 6 5 4 3 2 1

Contents

Dedication

This book is dedicated to buyers, future buyers and all those who aspire to work in this complex yet exciting and rewarding industry.

Special Thanks

Patrick Chai - Eut Marketing
Leng Peng® Fashion Book Centre
Arthur Yen
Kelvin Quek - Goldlion
Deirdre Ball

ACKNOWLEDGMENTS

To my friends Arthur, Adela, Doy, Aileen, Franco, GK, Jana, Kelvin, Patrick, Vish and Yoka: no formal introduction needed; you are my best.

To my husband Steve, who believes that books and friends should be few but good. Thanks for believing in and supporting this project.

To all the buyers, assistant buyers, merchandise managers, sales managers and dedicated sales staff with whom I have had the pleasure of working in the past 28 years: you have made me laugh, inspired and thrilled me, at times exasperated me but, most of all, imprinted wonderful memories that I will cherish always.

To my great friend Franco Guidotti, who shared with me his vast knowledge of Italian fashion, products, food and the Italian way of doing things. You have been a constant source of inspiration, and given me insights into design, sophistication and splendor.

The Art of Retail Buying

INTRODUCTION

As competition continues to escalate at a significant rate, retailers must utilize all their knowledge to keep pace with other merchants in the marketplace. Being able to forecast accurately the needs of their customers and satisfy them with the appropriate merchandise takes a great deal of experience and know-how. Perhaps more than anyone else in a retail organization, it is the buyers and merchandisers who are responsible for ensuring that the store's merchandise mix has the appeal to turn browsers into shoppers.

Although the sophisticated technology available to retail organizations today is an enormous help to buyers and merchandisers, their task still requires a great deal of knowledge and hands-on experience.

This book enables readers to examine the role of buyers and merchandisers, the qualifications, qualities and abilities required for the job, and how their decisions affect the business. Buyers who want to be successful must understand the climate within which they work. This environment consists of numerous components such as customers, types of retailers, the strategic planning process and the organization within which the buyer operates.

At one time or another, you have probably heard someone say: "Retail isn't rocket science. All you need to do is buy stuff and then sell it!" To the outsider, it may seem easy enough but those of us in the industry know better. Sure, the basic principles of buying can be learnt, particularly the general knowledge needed by all buyers in their day-to-day activities. But mastering the art of buying is something else.

What makes retail complex is that there are literally billions of buying options open to buyers. Take the approximately 195 countries in the world, multiply this by the number of manufacturers in each, and then multiply that by the number of items each makes just in that particular segment of the buyer's business and it gives you a pretty good idea of the complexity involved.

The tricky part is to sift through all these offers to find the right items that suit the retailer's customers. The task of selecting catalogs of merchandise the buyers anticipate will sell is only the first step. Then come the decisions of how much, in what colors, in what sizes, delivered in which months and placed in which locations, for all of these components to make a profit.

Retail is not for the faint-hearted. It takes a lot of hard work, dedication and the will to win customer loyalty. To gain and retain customers, you must first position yourself as the retailer of choice in the consumers' minds. This can be achieved by having the right merchandise of the right quality at the right price in the right location at the right time. There has been much talk about giving customers excellent or outstanding service but, unfortunately, not enough emphasis has been given to the core of the retail business: its products.

Retailers will, no doubt, agree that buyers are required to understand and use quantitative analysis in their day-to-day decision-making. Statistics on business performance are linked to consumer-spending behaviors which, in turn, are linked to strategic processes in selecting merchandise that will drive people's ability and willingness to buy.

Retail is BIG business. Worldwide retail sales are estimated to exceed US$7 trillion and 30% of these sales are generated by the top 200 largest retailers. So staying ahead of the game requires today's retailers to be smarter in managing and controlling what goes on their shelves. It is essential for professional buyers to focus on their product selections, and ensure that these selections are products that will satisfy consumer expectations and demands. In essence, professional retail buying is about being able to anticipate consumer demands and create ideas that combine and combust into exciting products that fulfill the consumer's desires.

The Art of Retail Buying shares with you some of the secrets of the trade, including how to build a range of products and why some products are selected over others. Whether you are currently working in the industry or are looking to become involved in buying, I hope this book will prove both inspirational and informative. Even old dogs can learn new tricks.

In the summer of 2006, I was approached by People Skills Asia to create a syllabus on retail buying for buyers in Asia. There was a need for a professional buying course applicable for Asian retailers that would tackle issues particular to the Asian region. People in the retail industry found that the courses available were too academic and theoretical for practical implementation.

What was needed was a course covering the how-to, the what-to and the when-to, with easy-to-understand material and case studies that would enhance their buying skills and facilitate the management of their daily activities.

From my 30 years of extensive retail experience—15 of which had been spent as General Manager Merchandising with one of Singapore's leading retail groups—I understood only too well the many challenges facing retailers and it took very little convincing for me to become involved in the project.

Throughout my career, I have always tried to make enhancing people's buying skills an enjoyable and rewarding task. So when I was asked to write a syllabus on retail buying, I felt I had much to contribute. Such was the success of the course, launched in Bangkok in the autumn of 2006, that I was prompted by many participants to turn the syllabus into a book because, they said, not all retail companies were willing to invest in training their buyers and many would benefit from having such a book at their disposal.

Retailers should recognize that without talented and knowledgeable buyers, they risk losing market share, customer loyalty and competitiveness—all of which translates into profit, or the loss of it. Training and enhancing buyers' skills is a vital part of staying ahead.

Retail buying is a demanding job that requires a creative flair, a strong awareness of fashion and lifestyle trends, as well as good interpersonal and team-working skills. Buyers and merchandisers have to ensure that the right merchandise is being sent to the right stores, at the right time, in the right quantities. This takes a blend of forward planning and rapid response to consumer demands. In combination with the other areas of the business, success comes from maximizing profit, which is achieved through anticipating customer needs and responding rapidly to immediate issues. It involves complex data analysis, liaison with the store's operation teams and balancing store stock levels.

To succeed as a professional buyer, you will need strong analytical and numerical skills, an interest and understanding of consumer demands and strong commercial awareness. A buyer also needs to have the ability to understand and prioritize issues quickly and this can be achieved through good time-management by tending to issues that have an impact on the business performance. Progression into the merchandising function also involves the ability to manage change. The better equipped you are in your buying function, the better you will be able to adapt to these changes: and the best change of all is to graduate from a good buyer to an excellent one!

As a norm, retail management will be expecting buyers to deliver higher year-after-year sales and profit projections, and it is not uncommon to hear buyers lamenting and wondering how they are going to match their management's expectations. The answer lies in re-thinking and re-strategizing your buying plans, as in how and why certain products are being bought, and by reviewing your vendor portfolio and asking if all are performing to expectation. Once this is established, the next natural step is to apply the Pareto Rule of 80–20. This principle implies that 80% of your sales are usually generated by 20% of your vendors: as such, some of that percentage growth can be found in building on your top-performing vendors and replacing weaker ones. I call this "the art of knowing what to keep and what to grow," or "the art of knowing what to keep and what to throw."

Why do people buy a new cookbook? For some, it is to learn how to cook; for others, it's to find better and more delicious ways to prepare food. Likewise, *The Art of Retail Buying* is meant for students aspiring to enter the retail industry and anyone in the industry looking for self-development, inspiration and growth.

Predicting consumer demands starts with understanding and responding to consumer trends. The prime objective of the buying function is to anticipate the needs and wants of customers by being ready to gratify their product desires, and this can only happen if you, the buyer, spend time on the selling floor interacting with your customers!

From the outset, a good buyer needs to be equipped with the right sets of tools. The skills required can be learned and/or improved at any time, and what better time than now to start expanding your proficiency.

Welcome to *The Art of Retail Buying*, your insider's guide to the best practices from the retail industry.

Chapter Flow

The chapters are sequentially linked to a buyer's role and in the order in which a buyer would get on-the-job training. It starts with describing the industry, what the job entails and what is expected. The next sections are the tools of the trade, the insight into how to become an excellent buyer.

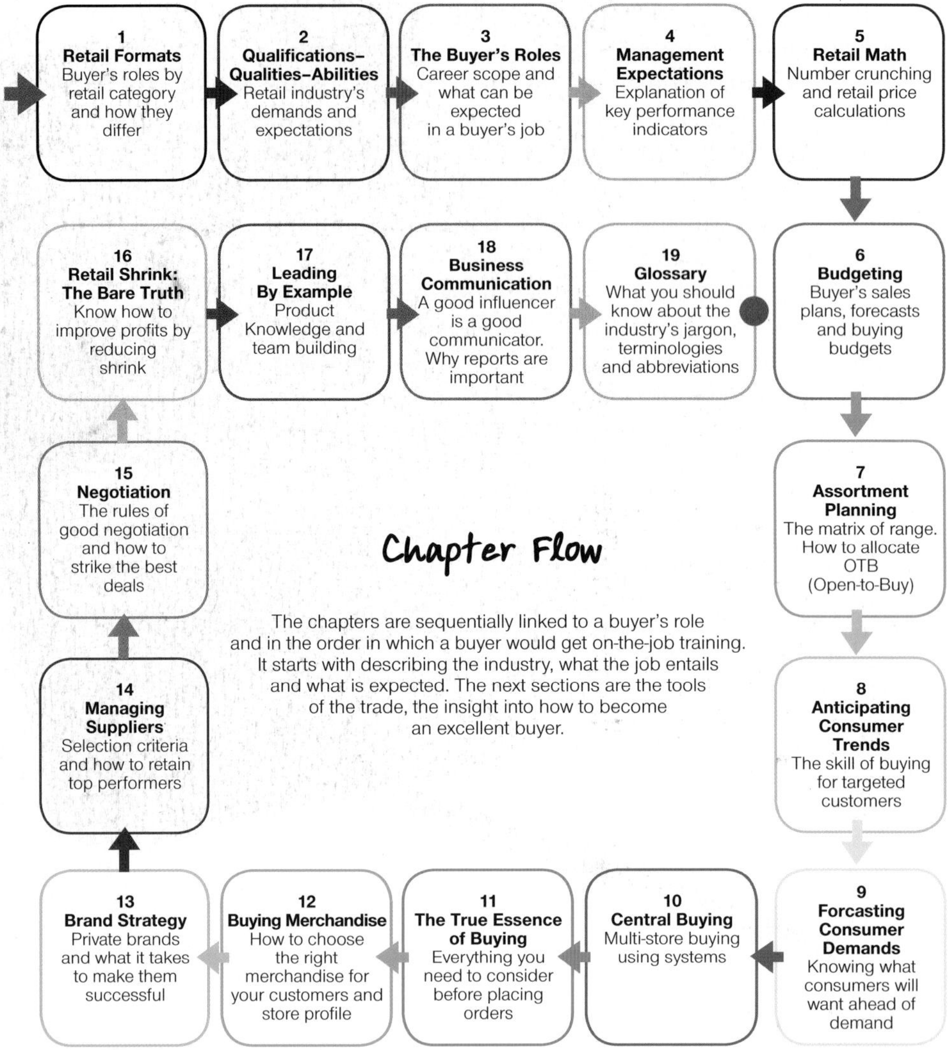

The Art of Retail Buying

1 RETAIL FORMATS

WHAT IT TAKES

Before we look at the various organizational structures within which buyers are called upon to operate, it might perhaps be useful to say a few words about the personal qualities and characteristics that contribute to making a good and successful buyer.

In my experience, anyone wanting to engage in a retail buying role should have a creative and extrovert personality, be a natural problem solver and be able to handle a high level of multi-tasking. Retail buyers must be able to understand and predict customers' needs and the saleability of a wide selection of products based on cost, style, function and quality while, at the same time, comparing these to other similar products available in the market. This is a significant task because they must order items months ahead of time, which requires a great deal of calculated risk based on experience and, more often than not, on sheer gut feeling.

Buyers need to put aside personal tastes and preferences and focus solely on what they anticipate customers will buy, in what quantities and at what premium. In making these choices, they also have to do so within specific purchasing budgets. A great deal of self-confidence is needed. Buyers eventually become experts in the merchandise categories they are buying for. After an initial trial-and-error period, they come to know what to buy, how to buy and where to buy, narrowing down wide selections of resources and knowing the best places to buy.

A retail buyer works in a dynamic but sometimes stressful atmosphere where decisions are made hourly. There can also be long and irregular hours, especially during holidays. Work is always fast-paced and competitive, and the buyer must quickly estimate the potential profitability of many products.

These conditions may vary, depending on the size and type of the organization for which the buyer works. Large department stores and chain stores require a buyer to plan, buy, and ensure that the sales staff is knowledgeable about the products. The role is, however, supported by back-office roles such as assistant buyers, visual merchandisers and other operational functions.

In a small store, a buyer may hold more than one position which, besides buying, may include advertising, floor and window displays, hiring new employees and training.

The roles of the buyer can be many and varied, being determined by factors such as the size of the company (the number and locations of outlets); the number of staff; the yearly revenue; and the merchandise classifications. Set out below are some of the many types of retail organization in which buyers may choose to shape a career.

RETAIL FORMATS

• Hypermarkets/Supermarkets

Hypermarkets are big business and growing fast in Asia. Asian consumers have changed their shopping habits, moving away from traditional wet-markets to the comfort of hypermarkets/

supermarkets, which provide a wide selection of goods in pleasant surroundings, and where the freshness of meat and vegetables is assured.

Hypermarkets in Asia can be home-grown like Mydin in Malaysia, or local start-ups such as Dairy Farm that grew to regional reach, or imported concepts such as Tesco, Carrefour and Jusco.

What they all have in common is that they sell "general" merchandise that includes perishables, household items, hardware, toys, small electronics, clothing, toiletries, cosmetics, furnishings and furniture, and more. They all boast of either being the cheapest or, at least, of offering the best value for money.

• Discount stores

Discount stores are stores that sell local or regional brands at lower than market price points. They can have a wide mix of goods or concentrate on specific merchandise types. More often than not, they will buy season-end merchandise, job lots and/or secondary brands. Merchants are required to hunt for deals regionally and buy in bulk to get the lowest price possible.

Factory outlets have been developed by the brand owners to release their own discounted season-end goods. The benefit lies in the control of the retail price this gives and thus leads to better profits.

What, then, is the difference between a hypermarket and a discount store? Comparative research has shown that the hypermarkets tend to have higher mean prices, but use promotional tools more often and more widely than the discount stores. Hypermarkets use promotional areas with strong signage that gives the impression that they are cheaper because they have the muscle to buy big and are thus able to offer bigger discounts. The advantage hypermarkets have is in the depth and width of the products on offer, which make it practical for consumers to shop there.

• Department stores

Department stores come in two types: those with a full-line designation, which carry a wide range of merchandise, from health and beauty to fashion/softgoods and accessories, to household and small electrical items/hardgoods and, occasionally, specialty gourmet foods; or those dedicated to specific brands or products. Department stores may have stores within the store, like shop-n-shops, ID-shops or specialist sections.

Because the department store serves as "the umbrella" for a wide assortment of goods, it is deemed convenient for customers to shop there.

While some department stores may concentrate on specific merchandise types, such as apparel and accessories, in the majority of cases they, like other retailers, need to decide which customer profile they intend to pursue and buy accordingly.

The vulnerability of today's department stores is that they have a hard time competing with true branded stores (see below). Customers are becoming increasingly fussy, and without very good service and merchandise that can give them points of differentiation, department stores may lose their edge. To maintain customer loyalty, some stores have adopted store credit cards and created special card-member events with special offerings or discounts to reinforce loyalty and consumer spending. The balancing act, though, is not to use such marketing tactics too often; otherwise, consumers can become blasé with yet another discounting event.

- **Branded stores**

Branded stores are those that carry single known brands. These may be globally or nationally renowned brands such as Nike, Adidas, Esprit, Mango, Zara, Timberland, Levis', and H&M; or "high-end" brands such as Gucci, Prada, Fendi and Burberry. These stores are either operated directly by the brand owners or through a franchise agreement.

The merchandise, price points, store layout, store design, store locations and merchandise displays are usually strictly spelt out by the Master Licensee or brand owner. Customer service is high and specialized. These stores are usually located in "choice" areas, streets or malls, with the stores designed specifically to encapsulate the mood of the brand. Customer loyalty is linked to brand loyalty which, in turn, gives the consumers a sense of identity with the brand. Branded stores lose their customers when they start losing their luster. I call these "sunset brands": in most cases, the brand has either lost touch with its customers, or the customers have graduated from them and moved on to other brands that are more in tune with their lifestyle.

- **Single-unit independents**

This trend is still big business in retailing. There are still many entrepreneurs who wish to be their own boss. Many of them are very successful, as they are able to cater very specifically to their customers' needs and give them personalized services.

The merchandise, similar to that in specialty stores, is usually limited in choice but appealing nevertheless. The "boutiques" can carry ranges of shoes, jewelry or apparel, which are usually higher-priced goods and sometimes custom-made.

Initially, the owners themselves usually act as the buyers but, as the business grows, they may expand this role to incorporate hired professional buyers.

- **Specialty stores**

Specialty stores are, as the name suggests, stores that specialize in specific types of merchandise, with a specific lifestyle offering. These can vary from luxury goods to mid-priced high-quality goods at commercial price points. Examples include sports shops, dive shops, telecoms shops, book stores, branded cosmetics (a new trend in the health & beauty industry), antique shops, oriental carpet shops and shoe shops, to name but a few. Here the attraction is that customers shop these stores as a destination shopping trip. The expectation is that they must have a wide choice of merchandise within their respective specialist categories and very knowledgeable staff who can recommend the right items.

The specialist stores are vulnerable to competition from general merchandising retailers who may opt to have some specialist sections for which they are sometimes able to buy in bulk and sell these items quite cheaply, creating price mayhem with point-of-no-return price levels (the point at which an item has been discounted so often that it can no longer command its original price). For example, pashmina shawls used to retail at $500 when they first came on the market. Big retailers then bought these in bulk and sold them at $300; other retailers discounted them further to $200, and today they can be as low as $150. In such circumstances, they can no longer command their original value of $500: the price has gone down to a point of no return.

Specialty stores are compelled to know a great deal about their customers and their individual requirements. There is usually a great deal of customer follow-up and special purchases on customers' behalf.

- **Franchised stores**

When the owners/developers of a concept or brand wish to expand the business into other territories or countries, they often adopt the franchising business model under which, for a fee, the franchisee is given the right to operate the retail concept in very specific locations (regions). This retail operation is conducted under specific rules and regulations that have been set out by the owners (the franchisors).

Franchises abound in the fast-food industry—McDonald's, Wendy's, Kentucky Fried Chicken, and Starbucks—but are also found in the fashion industry—Zara, Mango, Debenham's, Tommy Hilfiger and more.

- **Catalog retailing**

Catalog selling is still very popular, especially in the United States. Examples in Asia include Ikea and Lands' End.

Some department stores feature merchandise that is only available through this channel and thus will have separate buyers purchasing for the catalog business.

Some retailers in the United States use only catalogs as a means to reach their customers, with the exception of a few factory outlets to dispose of slow-moving merchandise.

- **License stores**

Licensing is similar to franchising, with the main difference being the start-up fee. Some of the best-known of such arrangements include Benetton—the largest retail licenser in the world—Ralph Lauren, and Marks & Spencer.

Here the licensees are required to follow the merchandising philosophies established by the licensors, and the buyer's role is quite different from any other retailing format. The merchandise sold is either produced completely by the licensee—in which case the buyer needs to be able to do product development—or purchased directly from the licensor (the original brand owner) by the licensee's buyer for distribution to the individual units. Generally, the individual stores have no buying responsibilities. Today, increasingly, licensors adopt a "push-model," under which the licensee gives the licensor an open-to-buy (OTB) budget (OTB being the difference between planned purchases and stock already ordered, or the value of merchandise that a buyer can order for a particular period), and the licensor selects all the merchandise to that value. Under this business model the licensee does not require a buyer. Though convenient for the licensor, it is riskier for the licensee.

Ideally, it is best when the licensees have some say in the assortments they carry, as these would be bought with their particular customer profile in mind. Benetton, for example, has as many as several thousand styles each season, and the individual licensees have the right to buy or select what they deem best for their stores.

• **Chain organization**

Chain organization is defined as multiple outlets under a common ownership. These can be general merchandise stores, limited-line stores, specialty stores or stores with different concepts but under one group. They can vary from discount stores and value-oriented stores to private brand stores or even off-price stores. Off-price stores are stores that sell only discounted merchandise. Unlike factory outlets, which sell only a specific brand, off-price stores can sell a wide range of merchandise. Buyers, in this case, would be looking for factory over-runs, season-end goods or job lots.

BUYERS' WORK ACTIVITIES

Typical work activities can vary according to the season, particularly for those working in fashion. Out of season, the majority of the time will be spent in the workplace (in the office and on the shop floor). During the buying season, a significant amount of time will be spent away from the workplace in assembling a new collection of merchandise.

Throughout the year, tasks typically involve:

• Analyzing trends; regularly reviewing performance indicators with sales

• Managing plans for stock levels; reacting to change in demand and logistics

• Meeting suppliers and negotiating terms of contract

• Managing relationships with existing suppliers

• Sourcing new suppliers for future consumer demands

• Liaising with other departments within the organization to ensure projects are completed

• Attending trade fairs/trade shows, locally and abroad, to select and assemble a new collection of products

• Participating in promotional activities

• Finding time to interact with customers

• Writing reports and sales forecasts, and analyzing sales figures.

In my many years in retailing, the one thing that has been consistent, regardless of the company I have been working for, is the buyers' lack of enthusiasm for writing reports, which are often handed in late, some incomplete, or worst of all, inaccurate. The main reason for this is that these buyers are not intimate enough with what is going on in their departments or areas of responsibility. As they are rarely on the selling floor, they do not have first-hand information on customer reaction to the merchandise and do not relish reading tedious computer-generated sales and profit analysis reports. The result is that many reports are scantily done.

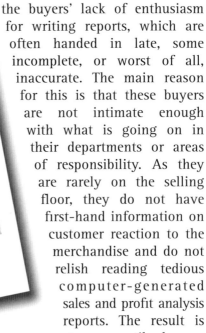

What many of these buyers have failed to understand is that poorly written reports connote poor job performance. How can management have confidence in buyers who cannot summarize their weekly or monthly trade clearly and cogently? Time spent in learning how to construct reports properly is time well spent. It will not only help you comprehend your business better, but will also signal to management that you are a professional, you know what is happening in your business, and can therefore recommend plans of action which will more than likely be accepted and supported.

Great influencers are always great communicators!

The Art of Retail Buying

2 QUALIFICATIONS QUALITIES ABILITIES

REQUIREMENTS FOR A BUYING CAREER

At one time in the retail industry, it was common for people to start at the very bottom of the ladder and make their way up, in some cases even to a senior management level. While there are still many such stories, this is no longer typical.

Today's buying hopeful must possess leadership, management and decision-making skills to meet the challenges of a career.

The following requirements are universal in the retail industry. The abilities listed are necessary for a successful buying career irrespective of the store's location. The bigger the market, the higher the stakes and demands on the buyers to buy merchandise that will keep their store competitive.

As you progress through the book, you will find that most of the subjects are catering for stores that buy a very wide range of merchandise for many different store formats. However, those of you who are operating with specific brands only should also read on: the fact of the matter is that your brand is in heated competition with all the other retailers out there.

If you also think that you don't have much influence on the ranges that your principals are showing you, think again. You do, and in more ways than one.

Think of it this way: the retail market is like a great big jigsaw puzzle of the ocean. Each piece may look the same but each has its specific place. Buying merchandise is a bit like that—similar yet different, because each serves a specific customer requirement, desire and demand. Your job will be to find that piece and place it exactly where it's supposed to be ... on your shelves: if you anticipate that requirement, desire and demand, the piece will fit just perfectly.

THE 12 QUALIFICATIONS—QUALITIES—ABILITIES REQUIRED FOR A BUYING CAREER

1. Education

A college education—preferably a degree majoring in retail management, marketing or business administration, or a degree from a fashion merchandising school—is considered a must for a buying career. Liberal arts graduates who show interest in retailing can also be considered.

The reason for this is the amount of work involved in analyzing company reports, financial statements, inventory listings, open-to-buy positions, unit sales summaries, and so on.

There are some retailers who are willing to offer tuition and courses to further enhance the skills of their buyers or buyers-to-be. Investing in education is good for both company and staff, improving individual productivity and translating into better merchandising management.

We are all constantly on a learning curve. Even without a college degree, you can continually expand your knowledge.

I believe that this book can help you improve your current processes and inspire you to take a fresh look at the way you do things.

2. Enthusiasm

When retailers are faced with two candidates who have similar education and experience, it is the more enthusiastic candidate that is most likely to be hired.

A buyer needs to interact with assistant buyers, department managers, selling staff and back-end staff, and should have an enthusiastic attitude to motivate them in their jobs.

This same enthusiasm can be felt by customers thinking about making a purchase. In my experience, buyers who take time to talk to customers will most likely be the best at "guiding" them in their buying decisions. Customers are usually thrilled to have the opportunity to talk with the buyers, and share their ease or difficulties in finding the right products.

3. Analytical excellence

Buyers have constantly to make decisions on such things as colors, prices, styles and sizes. Without a solid analytical ability, their decisions are at risk of being faulty. Analytical excellence is vital for measuring and evaluating situations and trends, for forming sound judgments and for making the right decisions.

The first and best step in the decision-making process is to analyze sales and any other available data. Remember, though, the data can only reflect what is happening with the merchandise you have bought; it will say nothing on missed opportunities.

4. Ability to articulate

By the very nature of their job, buyers are continuously interacting with people, both inside and outside the company.

Internally, you need to be able to articulate well when you are requesting a bigger budget or making a merchandise presentation on ranges you propose to buy. Good communication is necessary with a buying assistant who helps you carry out delegated responsibilities, or with selling staff when you guide them in how to place the merchandise on the selling floor.

Externally, when visiting vendors, buyers have to clearly express their views on ranges, quantities and price, as well as negotiate the best terms possible. Articulation skills–spoken, written and, in many cases, drawn–are necessary tools of the trade.

5. Product and market knowledge

Buyers are required to have full information on the product portfolio for which they are responsible. Without it, it is not possible to evaluate whether the offering is the best available.

While vendors are a great source of information, great product intelligence can also be generated by trips to factories and buying agents.

With constant changes in merchandising and product lines, it is essential that buyers keep updating their knowledge on a regular basis. Good product knowledge makes a solid base of information on which buyers can make accurate decisions; which, in turn, helps maximize profits.

To ensure that the best possible merchandise or product is chosen for the store, buyers are required to be fully conversant with the wide selection of resources available. This includes where the best deals can be made, the best terms and conditions, the best deliveries and, if needed, exclusivity terms.

The buyer may select the best product, but if the vendor is known to have delivery problems, the goods might not prove to be successful sellers because they arrive later than planned, taking up precious OTB that might otherwise have been placed elsewhere. On-time vendors are just as important as best-buy vendors.

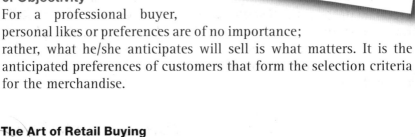

Buyers should have a set of basic requirements when dealing with new vendors from existing markets or vendors from new markets.

6. Objectivity

For a professional buyer, personal likes or preferences are of no importance; rather, what he/she anticipates will sell is what matters. It is the anticipated preferences of customers that form the selection criteria for the merchandise.

Whatever the product portfolio, objectivity must prevail. The choices and selections must be based on your store's customer profile, historical sales data, market sensitivities, trade paper forecasts, market representatives or any other objective sources.

Without total objectivity, the store may be left with shelves of unwanted merchandise rejected by the customers. These "rejects" cost money and ultimately reduce profits.

7. Forecasting

One of the more difficult tasks for buyers is to be able to predict the direction in which the consumers' merchandise preferences are heading. In-house forecasting formats or budget forms are available as tools to use within the budget guidelines set down by management, but the merchandise mix and variables are the buyer's responsibility.

Buyers purchasing staple items such as food, appliances, household items and the like are exposed to fewer risks than a fashion buyer. Fashion buyers are faced with many more, constantly changing, variables such as colors, trends and styles, and fabrics, which require an in-depth knowledge of the consumer profile and trends—together with a good dose of gut feeling thrown in—if forecasting is to be accurate.

Forecasting becomes even trickier when the buyer needs to buy six months or more in advance, taking the possible risk that the color emphasis may change in the interim. While past sales combined with fashion forecasters' predictions are helpful, the buyer always needs to exercise sound judgment.

8. Dedication

Working long, irregular hours is typical for buyers. Buying trips where the day's orders need to be reviewed; vendor visits; fashion shows; market-week (a fixed period when all vendors show their new collections for the coming season, enabling buyers to make comparisons and vendors to assess the volume of production required)—all add up to long, full days, especially when the associated administrative work has to be completed as well.

Managing peak festive periods or season-end sales, where the buyers are required to be on the selling floor, or opening a new branch or store where stock deliveries and inventories need to be presented in the best possible manner are all part of a buyer's responsibilities.

Only the truly dedicated can endure these long days, and this is where the *passion for the job* makes or breaks an aspiring buyer.

9. Honesty/Integrity

This is one of the most important qualities that any retailer should seek in its buyers and merchandisers.

Wherever beautiful products are on display, the temptation to pilfer is high. To overcome this, many retailers offer high staff discounts.

There will always be people who will try to entice buyers to favor their products. This can be through offering a direct monetary bribe, goods in kind or lavish dinners and outings.

Call it what you like—bribe, backhander, sweetener, kickback—it's corruption all the same. How does it all start? Amongst experts on the subtle, sometimes manipulative, power of gifts views vary as to what constitutes a bribe. In the absence of explicit policies governing what is acceptable, individuals in positions of responsibility and trust can sometimes cross the line and become entangled—perhaps tragically—in questionable activities. However, even where there are no clear guidelines, there are usually tell-tale signs where something is amiss, if you pay attention. In some Asian countries, declining a gift may be considered rude; in most, however, there is a fine but perceptible line between politeness and bribery.

I hold the view that a gift becomes a bribe when something specific is expected in return. For buyers, this may entail buying higher quantities from the source, paying more for the goods or giving more space on the selling floor than the product deserves. I would suggest that, as a rule of thumb, a gift—in whatever shape or form—be considered a bribe whenever there is a condition attached to it. Learn to know the difference; otherwise you may jeopardize your reputation and your job.

It is not only morally wrong to engage in such practices but if/when caught, the likelihood of being thrown out of the industry is very high. Over the years, I have seen many bright buyers lose their job and their entire career in the retail industry because of this.

You should, therefore, never let anyone take advantage of you by putting you and your job in jeopardy. It is just not worth the pain that goes with losing everything you worked so hard for. You have to be constantly alert to this because, as someone once said: "Opportunity may knock only once, but temptation leans on the doorbell."

10. Time management

Time management is important if you are to juggle the multi-tasking that is required in a buyer's job. Many buyers fail on this one count alone. They find themselves stressed out and reports start to get sloppy and late.

Effective time management entails the ability to prioritize work to enable you to be more productive and clear-headed in managing your analytical reports, which then enables you to be more creative. Stress, on the other hand, will hamper your creative thinking, your communication and your health.

11. Appearance

The old saying "Never judge a book by its cover" doesn't hold true for a fashion buyer. They are expected to dress fashionably or, at least, very professionally. Buyers are business people who interact with customers, vendors or business associates most of the time, and being properly attired will make a good impression.

A well-groomed buyer serves as a role model for aspiring assistant buyers, department managers and sales associates.

12. Negotiation skills

Good negotiation skills are such an important and fundamental part of a buyer's job that I have dedicated a chapter to this subject. Chapter 15 outlines the eight golden rules of negotiation, how to negotiate favorable terms and the factors to be aware of when negotiating.

RETAIL RECRUITMENT ADS

The following examples illustrate the qualities, qualifications and abilities retailers seek when looking for a new candidate to fill a buyer or merchandise manager's position. The first example is from Macy's (USA) website.

Job description for a buyer

Job overview

Maximizes sales and profitability of a given area of business through the development and implementation of a strategy, analysis and appropriate reaction to sales trend. Lends overall support to the company sales, gross margin, and turnover objectives.

Core responsibilities

- Train, motivate and develop team to ensure effective performance and growth through consistent on-the-job training.
- Establish department direction and priorities, and communicate effectively to merchant team.
- Develop and execute seasonal merchandise plans and pricing strategies.
- Complete accurate forecasts evaluating financial components based on current trends, and accumulate information leading up to future events that will

have an impact on the business, specifically events that may influence the general cost of living or changes in people's lifestyle.

- Develop assortment plans which support the departmental goals and key item focus.
- Profile target customer to ensure customer satisfaction.
- Partner with the planner on the development of assortment plans.
- Manage vendor performance to maximize profitability and achieve financial objectives.
- Communicate with Macy's Merchandising Group for direction and recommendations to maximize division performance.
- Determine marketing plans and promotional calendar.
- Reconcile marketing plans with assortment and financial plans.
- Develop visual presentation guidelines for the stores to support seasonal strategies.
- Maintain collaborative partnerships and negotiate effectively with vendors and internal colleagues.

Skill summary

- Minimum of 1–2 years' prior buying experience in a department store or specialty store environment.
- Experience with planning, forecasting and allocation.
- Strong analytical and PC skills.

- Strong negotiation skills.
- Sense of urgency.
- Excellent written and verbal communication skills.
- Ability to develop, plan and execute strategies.
- Ability to deal effectively with all levels of management.

Job description for a merchandising manager

Job overview

Responsible for developing strategies to maximize business performance and profitability, promotional strategies, competitively dominant merchandise assortments, by business profit maximization, and customer satisfaction by meeting demographic needs. Oversees the execution of merchandise selection and procurement for related families of business. Sets the merchandise direction to ensure a focused continuity on the selling floor across families of business.

Key accountabilities

- Manage, coach and develop buying staff.
- Foster an environment that promotes personal development of divisional merchandise manager (DMM), buyers and their businesses. Build and maintain high morale amongst entire buying team and personally set the example for development.
- Set the overall strategy and merchandise direction for a pyramid of businesses.
- Direct DMMs to develop assortments that support the needs of the customer and the financial objectives of the merchandise division.
- Ensure that pricing, promotional strategies and marketing support the financial objectives of the merchandise group.
- Work with the planning organization to develop assortment plans that support overall strategy of in-stock positioning for key merchandise categories, important merchandise classifications and key vendors.
- Work with the General Manager Merchandising to strengthen market relationships and knowledge of market trends, strengths and weaknesses.
- Understand competitors' strengths, weaknesses and strategies.
- Facilitate and promote timely communication and cooperation between stores, merchandising functions and resources to accomplish sales, margin and service objectives.

- Support buying staff with the vendor community to ensure that Macy's, Inc. obtains merchandise exclusives, product launches, best deliveries, and the desired sales, turnover and margin plans.
- Establish department direction and priorities, and communicate effectively to merchant team.

Skill summary

- Successful completion of multiple buying and/or management assignments in a full-line department store, or equivalent.
- Strong leadership profile.
- Highly organized and have the ability to adapt to quickly changing priorities.
- Excellent written and verbal communication skills.
- Strong negotiation skills.
- Ability to work well with all levels of management, build partnerships and direct teams.
- Ability to develop and empower a team.

RETAIL JOB SEARCHES

There are several avenues open to someone looking for a job in retail, including visiting the websites of big retailers to check their current job availability, as illustrated above; checking newspaper recruitment ads; and contacting specialist recruitment agencies.

Recruitment agencies have the advantage of having a retail client base for which they source talent. They are well versed in their clients' company profiles and the types of future employees they are seeking. The disadvantage, especially for someone starting a career in retail buying, is that the agencies' main focus is on finding candidates with experience and good track record rather than proposing an inexperienced candidate with potential.

Visiting the websites of recruitment agencies is interesting in that they list catalogs of jobs by industry—retail, wholesale, FMCG (fast-moving consumer goods), manufacturing, electronics, IT, telecoms, and so on; by job type—sales, marketing, merchandising, management, HR, accounting, warehousing; by job title—retail sales assistant, buyer, merchandiser, sales manager, marketing manager, general manager; by salary range; and by country.

The screening process for many recruitment agencies is also worth mentioning. The high volume of applications is screened automatically, using computerized systems which pick up key words that fit the job requirement and identify these resumes for further screening by the recruiter until they have a short list of suitable candidates to interview. The interview process then reduces this list to two or three candidates who best fit the retailer's criteria.

The other, and probably the best, option for someone fresh out of school is to send particulars direct to the retailer's HR department and follow up with a phone call. Many retailers have management trainee programs that are not advertised and this could be a good starting point for someone who desires a job in merchandising.

The websites of the following recruitment agencies might prove a useful starting point for those looking for jobs in retail:

- Michael Page International
- Robert Walters
- Hudson
- Kerry Consulting
- Boyden Executive Search
- Monster

case study

An exceptional buyer

This is about a buyer who developed 11 of the 12 most sought-after qualities that retailers look for in a buyer.

I had a buyer's job opening for one of my ladies' wear departments. It was one that would require a great deal of product development. After considering all the applications, I set up interviews for the three best candidates. Two were all right but the third was special, exceeding the other two on several criteria. She said the right things, answered all questions correctly, showed a passion for the industry, had had years of buying experience and had done product development before. Yet, despite all of these good things, I was still a bit apprehensive: the position was for a *fashion* department and this candidate was simple-looking, chubby and softly spoken ...

So I asked her to draw a few sketches of blouses, knit-tops, pants and a jacket, with a view to meeting again the following week to look at what she had done and to see where we would go from there.

When she presented her drawings, I had to admit they looked good: the styles were fashionable yet commercial enough for our type of store positioning. So I hired her.

She already had a great attitude, was naturally drawn to the selling floor, had good communication skills, was good at analyzing her business, and could thus forecast well. As with all my new buyers, I took time to mentor her in the areas that she had not been exposed to: in this case, creating fashion concepts and commercial ranges of coordinates, working European trade shows and dealing with European vendors—which included how to select ranges to suit the department store's customers and enhancing her negotiation skills with foreign vendors.

She was a fast learner, like a sponge, and didn't miss a nuance of what was being taught. Not only did the department excel under her charge, but she became our European vendor's "little darling." Why? Because she had an irresistible sweetness about her that was infectious and, at the same time, was amazingly astute as far as market trends were concerned. The market had a lot of respect for her. She would get the most amazing deals out of them and I would hear time and again: "We normally don't give such and such; but for you, how can we say no?" They valued her opinion on the ranges, and the fact that she was spot on and decisive with her selections. One thing she always shared was her sellthrough—the sales performance of the merchandise she purchased from them—and would go to great lengths to explain how the business could improve. As far as her in-house development went, two brands—MLM and Gina Rossi—had outstanding sales and profit results, becoming departments in their own right and extending to sub-brands such as MLM Sports, MLM Resort, MLM *Classic* and MLM *Couture*. Gina Rossi expanded to Gina Rossi-Urban.

She has shown herself to possess 11 of the 12 attributes and, as the saying goes, "Beauty lies in the eye of the beholder."

case study

Learning the importance of time management

As you will have gathered by now, a buyer's role is multi-tasked and involves a great deal of paperwork. I had a buyer once who had a serious time-management problem that affected her overall productivity. Because she failed to keep up to date with her paperwork (which included such things as issuing purchase orders (POs), maintaining proper records for stock-keeping units (SKUs) and OTB planning, and data analyses on sales, intake margins and vendors—all key indicators that enable buyers to write concise and accurate monthly reports—it eventually put her in a position where she had overbought merchandise.

In this case, late deliveries were not shifted in the system, cancellations were not updated and removed from the system, and the new purchases were late in being added into the system. Though such tasks are time-consuming, neglecting to do them can have a snowball effect over a longer period of time and can cause an acute problem; which it duly did. The buyer was subsequently given time-management training, which helped her greatly.

I bumped into her a couple of years after she left the company. She was now holding a very responsible job with a chain store. During our conversation, she admitted that after she left us, she went back to her old ways, giving her the same problematic outcome. She admitted that had she been more conscientious in practicing good time management, it would have saved her a great deal of hardship and embarrassment. How was she doing now? Fabulously! "I learned the hard and long way. You gave me an opportunity to improve myself and I just couldn't see it at the time. I have learned to do one task and finish it instead of getting distracted and trying to do 10 different things and not finishing any of them."

I have to admit that this made me very proud.

case study

Development, in more ways than one

There was a time where I was asked to run the children's division of the Singapore department store. The buyer was a bubbly sort, and you could also say that she had the gift of the gab. The type of buying she had been used to incorporated a certain amount of standard line buying from vendors and, to a larger extent, consignment business, under which, for a fee, vendors are assigned part of the store in which they can sell their own merchandise direct. As the margins for this were low, it was natural for me to explore outright purchase opportunities.

We started to buy lovely ranges from Italy and the United States covering most age groups. The sellthrough was great. With more confidence, more lines were bought and the outright margins started to pay off. The next step was for us to explore in-house development. She had never done any development, so her level of confidence was quite low. I sat down with her and started to develop some concepts based on the types of merchandise we were having success with.

The first lines were developed in Malaysia under a brand called "The Munchies." We registered the name and had our first launch with casual coordinates for girls and boys aged six to 12. It took off like a rocket! The next programs were for toddlers to age 16. Our size ratio was also special. The ranges from size 8 and above were cut for plus-sizes (for chubby kids), and this became a great sales niche as no one else in Singapore had clothes that could fit these kids. The renowned indulgence of doting parents meant that Singaporean children tend to be quite large and, knowing that trend, we made sure that our clothes could fit.

The next program was for underwear and socks, and we were the first store to launch pre-teen bras, which also became a "must buy" item.

The buyer went on to develop a second brand—Hardy Kids—with one of her key suppliers, and had her biggest ever launch, with children's partywear from Europe, for the Millennium Christmas and New Year in December 1999. As few stores in Singapore carried such lines, it was a great hit with our customers.

Asked a year later how she felt she was progressing, she said: "I never thought I had the talent to do development. I feel privileged that you took the time to teach me." To this, I replied: "Stick around kid, there's more to learn!"

The Art of Retail Buying

3 THE BUYER'S ROLES

Buyers play an important role in the retail industry. The skill with which they select and order merchandise has a direct effect on the store's sales volume and on its share of the total retail market.

They may buy for a department, an entire store, or a chain of stores. Those who work for larger retail businesses often handle one or a few related lines of goods and are referred to by the type of goods they purchase—a sportswear or a dress buyer, a men's wear buyer, a toy buyer, and so on.

Buyers in small stores often manage several departments for which they buy. In addition, they train and supervise sales and clerical staff. They may also plan advertising, displays and sales promotions. It is important that buyers maintain a balanced inventory and a budget agreed upon between themselves and the store or merchandising manager. Although computers are useful in helping to maintain inventory records and analyze customer purchasing preferences and trends, buyers still have to make key decisions concerning style, taste and customer motivations.

Central buyers work for chain stores and mail-order houses. They may be located in divisional headquarters, the parent store of a chain, or in offices in wholesale market areas. **Resident buyers** may be employed by one firm or they may sell their services to many firms. Buyers are often located in major market cities or, in some cases, overseas. They may place orders for stores, and prepare information bulletins for the branch buyers they serve.

If you are already a buyer, then you understand that the challenges and demands are significant. Your decisions must be accurate so that your company can turn acceptable profits. As a buyer, you are ultimately responsible for selecting merchandise from a vast number of sources. When a professional buyer makes a final decision, personal taste is of little importance: customer satisfaction and company profitability are the only barometers by which a purchase is judged. Accordingly, a great deal of the company's profitability is in the hands of the buyer.

A buyer's job can be lonely at times. You have a specific portfolio to buy for and few people you can discuss matters with, bearing in mind that buyers may be competing with one another. The best place to release that pent-up lonely energy and to find answers to many of the questions you may have is on the selling floor, interacting with customers.

WHY BECOME A BUYER?

Many who wish to embark on a career in retailing probably do so with the perception that the job provides a great deal of excitement and glamour. A buyer for hard goods may not have such high expectations, but a would-be fashion buyer often believes this comes with the territory and has visions of attending fashion shows and designer exhibitions, trips to exotic foreign destinations, dining with vendors in elegant restaurants, and enjoying generous staff discounts or clothing allowances. The reality is quite different: at times, it can be hard work, rigorous and challenging. That's why having an enthusiastic and positive attitude goes a long way in this business.

To be a buyer, you must have a strong retail background, preferably in sales, but otherwise to have started your career as an assistant buyer. It is at these two points that the fundamental conditions of this industry are learnt.

While acquiring practical experience, other skills are being developed. One of the most important requirements of this industry is to develop great people skills, which will be needed in the buyer's many dealings with staff from other departments/divisions, in communicating with management and in negotiating with suppliers.

There are a few direct-entry training schemes into buying. These tend to be aimed at graduates and are generally in the fashion retail sector. Many large retail organizations offer general store-management training schemes, with the opportunity to specialize in buying after the general program has been completed. This training provides an opportunity to gain experience and skills in all aspects of retail.

Because of the high level of competition, buying is not usually a first job in retail. If you are unsuccessful in gaining entrance to a training scheme, it is possible to work elsewhere in retail, such as on the shop floor, and then gain an internal promotion to retail buying.

Buyers must have the flexibility to travel and sometimes relocate. The job entails visiting branch stores and sometimes foreign markets, and buying trips can be physically and mentally demanding. Buyers work closely with managers, sales staff, and advertising and systems personnel.

Buyers must monitor general economic conditions to anticipate consumer buying patterns. In addition, they must keep abreast of style and manufacturing trends, read fashion and trade magazines, follow ads in newspapers and other media, and check retail competitors' sales activities.

BUYERS AND ACCOUNTABILITY

Merchandise managers (MMs) or divisional merchandise managers (DMMs) are the team leaders managing the buyers to excel and reach higher retail success. They are the ones in the driver's seat when it comes to the entire division's sales results and profitability.

Buyers are accountable for every item appearing on their department's stockholding. The MMs and DMMs are accountable for the overall assortments and composition of the buyers' areas, ensuring that they are in line with the store's image, guidelines and forecasts. Importantly, they are the custodians of the business and have to be vigilant to ensure that all goes according to plan.

A good MM/DMM will do everything in their power to support and guide the buyers, involving themselves with the various steps the buyer needs to go through until such time that the buyer is able to do the job with confidence and assurance.

The MM/DMM takes an advisory and mentoring role to help new recruits develop the necessary leadership, decision-making, delegation and communication skills, as well as ensuring that they become effective in their use of analytical data and other available reports. The purpose of this on-the-job training and guidance is to prepare the individuals for an elevated level of personal and professional competence within that particular retail company. Enhancing the buyers' skills, traits and behaviors is the foundation for the retailer's success: there is just no room for mediocrity in this competitive industry.

Once the buyers are deemed equipped and skilled enough, they are left to do their jobs, reporting back to their MM/DMMs on a weekly basis or on a case basis, depending on the activities on hand.

The merchandise, concepts, prices and everything else expected of the role become the buyer's full responsibility, and they are accountable for the budgets and profitability of the areas of which they have been put in charge.

BUYING AND MERCHANDISING

Under the guidance of the MM/DMM, and within the company framework, the buyer is asked to develop a merchandising strategy for the department, division or store(s); analyze and understand targeted consumer demands; segregate merchandise classifications (fashion & trendy assortments, basic assortments, novelty assortments); improve on resource structures; maintain good relationships with key vendors; set pricing policies that fit the company structure; analyze trends; and regularly review performance indicators with sales.

The buyer's other major duties are finance-based and include preparing sales and gross profit budgets, as well as stock-holding levels by department or by brand (and, in some companies, by SKU), and mark-downs and discounts. These will be covered later in the book.

Managing plans for stock levels also involves reacting to change in consumer demands and, at times, pre-ordering merchandise based on stock sheets. Pre-ordering is designed to ensure that certain basic items are always on hand. While this can be done through the company's computerized systems, it often requires the assistance of the selling staff where a manual count is called for.

Pre-ordering is generally based on historical sales data, which enable the buyer to pre-book items with vendors. Let's say, for example, that a buyer is working in a store in Southeast Asia (where there are no seasons/winters) and is responsible for a winter-wear department for customers traveling to cold climates. She has in stock thermal underwear that is sourced out of Italy. Twice a year, she would have placed orders with this vendor but, at the same time, would have arranged for "block orders" for basic styles and popular sizes to be sent mid-season as and when needed.

Another ongoing duty is to meet suppliers and negotiate prices and margins and, at times, terms of contract. This is an area that requires both skill and tact, and in which the buyer needs to be clear and concise in explaining what she wants without being too forceful or too arrogant.

Maintaining relationships with existing suppliers and sourcing new suppliers is another key function and the basis for growing the business: the better the buyer–vendor relationship, the stronger the commitment from the vendor.

These relationships are a two-way arrangement. On one side, the buyer will seek out vendors who are progressive and innovative in meeting the needs of the company and its customers. On the other side, the vendor will look for a retailer that offers the best platform to sell his products. (Buyers come and go, but the long-term stability and continuity stays with the retailer.)

Some buyers will have the chance to travel, attending trade fairs, meeting foreign suppliers or manufacturers. Interestingly, I have found that not all buyers (even those with no apparent family commitments) are keen on traveling. This can be a huge handicap. I always make it a point to ask new recruits how they feel about traveling and I expect prospective new buyers to be honest about this. While travel is often important, it may not always be necessary, as the following example illustrates.

I had a buyer who had luggage and men's underwear as her portfolio. She did her job well, her sales figures showed steady single-digit growth, but whenever the subject of traveling came up, she gave all kinds of excuses to avoid it. Private labels being a growing business for our company, I gave her the task of developing a range of men's underwear and a travel series of soft suitcases. The quality had to be superior or at least comparable to national brands; the retail prices had to be lower; and naturally, the margins had to be 20–25% higher than her current brands.

When the time came to present her ranges, I was curious to see what she had prepared, as she had not applied for any overseas trips. To my surprise, the concept, design, quality, price and margin were exactly what I had asked for. I asked how she had managed to do this without leaving the country, and she told me that she had commissioned her key suppliers in each category to source the merchandise for her. I knew that these same suppliers were always sticky on margins and inflexible in giving us exclusive ranges, but she had worked out a reasonable stockholding with them and did not need to keep very high inventory. I could not deny that she had done an excellent job, and complimented her on her work.

I concluded that her dislike of traveling was so great that it made her think outside the box to find someone that could fulfill the requirements. I also learnt that sometimes the source is closer to home; you just have to look harder for it.

Besides buying, a buyer has several other routine duties that entail liaising with other departments. For example, a buyer would be in contact with her shipping department to check the status of merchandise or assist in cases when goods received do not tally with goods bought. Some buyers may have to be in daily contact with their warehouse to liaise over certain stock replenishments, changes of price tags or stock returns.

Buyers would be in contact with the finance department as and when payments to vendors are held up or a vendor's credit note is late in arriving. With the marketing department, buyers would be responsible for arranging samples to be sent for photo shoots, for submitting information on the products or for arranging meetings prior to any promotional events. The highest level of contact, however, should be with the selling department or operational staff.

In addition to the above, buyers in most retail companies are required to participate in promotional activities, liaise with shop personnel to ensure product/collection demand is met, seek merchandise feedback from customers, train and mentor junior staff, write reports and sales forecasts, as well as analyze sales figures.

As the buyers gain experience in juggling these many functions, the level of business has the potential to grow to new heights. Good buyers are able to significantly increase year-on-year sales, help achieve higher customer retention through better merchandise mix and ranges and, as a result, lift profitability levels.

The challenge retailers face is in their ability to retain good talent. Buyers don't usually leave a company just to earn a few extra dollars; they do so because they aspire to reach the next level. So, if they want to keep good talent, retailers should develop career opportunities that will benefit both the individual and the company.

To be successful, a buyer will require a great deal of lateral thinking as well as analytical ability because the nature of the retail business is constantly changing in line with customer trends and demands. The old saying "find a need/niche and fill it" is readily applicable to retailers. This is where the process of lateral thinking comes in.

LATERAL THINKING VS. PROBLEM SOLVING

Edward de Bono, who pioneered the notion of lateral thinking, points out that the term "problem solving" implies that there is a problem to respond to and that it can be resolved. It overlooks situations where there is no problem, or where a problem exists that cannot be resolved. It is only logical, however, to think about making a good situation, which has no obvious problems, into a better situation.

Sometimes, it may not be possible to remove the immediate cause of the problem and a different way forward has to be found. For example, a retailer may find that the distance between the store and the warehouse is having an adverse effect on the speed at which he needs to replenish his stocks, especially at peak times. He could change warehouse, but that would involve divesting himself of the existing warehouse and finding a suitable replacement without incurring greater expense. Alternatively, he could explore other ways to work around the problem, such as getting local vendors to deliver direct to the stores. This, however, would entail higher costs for the vendors and would need to be negotiated. He could instill higher replenishment disciplines with his buyers or perhaps change the delivery roster to include night deliveries. The location of the warehouse is still the problem, but a plan that incorporates some or all of the above alternatives might help reduce the trouble it is causing.

De Bono[1] has detailed a range of "deliberate thinking methods"—applications emphasizing thinking as a deliberate act rather than a reactive one. In some circles, it is called **thinking outside the box.** This is a cliché or catchphrase used to refer to looking at a problem from a new perspective without preconceptions, also called a process of lateral thought. The catchphrase has become widely used in business environments.

PO (short for Provocative Operation) is a notation used in lateral thinking, and is used to propose an idea which may not necessarily be a solution or a "good" idea in itself, but moves thinking forward to a new place where new ideas may be produced.

- **Examples of provocative operation**

"The problem is that Tom won't come to the mountain."

1. PO: The mountain must come to Tom (the classic answer).

2. PO: Use a video conference (an IT idea).

3. PO: Use an intermediary.

4. PO: Ask him what he wants in exchange for coming to the mountain (a deal).

5. PO: See if he'll accept a free timeshare slot in a holiday home (which just happens to be on the mountain).

6. PO: Wait until he changes his mind.

7. PO: Cut your losses and tackle a different problem.

---

[1] The following books by De Bono should prove useful to buyers: *Lateral Thinking*, Penguin Books, 1970; *Po: Beyond Yes and No*, Penguin Books, 1972; *Serious Creativity*, Harper Business, 1992.

8. PO: Negotiate with him.

9. PO: Force him.

10. PO: Ask Tom to go near the mountain if not to the mountain.

11. PO: Lure, deceive or blackmail him.

12. PO: Make him an offer he can't refuse. Leave him no alternative.

These are all provocative operations and characterize a stage of lateral thinking where the ideas generated need further work in order to become practical solutions.

Such thinking can prove very useful to buyers, who need to be able to think quickly on their feet. Faced with so many different aspects of the job—buying, developing, coaching, organizing, negotiating—lateral thinking will always be a buyer's best asset.

The Art of Retail Buying

4

MANAGEMENT EXPECTATIONS

HOW MANAGEMENT EVALUATES BUYERS

Buying is the lifeline of retail, and success as a buyer is determined by results. You may have great personal qualities but if you are not productive in providing a suitable return on investment (ROI), your future value to the company may be limited. Your results will depend on how well you can translate consumer trends and gear your buying accordingly. This requires that the buyer has an insight into who the consumers are, what they buy and why they buy, a subject that will be explored further in a later chapter. For the moment, let's have a look at the 14 key evaluation measures that are used to gauge a buyer's success:

1. Sales against budget and against previous year (the top line)

Management will be expecting year-on-year sales growth, and the budgets are the indicators of how much more sales the company is anticipating to generate against the previous year. These forecasts will normally take into account market trends, political stability, commodity price hikes, changes in taxes or any foreseeable trends that may affect consumer spending. Achieving the previous year's levels but without reaching the current budgeted sales may, in some circumstances, be acceptable; however, performing below both of these levels spells trouble. In my experience, the problem almost always lies in poor merchandise assortments.

2. Gross profit margin against budget and against previous year (the bottom line)

For most retailers, achieving the planned gross profit margins has an even greater importance than over-achieving planned sales. This is because all budgeted expenses are in line with the profits expected. Growing the top line is fine but, at the end of the day, it's the profits that pay the bills.

3. Accumulated sales and gross profit for year to date

These are the markers or the global overview of the business being generated by the buyer. Though each month's performance is probed individually, if the accumulated sales and gross profits are behind plan, management will want to explore the cause of these discrepancies and assist the buyer in closing the gap.

4. Sales per square foot

A sales-per-square-foot figure allows management to assess if a product line or a brand is generating sufficient business on a given sales area. In a cosmetics department, for example, sales per square foot will always be better than in a fashion department, simply due to the nature of the products sold. Thus, each segment of the business will have specific requirements in this regard based on whether the management judges the products or brands to be performing up to expectation. Their respective locations on the selling floor will also be taken into account.

5. Gross profit margin per square foot

While the cosmetics department in our example above enjoys greater sales per square foot, against this productivity measure, the fashion department will have the advantage. While cosmetics usually offer between 25–29% margins, fashion should command 40% and above.

6. Actual stocks against planned stocks

A stock holding against plan reflects the efficiency of the products bought. If a buyer is over plan, it could indicate that goods are not selling as well as anticipated, more goods were bought than were planned for, or goods were brought in early to prepare for a big sales event. The last of these is acceptable, as long as management is informed and there are good reasons to justify the early deliveries. More critical is when goods are selling below expectations, or if a buyer has over-bought. Such circumstances usually lead to mark-downs and loss of profits.

7. Stock turn

A stock turn is a ratio of sales to average stocks. The stock turn measures the efficiency of the inventory, the retailer's main source of operating profits. It determines the effectiveness of the merchandise planning and controls in place. The higher the stock turn of the inventory, the more profitable the operation will be. A stock turn below plan is costly. In retail, we estimate that an excessive inventory can cost the company as much as 3% per month as a result of increased expenses in storage, interest, insurance, internal transfers, and, ultimately, devaluation of the merchandise with mark-downs.

8. Gross margin return on inventory (GMROI)

The GMROI assists management in evaluating whether a sufficient gross margin is being earned on the products purchased in relation to the investment in inventory required to generate it. This can be worked out by calculating the gross profit margins of the average inventory at cost and dividing this by the average cost of inventory. The result is a ratio that indicates the number of times gross margin is earned from the inventory investment.

9. Conversion rate

Conversion rate takes into account the number of customers walking into the store vis-à-vis the number of transactions being processed. It provides another tool for measuring the efficiency of store locations, merchandise categories, and the staff's selling skills in turning potential shoppers into actual customers.

10. Average selling price against the plan

The average selling price (ASP) is the price at which a particular class of merchandise is typically sold. This varies according to the type of product and its expected lifecycle. Products such as silverware, crystal ware, watches and jewelry tend to have a higher ASP than garments and fashion accessories. In the latter part of its lifecycle, a product becomes less attractive as the novelty wears off and is replaced by newer styles, or, more likely, is saturated with competitors, thus driving the ASP down.

If an average selling price goes below plan, it is usually caused by the buyer underselling products before the end of their lifecycle, or by introducing higher-than-planned levels of low-priced items. Having aggressive price promotions or ill-managed discounts is a sure way of lowering the perceived value of a given product, and therefore driving down the ASP.

11. Monthly mark-downs, accumulative mark-downs and mark-downs against budget or previous year.

Mark-downs are planned for by month, and typically involve a standard set of mark-down percentages implemented on a standard schedule, across all departments or stores. These plans, however, do not take into account store-specific consumer demand, inventory on hand, and sales velocity. They are allocations as a percentage to sales for clearing oddments and limited levels of slow-selling merchandise during the season. Whether correcting a bad buy or clearing merchandise at the end of a product's lifecycle, buyers are expected to control and manage their mark-down allocations. Excessive use of mark-downs always equates to loss of profits. Astute buyers can often negotiate cooperation or compensation from vendors on mark-downs as part of their purchasing deal.

12. Stock obsolescence (OBSL)—year to date

Stock obsolescence reserves are financial tools based on historical mark-down data that enable retailers to factor into their calculations a certain percentage of mark-downs against sales to clear aged, or problematic stock holdings at the end of each season. The reserves can typically be a reduction of 40% on an inventory that is older than seven months, and 80–90% off for inventories that are older than a year. The percentage allocated will normally be higher for fashion departments than for homeware, which has a much longer lifecycle.

The OBSL reserves are made accessible after the stocktake result is known. These mark-downs are then utilized to clear any old stocks during the store's season-end sales. As a result, the newer the buyer's inventories are, the more management saves.

13. Shrinkage (due to theft or spoilage)

Many retailers plan shrinkage arising from theft or spoilage as a percentage of sales. Though minimizing shrink is an operational duty, any help rendered by the buyers to reduce these losses is greatly appreciated by management.

14. Return on investment (ROI)

In retail, the ROI will calculate the profit returns generated by the inventory invested and is usually expressed as a percentage. For instance, a $1,000 investment that earns $50 in interest obviously generates more cash than a $100 investment that earns $20 in interest, but the $100 investment earns a higher return on investment.

- $50 ÷ $1,000 = 5% ROI
- $20 ÷ $ 100 = 20% ROI

ROI enables management to evaluate the relative efficiency of the profits generated by the merchandise bought.

EXPECTATION OVERVIEW

- **Sales performance**

Sales performance is the first factor that management looks at daily, weekly, monthly, quarterly and at full-year end in gauging where the profits are heading in relation to planned margins. The actual profit results are only available at month end, when all items have been factored in. These may include new deliveries and their intake margins, goods returned, mark-downs, mark-ups, and more.

Though operations are directly involved in making the sales, buyers are made responsible for overall sales performance. You may have a department that is achieving or exceeding sales targets, but if the gross profit margin is below plan, there will be a lot of explaining to do because all operational costs are pegged against the store achieving a certain gross profit margin. Higher sales at lower-than-planned margins are costly.

Accumulated sales and profits are an indicator of how the quarters are stacking up. This helps retailers decide if they will need to inject an extraordinary event in the form of a promotion or a store-wide discount should their performance come short of plan or of the previous year's actual figures.

Sales and margins per square foot are other important measures used in deciding whether to expand or reduce selling space in a given department. Should a division be expanding at an exceptional rate, attempts would be made to find additional space (most likely from another department that is underperforming) to accommodate that growth.

But expansion may not always be due to margins per se. The determining factor may be the high overall sales and margin per square foot. As we saw above with cosmetics, for example, margins can be low but the products sell at relatively high prices and take up very little space, making returns and sales per square foot the highest in the store. It may be, too, that management is following consumer trends and wishes to expand these merchandise categories.

- **Profitability**

The components that constitute profits generated from the investment or inventory are as follows:

Mark-up: calculated by dividing the retail price by the cost price

Realized gross margins: the final retail price less cost of goods sold (includes discounts and price changes)

Controllable realized margins: gross margins minus direct department expenses (some stores also include warehouse expenses)

Operating profits: gross margins minus expenses chargeable to the selling department. In some cases, a department store may choose to charge the individual departments for operational expenses that might include delivery and warehouse charges, charges for visual merchandising services or for extra sales staff.

Generally, profit margins are calculated as a percentage of sales. Both the cash margins and the percentage ratio are important and some retailers evaluate their buyers against the gross margin per dollar of cost inventory.

- **Stock turn**

Stock turn is, as explained earlier, very much a buyer's responsibility. If the plan is a stock turn of 4 and a buyer is achieving 3.3 (see "Productivity" section on page 48), this gives management a clear indication that the buyer's purchases are off-balance. This can be due to a number of factors, including over-buying or buying over the planned OTB, or having slow-moving merchandise which produces a domino effect (where existing goods are not moving and new arrivals are inflating the stockholdings).

The higher the stock turn, the healthier the merchandise investment. Stores that carry high levels of consignment or concessionaire goods will have high stock turns. In such cases, the company's stock turn will need to be calculated separately on the basis of its own outright buys to assess the health of the stockholding turnaround.

- **Conversion rate**

This is a measurement used to assess the number of purchases made against the number of people who come into the store. Some companies may do random manual counts of the numbers entering their stores, but automatic counters, offered by several electronics and loss-prevention companies, are becoming increasingly popular.

The customer-to-sales ratio is determined by the store's management. Even if there were an industry standard, retailers would be sensitive to their own situation and the locations of their stores. A suburban store, for example, would not expect to have the same high traffic as a store in the city center, but may expect to have a higher customer-to-sales ratio because its customers are less likely to be browsers and more likely to be shoppers (or vice versa, depending on the country and its habits).

Once the customer-to-sales ratio has been determined, management will analyze the factors that influence their current ratios. Factors which can lead to lost sales may include having inadequate staff to attend to customers; having staff who lack the necessary skills and standards of service; or offering merchandise that is not appealing, is deemed too expensive or simply out of stock.

While a store may be located in a high-traffic location, this does not necessarily lead to a higher conversion rate automatically. It may be that the store is merely being used as a shortcut into the mall or subway. Quantity is no guarantee of quality and management would need to find ways to convert these "pedestrians" into actual shoppers.

- **Average selling price (ASP)**

Most companies aim to keep their average selling prices stable. Attempting to boost sales by introducing too many low prices is a dangerous course to take, and there are several examples of how the lure of high returns with decent margins has made some retailers lose their heads. The long-term danger comes from selling too low, too often; after a while, the merchandise's ASP is obliterated and, once this happens, it is difficult to regain.

Stores that are tempted to introduce more sales, more promotions, more card-member discount days, and more store-wide discounts are putting the company at long-term risk. While sales may experience high spikes during these events, the trouble is that they will be around again the following year (since sales budgets and forecasts are based on the previous year's performance). Once a vicious cycle is started, it is hard to stop.

The big danger of these price events getting out of hand is the damage they can cause for the "brand" or the store's good name. The company is at risk of losing credibility, and once that credibility is lost, so too are its customers.

- **Mark-downs and stock obsolescence**

Most retailers will have monthly mark-down allocations to clear oddments or slow-selling merchandise and, in my view, it's best to use them. The first mark-down is always the cheapest. A slow-selling item will have even less appeal three months down the road than when first identified as being a problem stock.

Over-usage of mark-downs and price changes to clear problem stock will, however, erode profits. Being overstocked with slow-selling merchandise can eat up big chunks of hard-earned profits.

The best advice is to always try to keep OTB buffers to buy small and often. This will also help you increase or decrease merchandise types within the season, with a lower risk of overextending.

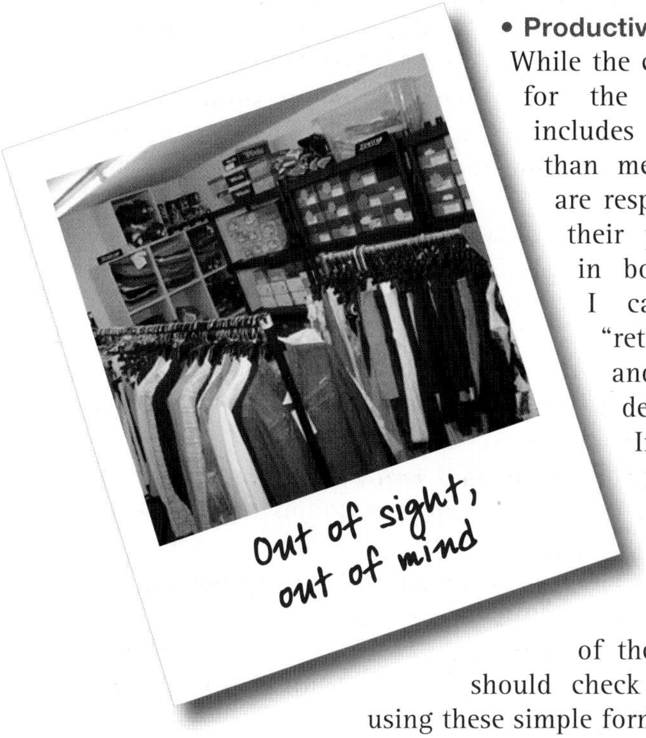

- **Productivity**

While the company is responsible for the overall ROI, which includes investments other than merchandise, the buyers are responsible to make all of their purchasing productive in both sales and profits. I call this the buyer's "return on inventory" and it is linked to the department's stock turn. In other words, the faster the inventory is moving, the faster the return is generated on these purchases. To check the health of the inventory, the buyer should check their stock turns by using these simple formulae:

Stock turn = yearly sales ÷ average stocks

or

Stock turn = monthly beginning stocks + monthly end stocks ÷ 13

or

Stock turn = monthly cost of goods sold ÷ average inventory cost

The ideal is to keep inventories low without compromising sales.

PRODUCTIVITY MEASURES

- **Stock-to-sales ratio (STSR)**

Another way to measure productivity is by calculating your stock-to-sales ratio, as follows:

STSR = Beginning stocks ÷ total month's sales

Example: Beginning stocks: $20,000 Sales: $5,000

STSR = 20,000 ÷ 5,000 = 4

- **Gross margin return (GMR)**

If your sales for the year are $100,000 at 37.5% (that is, $37,500), and average inventory at cost is $15,000, the gross margin return for each $1 investment is $2.50, calculated as follows:

(Margin) $37,500 ÷ (cost of goods) $15,000 = (GMR) $2.50

- **Realized gross profit margin**

A buyer has a sales target of $500,000 and a budgeted margin of 30% (that is, $150,000). The buyer stages a promotion that generates $600,000 at a margin of 25%, will ring up $150,000 in gross profits. The question to ask here is whether this is a satisfactory result.

The answer in this case is probably "No" because the buyer has broken away from management's intention to operate at a higher margin, and has, in all probability, increased expenses considerably. This is because there is an increase in the cost of moving an additional 29% physical volume of merchandise without the additional margin to support it; which means more work and less efficiency to generate the same profit. The calculation is as follows:

Gross margin per dollar of cost inventory

- Management will always measure on a percentage-to-sales basis.
- Profit dollars are important, but should be viewed as the result of achieving sales at the budgeted ratio of a given margin.
- EXAMPLE:

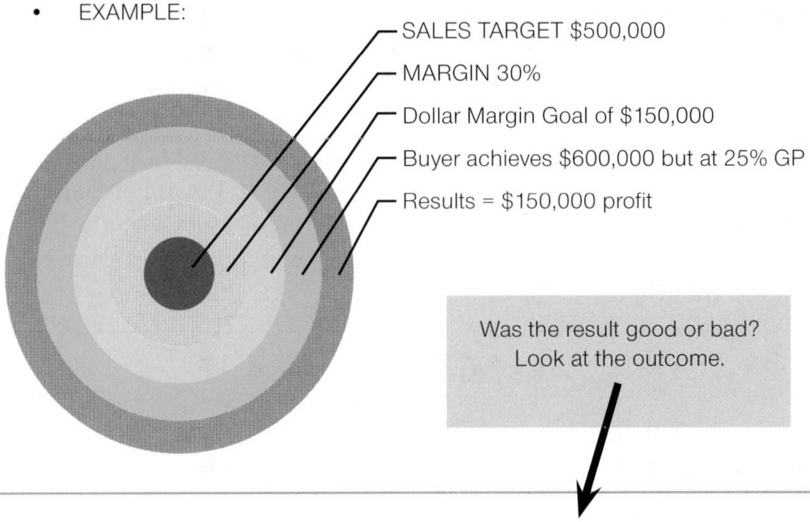
SALES TARGET $500,000
MARGIN 30%
Dollar Margin Goal of $150,000
Buyer achieves $600,000 but at 25% GP
Results = $150,000 profit
Was the result good or bad?
Look at the outcome.

The effect of lower-than-plan margins

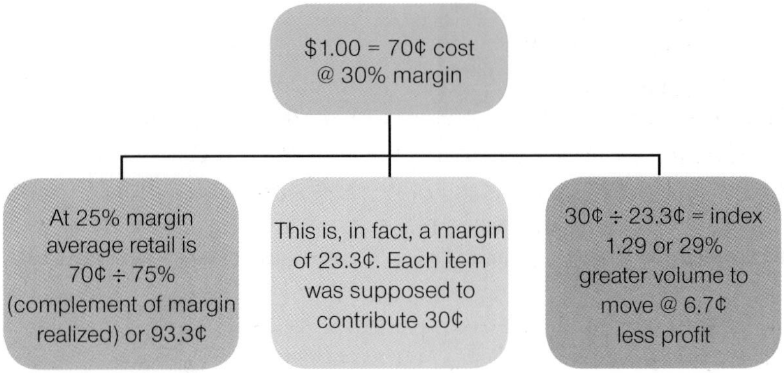
$1.00 = 70¢ cost
@ 30% margin
At 25% margin
average retail is
70¢ ÷ 75%
(complement of margin
realized) or 93.3¢
This is, in fact, a margin
of 23.3¢. Each item
was supposed to
contribute 30¢
30¢ ÷ 23.3¢ = index
1.29 or 29%
greater volume to
move @ 6.7¢
less profit

Buyers are responsible for achieving planned margins. Though margins can fluctuate from within the total merchandise assortment, the grand total by month end must hit budgets.

PERFORMANCE BEYOND YOUR STORES

Retail performance goes far beyond the individual store or the individual company. Industry-wide statistics enable retailers to compare their performance against the industry standards and to determine whether their merchandise mix is such that they meet, exceed or fall below those standards. These statistics are also a good indicator of which retail formats are on the rise and which ones are in decline. It has to be remembered, though, that these trends are very much tied to consumer demand, as illustrated in the charts below.

It is clear from the top-left-hand chart below that the department store format seems to be losing market share to the apparel specialty stores. In such circumstances, the department stores would have to re-look at their fashion offering and come up with a strategy to regain their market share.

Retail Statistics

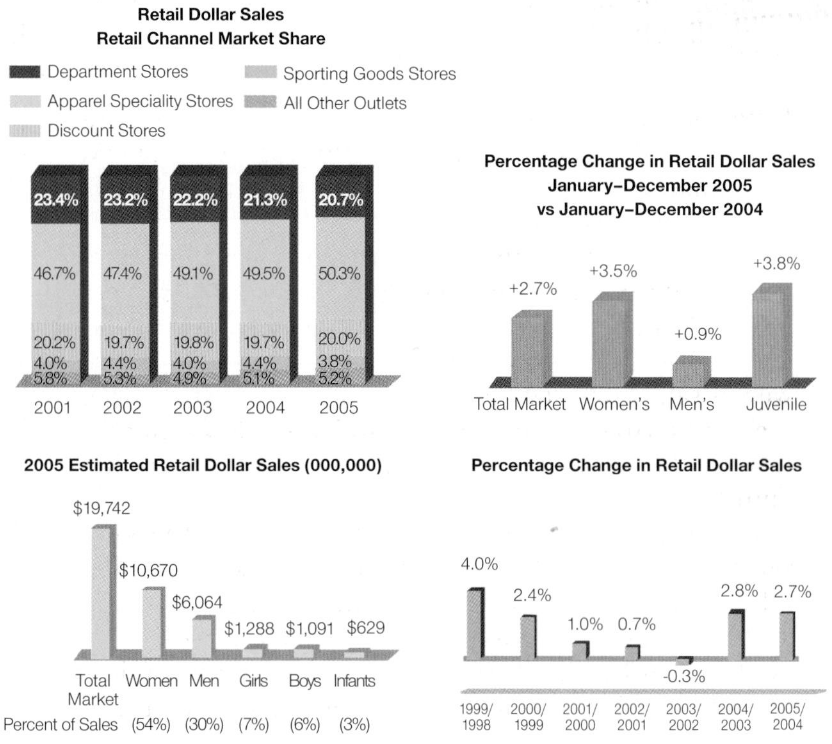

Source: www.gdsourcing.com/works/tradestatscan.htm

The next chart shows that the shift in retail spending is mainly in the women's apparel and juvenile segments, which again may provide management with an opportunity for further growth. Some, however, may not choose to follow this trend, preferring to follow a different strategy. If their particular store's growth is in the area of men's wear, they may deem the lower statistical growth in this area an advantage: while everyone is chasing after the women's and juvenile business, they may want to focus and grow their men's wear further while maintaining decent growth in women's wear.

Retailers have to make a choice. They can be generalists and have a decent range of everything, or be a specialist and outshine competitors in certain segments of the business.

case study

Management expectations vs. buyer's application

I mentioned how important it is to maintain budgeted margins. This case is about a zealous buyer who did everything in her power to do just that. The catch here is how far she went to accomplish it.

We had a very good vendor who sold us his usual ranges and participated in doing some product development for us. As our in-house brands grew, so did the levels of purchases. This vendor was supplying regular ranges as well as sales lines, the units for the sales lines being in the thousands. Granted, not all outright buys will sell equally well and the buyer convinced the vendor to take back her outright sales buys as some styles did not have a fantastic sellthrough. He did so on condition that she would be taking the goods back. Months went by and no POs were issued to take the goods back. When the vendor pressed her to take back her goods, she asked him to bear the mark-downs. So, not only had he warehoused the goods for more than six months, she now demanded a reduction in cost. The reduction meant that he would re-sell her the goods at a pretty hefty loss.

The case came to my attention and we met up with the vendor to sort things out. My buyer was obviously in the wrong on several counts. She was forcing the vendor to warehouse our merchandise, which meant that even if she took the goods back, these would come in with a new entry date, as if they were newly purchased items. It all equated to tactics that put a strain on the vendor–buyer relationship:

(1) By re-purchasing these goods, the delivery code marked a current age, though the merchandise was more than six months old.

(2) Bullying the vendor into keeping the goods and forcing him to bear her mark-downs, which he refused to do, created an unnecessary confrontation.

(3) The other part that surfaced was contribution to advertising, for which she had billed him. Not that he minded participating, but the amount she was asking was huge!

Three wrongs do not make one right. Lesson learnt: always make a win-win deal. I'd rather lose a deal once in a while than lose a productive vendor that represents big business in the long term. The buyer's zeal in securing her margins and planned stocks almost cost us a valued vendor.

You may find retail math a bit dry, even boring. But without an understanding of the basic concepts, it will be difficult to become a buyer. The good news is that it is pretty straightforward and easy to apply. Once you know how these formulas work, they can easily be processed on normal Excel spreadsheets.

This section should give you a feel of how merchandise is priced with profits in mind. The examples given are applicable to most types of merchandise in most types of retail formats.

SELLING PRICE, GROSS MARGIN AND MARK-UP

For many products, price is often a function of the cost of the product and a desired level of mark-up. When price is determined by the level of mark-up desired, this is often referred to as cost-plus pricing, mark-up pricing or full-cost pricing. There are several schools of thought related to mark-up pricing. For example, some retailers may expect to price items at anywhere between 15% and 100% above their cost. There is, however, a fine line between the desired mark-up, the cost of the product and the price that the market will accept.

All of these elements must be fully understood. In retail, a selling price is often not only a function of what the market can tolerate but also a function of demand. If the demand is high, then a 20% mark-up may have a selling price that is deemed inexpensive in relation to the demand or to the desirability of the product. Branded goods and niche products often command a premium which exceeds the set mark-up, which is why it is important to evaluate the cost, the desired mark-up and market demand when establishing a selling price.

There are two important terms used when discussing prices: "mark-up" and "margin"; and the difference between them can be confusing. **Mark-up** is a percentage added to the cost price to get the selling price. **Margin** is that proportion of the final selling price that represents profit.

In retail buying, it is recommended that you work with margins because this enables you to know what percentage of your total income is profit. Obviously, profits calculated in this way are *gross* profits, and from these are deducted your overall retail expenses—wages, taxes, operational costs such as rent, electricity, and phone bills, stationery, bags, warehousing, and so on—to establish your *net* profits.

Having a 50% margin means that half the selling price is profit. In mark-up terms, this would be a 100% mark-up (you have added 100% of the cost price to make the selling price).

Imagine an item that costs $50. If you sell it with a margin of 50%, half of the selling price will be profit. Thus, if you sell it at $100, $50 of this is profit. If, on the other hand, you sell the same item (cost $50) with a mark-up of 50%, you simply add 50% of the cost price—$25—to give a total selling price of $75. A 50% margin is clearly higher than a 50% mark-up.

The formula for calculating a gross margin percentage is:

Gross Margin % = (Selling Price – Cost) x 100/Selling Price

Here is another way to work it out and, as you can see, there is a pattern:

For a 5% margin, divide the cost price by 0.95:
Cost is $10 ÷ 0.95 = retail price $10.52

For a 5% mark-up, multiply the cost price by 1.05:
Cost is $10 x 1.05 = retail price $10.50 (or 2¢ less)

For a 10% margin, divide the cost price by 0.90:
Cost is $10 ÷ 0.90 = retail price $11.11

For a 10% mark-up, multiply the cost price by 1.10:
Cost is $10 x 1.10 = retail price $11 (or 11¢ less)

For a 15% margin, divide the cost price by 0.85:
Cost is $10 ÷ 0.85 = retail price $11.76

For a 15% mark-up, multiply the cost price by 1.15:
Cost is $10 x 1.15 = retail price $11.50 (or 26¢ less)

For a 20% margin, divide the cost price by 0.80:
Cost is $10 ÷ 0.80 = retail price $12.50

For a 20% mark-up, multiply the cost price by 1.20:
Cost is $10 x 1.20 = retail price $12 (or 50¢ less)

For a 25% margin, divide the cost price by 0.75 ... and so on.

You will notice from this that as the margin/mark-up percentage increases, so does the gap between the retail prices realized by each. So, using the formula for a 95% margin would give a retail price of $200 ($10 ÷ 0.05). A 95% mark-up, on the other hand, would produce a very different result: $10 x 1.95 = $19.50 (that is, $180.50 less).

(Obviously, a 100% margin cannot be achieved because this would imply a cost of zero, which is impossible to compute. The mark-up possibilities, however, are endless. To achieve a 100% mark-up, for example, you simply double the cost price.)

DISCOUNTS ON LISTED COST PRICE

Many suppliers prefer to quote list prices less a discount. This is because that gives them and the buyer a base line to work from. Buyers love the idea of getting a discount just as much as their customers. But the buyer also needs to know how these discounts are going to affect the end selling price and if these discounts are attractive enough for, say, a promotion or a sale. In my experience there are three levels of discounts.

1) A meaningful discount that enables the merchandise to be sold during a sale. For an item to be attractive enough for a sale, the retail offer should be at least 30% off, and is best at 50% off.

2) A good discount that enables the buyer to sell the items during a promotion, when the price can be anywhere from 20%–25% off the normal retail price.

3) A small discount (below 6%) given by a vendor can be used by the buyer to lift the margin or used as mark-downs to clear obsolete stocks, as this level of discount is not sufficient to have any real impact on the selling price.

The formula normally used by the supplier to give his buyers a discount is as follows:

Net cost = list x (100 – discount)/100

where list is the original list price and the margin that he has been operating with, expressed as a percentage; and discount is the discount that he wishes to give his buyer, expressed as a percentage of the original list price.

Final discount is the maximum discount that he is willing to pass on to the buyer.

Interestingly, this does not mean that the buyer may not opt to give her customers a further reduction. For example, let's say that the vendor's final discount is 40%. The buyer deems this good, but not good enough for her planned sales event. She may then decide to offer the merchandise to her customers at 50% off, using a lower-than-planned margin in the process. In this case, she has topped-up the discount by reducing her margin.

Note: These kinds of merchandise decisions and price evaluations are very important in a buyer's job. The additional 10% off can, in many cases, be linked to the quantities she is buying. The higher the quantity, the more important it is that the retail price is deemed so attractive by the customers that her chances of achieving a very fast sellthrough are high, making this buy very productive.

As mentioned, the discounted cost price given by the vendor does not necessarily need to match the discounted retail price the buyer intends to give her customers. However, she will need to do some calculations to see how far she is willing to reduce her margin to meet the "ideal" discounted retail price. If, as in the example above, she decides to give her customers a 50% discount, she will need to calculate the effect it will have on her overall margin. The higher the quantities she is buying, the greater the effect on the margin. Next, if the special offer is from a vendor selling a product that has fairly fixed prices in that market (this could be a national brand, for example), she will need to get the vendor's approval to sell the merchandise at the increased discount.

Here is an example:

- Original list price $100 ÷ 0.40 = $250, giving you a 60% margin. $250 would have been your normal-original retail price based on the supplier's normal-original cost price.

New listed price (discounted cost) $80 ÷ 0.40 = $200. Your margin is still 60% if you decide to sell the item at $50 less.

> (1) cost = list x (100 – supplier discount)/100)
> Original cost $100 ÷ 0.40 (60% margin) = retail before discount $250

discounted cost ($100 – $20 = $80) or 20% off the original listed cost price

(2) selling = cost/(100 – margin)/100) (new cost $80 ÷ 0.40 (60% margin) = $200 retail)

(3) final discount = (1 – cost/selling) x 100 (new cost $80 ÷ $200 = 0.60 margin)

You decide that you want to give your customers a 40% discount. The original retail price calculated on the original listed price is $250 (40% off retail) x 0.60 = $150, or $100 less. The new cost price, however, is $80: $80 ÷ $150 = 0.533, or a margin of 46.66%. If you are comfortable with a 46.66% margin, then that is what you can offer. If you need at least 50% margin and still want to retail at $150, you will need to negotiate the cost price further to $75: $75 ÷ $150 = 0.50 or 50% margin.

SALES TAX

In some countries, it is normal for retailers to quote prices exclusive of sales tax (also known as VAT or GST in some places). To add sales tax/VAT/GST to a price where, say, the rate of such a tax is 17.5%, multiply the price by 1.175.

If you have a price that includes VAT at that rate and need to work out the ex-VAT price, divide by 1.175.

MORE ON MARK-UPS

The formula for determining a product's selling price using a desired percentage mark-up is:

Selling Price = Total Cost x (1 + Percentage Mark-up)

For example, a product costs $2 and you wish to know the selling price with a 30% mark-up:

Selling Price = $2 x (1 + 0.30) = $2.60

Mark-up percent is the proportion of total cost represented by profit. In some instances, the selling price may be set based on the comparison of the cost of a product with the price that the market will bear. For example, if a product offered to you costs $2 per unit and the market appears to support a selling price of $3 for a comparable product, then the selling price may be set at $3. These numbers can be used to determine the mark-up percent. In this case, the formula for determining the percentage mark-up is:

Mark-up Percent = (Selling Price – Total Cost) ÷ Total Cost
= ($3 – $2) ÷ $2
= $1 ÷ $2
= 50%

The notion of mark-up pricing should not be confused with profit margins and gross margins. The profit margin or GP margin is the dollar value difference in the selling price and total cost.

Therefore, the profit margin in the previous example is $1 per unit. Consequently, while the gross margin is usually thought of as revenue minus the cost of goods sold, the gross margin percent is the percentage of the selling price accounted for by the profit margin. Gross margin percent is calculated as the profit margin (difference in the selling price of $3 and the total cost of $2) divided by the selling price. The formula for this is:

Gross Margin Percent = (Selling Price – Total Cost) ÷ Selling Price
= ($3 – $2) ÷ $3
= 33%

Mark-up on the same would be selling price $3 ÷ cost price $2 = 1.50; that is, a mark-up of 50%. If you know the cost and want a mark-up of 50%, simply multiply the two to give you the retail price ($2 x 1.50 = $3). If you know the cost, and want to figure out your mark-up if you estimate that the item would sell much faster if it was priced at $2.50, divide the new proposed selling price ($2.50) by the cost price ($2.00), which gives 1.25 or 25% mark-up. The profit per item is 50¢ and the GP margin is 20% (retail – cost ÷ retail).

If a desired level of gross margin is known, the formula for gross margin can be modified to calculate the selling price. Using a desired percentage gross margin—in this case, 30%—the formula for calculating the selling price is:

$$\begin{aligned}\text{Selling Price} &= \text{Total Cost} \div (1 - \text{Gross Margin})\\ &= \$2 \div 0.70\\ &= \$2.85\end{aligned}$$

It is clear that the gross margin of 30% is different from the mark-up calculated earlier (25%), although both examples used a selling price of $3 and a total cost of $2. Mark-up and gross margins are often used in calculating and evaluating selling prices. However, they should not be used interchangeably for they are defined and calculated differently. What is noteworthy in these examples is that if the buyer only focuses on achieving her margin, say 30%, then the danger is that she may be happy enough to sell the items at $2.85. But, as mentioned earlier, if the market can take more, and $3 is just as acceptable, then without thinking, the buyer has lost a potential 15¢ each time this item is sold. It is always best to evaluate the item, determine what you think it can sell for, then calculate the cost to retail.

CALCULATION CLARIFICATION

- A mark-up is the percentage of the cost price which is added to it to get the selling price.

- GP margin is the percentage of the final selling price that is profit.

- Profit margin is the difference between selling price and total cost.

YET MORE ON MARK-UP

Mark-up or (mark-on) is an amount the retailer adds to the cost of goods to cover its operating expenses and the profit it wishes to make. Together, these three things comprise the final retail price.

Jacket	Cost of goods	:	$75
	Operating expenses	:	$15
	Profit	:	$10
	Retail Price	:	$100

The mark-up here is $25 and covers expenses of $15 and a balance of $10 as profit.

Mark-ups are often expressed as percentages; so, an item bought at a cost of $5 and sold at $10 has a mark-up of 100%. An item bought at $2 and sold at $3 has a mark-up of 50%.

- **Mark-up on retail**

In a buyer's terminology, most mark-ups are expressed as a percentage.

If a department sells goods to the value of $10,000 and these goods have an average mark-up of 35%, then the gross margin will be $3,500 ($10,000 x 35%) and the cost value is $6,500. Cost $6,500 ÷ 0.65 (35% margin) = retail $10,000.

If a shirt costs $20 and is priced to sell at $35, the mark-up is thus $15 (retail price – cost) and the mark-up percentage will be 75%. [Cost $20 x 1.75 (75%) = retail $35]

The margin as a percentage of the retail price is calculated by dividing the mark-up by the retail price: 15 ÷ 35 = 42.8%.

- **Mark-up on cost**

If an item costs $20 and the required mark-up is 15%, the retail price will be ($20 x 15%) + $20 = $23, a mark-up of $3.

FIND YOUR RETAIL PRICE

A figurine costs $75, to which you apply a mark-up of 55%:

Retail = Cost + Mark-up
= $75 + 41.25 (75 x 55%)
= $116.25

FIND YOUR COST PRICE

Your retail price is $80, which includes a mark-up of 40%. The cost price can be calculated in two ways:

(1) Cost = Retail – Mark-up
= 100% – 40%
= 60%
= 60% x $80
= $48

(2) Mark-up = 40 x 80/100
= 32
Cost price = 80 – 32
= $48

CUMULATIVE DEPARTMENTAL MARK-UP

When buyers buy an assortment of merchandise, the mark-up may vary from item to item. Buyers need to keep track of these mark-ups to ensure that, at the end of the month, the cumulative mark-up is well within plan. The cumulative mark-up is calculated as follows:

Mark-up on all goods bought = Retail price of all goods – cost of all goods

$$\text{Cumulative departmental mark-up} = \frac{\text{Mark-up on all goods bought}}{\text{Retail price of all goods bought}} \times 100\%$$

	Cost	Retail
Beginning stocks	$10,000	$15,000
Purchases	$5,000	$10,000
Total stocks	$15,000	$25,000

Mark-up = Retail – Cost
= 25,000 – 15,000 = $10,000

$$\text{Cumulative mark-up} = \frac{\$10{,}000}{\$25{,}000} \times 100\%$$
$$= 40\%$$

AVERAGE DEPARTMENTAL MARK-UP

The menswear buyer has an OTB plan to buy merchandise to the value of $24,000 at cost for the month. The purchase will be marked up with 38% on retail. His total retail price on the goods bought will therefore be $33,120 ($24,000 + [38% x $24,000]).

A couple of weeks on, he has placed his first set of orders for $11,000 at cost, which he will retail for $14,850.

Mark-up = $3,850 ($14,850 – $11,000)

$$\text{Percentage mark-up} = \frac{3{,}850}{11{,}000} \times 100\%$$
$$= 35\%$$

If he is to reach the overall retail price of $33,120, the balance of his OTB, $13,000, must be marked up to retail at $18,270 ($33,120 – $14,850), a dollar mark-up of $5,270. The percentage mark-up is therefore:

$$= \frac{5,270}{13,000} \times 100\% = 40.54\% \text{ (or 2.54\% more than the initial buys)}$$

The mark-up on the cost is $5,270 or 40.54%, which is what he needs to achieve if he is to complete the month's planned mark-up of 38%.

	Cost	Retail	Mark-up
Total planned buys	$24,000	$33,120	$9,120 (38%)
Purchases placed	$11,000	$14,850	$3,850 (35%)
Balance OTB at cost	$13,000	$18,270	$5,270 (40.54%)

The first buy, with a mark-up of $3,850, plus the second buy, with a mark-up of $5,270, gives a total mark-up value of $9,120, which is exactly what was planned for.

To make things a little more complicated, we also need to consider the department's opening stocks, which are added to the cumulative buys. So let's say that the buyer started the month with $2,000 worth of goods at cost, at a retail price of $2,800.

	Cost	Retail	Mark-up
Total planned buys	(+) $24,000	(+) $33,120	38%
Less opening stock	(–) $2,000	(–) $2,800	40%
Buys placed	(–) $11,000	(–) $14,850	35%
Balance required	$11,000	$15,470	40.64%

OVERALL MARK-UP

During the course of the season, it may be that some merchandise proves slow to move and has to be marked down. In such circumstances, the actual achieved mark-up is the overall mark-up.

Let's say that a buyer buys 100 frying pans at a cost of $20 each and marks them to sell at $50 each. The mark-up on each piece sold is $30 or 150%. At the end of the season, 20 pieces are left, and these are marked down to $30 each. What was the overall mark-up on this purchase if she sold the balance at $30?

$$
\begin{aligned}
\text{Initial mark-up} &= \text{original retail price} - \text{cost} \\
&= (100 \times \$50) - (100 \times \$20) \\
&= \$5{,}000 - \$2{,}000 \\
&= \$3{,}000
\end{aligned}
$$

$$
\begin{aligned}
\text{Initial \% mark-up} &= \frac{\text{initial mark-up}}{\text{original retail price}} \\
&= \frac{\$3{,}000}{\$5{,}000} \times 100\% \\
&= 60\%
\end{aligned}
$$

$$
\begin{aligned}
\text{Overall mark-up} &= \text{net sales} - \text{cost} \\
&= (80 \times \$50) + (20 \times \$30) - \$2{,}000 \\
&= \$2{,}600
\end{aligned}
$$

$$
\begin{aligned}
\text{Overall \% mark-up} &= \frac{\$2{,}600}{\$4{,}600} \times 100\% \\
&= 56.5\%
\end{aligned}
$$

In this case, the buyer's overall mark-up was 3.5% less than the original 60%.

PERCENTAGE CALCULATION MADE EASY

To find the percentage amount on a value, change the rate to a decimal and multiply by the base:
Percentage Amount = Rate x Base

Calculation 1

Find 30% of $200
Percentage amount = .30 x 200 = $60

Calculation 2

If during a promotion, you offer a 20% discount on a given item, how much discount will you be giving if the item retails at $299?

Percentage amount = .20 x $299
Percentage amount = $59.80
Actual sale price = $299 – $59.80
= $239.20

WHAT IS YOUR FACTOR?

Very often, a supplier will ask the buyer what her factor is. This enables the supplier to estimate what margins the buyer operates on, and figure out if his cost to retail will be commercial with this type of margin. He will not want the merchandise to be priced too high (and thus run the risk of selling fewer units), or too low (and thus run the risk of cheapening the brand in the consumers' eyes). Vendors will have an ideal price point in mind. By asking the buyer for her factor, the vendor can then calculate if the buyer's retail price fits his ideal price for the merchandise to be sold.

This is applicable regardless of vendor location. Both local and foreign vendors will want to know the "ballpark" retail price at which their goods/brand will be sold.

A factor is another way of expressing a margin. A factor of 2.5 (suggested industry best practice) indicates that the buyer operates with a margin of 60% and a mark-up of 150%.

Example: Applying a factor of 2.5 to an item costing \$50 gives a retail price of \$125 and a margin of 60% (\$125 – \$50 ÷ \$125). You can also say that cost \$50 ÷ 0.40 = retail \$125 and a margin of 60% (\$125 ÷ \$50 = 2.5). Once the buyer uses a factor of 2.5, she knows automatically that she is calculating the cost with a margin of 60%.

Another example would be: cost \$50 x factor 2.0 = retail \$100. \$100 – \$50 ÷ \$100 = 50% margin. So a factor of 2.0 = 50% margin. Once the buyer uses a factor of 2.0, she knows automatically that she is calculating the cost with a margin of 50%.

Applying a factor of 2.5 to a cost of, say, \$37.30 would give a retail price of \$93.25. This price is a bit odd and, customarily, the buyer might either round up to \$95.95 or down to \$89.99. If she opts for the latter, her margin will be: \$89.99 – \$37.30 ÷ \$89.99 = 58.55%. If, for the sake of this discussion, her budgeted planned margin for her division is 55%, she can comfortably use a rounded down retail price of \$89.99, in which case her factor will be 2.41 (\$89.99 ÷ \$37.30).

So when a vendor asks the buyer for her factor, she can comfortably say: "Anywhere between 2.2 and 2.8, depending on the item." (This translates to a margin no lower than 54.54% and no higher than 64.28%.) I would not recommend that buyers mention a factor of 2.0 because if their budgeted division margin is 50%, that becomes their threshold, and this information should not necessarily be discussed with the vendor for negotiation reasons. I urge buyers to always think in terms of buffers.

At retail for non-promotional items bought outright, the margin should be in the region of 50–60% to allow some margin buffer to mark down unsold balances later on. In my experience, buyers are not keen in utilizing full margins, thinking that if they use a lower margin, the merchandise will sell better, which is not true. *The price is right if the merchandise is deemed to have a high(er) perceived value vis-à-vis the price asked from the begining.*

CALCULATING GROSS MARGIN

You want to sell an item for $59.50, and the cost of the item is $35. What is your gross margin?

GM % = **$59.50 – $35** ÷ $59.50 = 41.1% margin

Quick mark-up calculation: $35 x 1.70 (mark-up)
= retail price $59.50

MARK-DOWNS

Mark-downs are used on goods that are slow to move and in hope that the new price will attract customers. Slow inventory ties up precious OTB dollars that could otherwise be used to buy productive lines. The degree to which prices are marked down will depend on how much has been sold at the regular price or, in other words, on the initial interest. The balance, the sizes and the time left in the season have some bearing on the estimated discount required to clear the goods.

DISCOUNTS

While discounts are also price reductions, they are viewed differently to mark-downs. In retail, a discount is calculated as a mark-down. For example, for a shirt selling at $69 and offered at less 20%, the discount of $13.80 at retail value will be registered as a mark-down. Discounts are often used to stimulate shoppers to buy and are often part of an event. It could be that the store is having a VIP (Very Important Purchasers) weekend, giving some discounts on selected items. Calculations are fairly straightforward. For example, a buyer for bed linen selects a range of imports for such a weekend event. His total inventory is $20,000 and will sell at a 15% discount during the weekend. All goods are sold.

$$\begin{aligned}\text{Dollar mark-down} &= \text{Original retail x percentage reduction}\\ &= \$20{,}000 \text{ x } 15\%\\ &= \$3{,}000\end{aligned}$$

$$\begin{aligned}\text{Sales value} &= \text{Original retail} - \text{dollar mark-down}\\ &= \$20{,}000 - \$3{,}000\\ &= \$17{,}000\end{aligned}$$

$$\begin{aligned}\text{Percentage mark-down on sales} &= \frac{\text{dollar mark-down}}{\text{amount sold}} \text{ x } 100\%\\ &= \frac{\$3{,}000}{\$17{,}000} \text{ x } 100\%\\ &= 17.6\%\end{aligned}$$

WEEKS OF STOCK ON HAND

To calculate your average stocks on hand, divide the retail value of the inventory by the average weekly sales for a specified period of time.

Let's say you have $10,000 worth of inventory in one product, and your total sales of that product for the previous six weeks is $15,000, the calculation would look like this:

$$\begin{aligned}\text{Average weekly sales} &= \$15{,}000 \div 6\\ &= \$2{,}500\end{aligned}$$

$$\begin{aligned}\text{Weeks of stock} &= \$10{,}000 \div \$2{,}500\\ &= 4\end{aligned}$$

This indicates that at the current rate of sales inventory will have to be replenished within the next four weeks.

LOCAL CONSIGNMENT AND LOCAL OUTRIGHT VS. INDENT MARGINS

The difference between a local margin and an indent margin (the margin on imported goods) is that the local margin is in most cases dictated by the vendors and this, in turn, will dictate the levels of profit margins their retail clients will have. This is usually because many of the goods will be on either consignment or concession terms. However, consignment or concession terms would include staffing and the inventory owned and managed by the vendor. This can be a benefit to the buyer, as shrinkage, mark-downs and staff costs are borne by the vendor.

In the case where the goods are bought on outright terms locally, the buyer will have some margin flexibility, though limited. This is because the same goods are usually sold to other retailers with a retail price suggested by the local vendor. The margin benefits from outright terms can be as much as 20% or more higher than goods on consignment. However, take note that outright terms mean that the buyer owns the inventory and has to use his own staff to sell the goods. The relative benefits have to be carefully weighed up.

An indent margin is higher because the buyer buys directly from the source and establishes the retail price, assuming full responsibility for the inventory and for providing the necessary sales staff. Depending on the store format, some retailers will operate solely with local vendors, others entirely with merchandise bought from various locations. Most retailers will have a mix of both. An indent margin is higher in most cases, primarily not only to cover the cost of importing the goods but also because of the "perceived" higher value these goods have compared with locally sourced merchandise. The other advantage is that these goods are, or should be, exclusive to the store importing them. For example, a blouse made in Singapore will have a "perceived" retail price while a blouse coming from Milan or Paris will have an entirely different value in the eyes of the consumer. Why? Usually, it is because of the styles, choice and quality of the fabrics used and, of course, the brand name.

I have seen many cases where buyers accept low margins from a local source and try to make up for it by loading on their indents. Indent merchandise comes at a cost—for travel, shipping and, in most cases, agents, all of which have to be factored into your margin calculations. Remember that exclusive indent is what management is looking for to secure points of difference vis-à-vis the competition and market positioning.

Indent goods should be given the best location on the floor and the sales staff should be given the best possible product-knowledge training. Anything less will result in poor sellthrough and lead to mark-downs which will have buyers conclude that buying locally is more profitable, which is not necessarily the case if the outright buys are managed properly.

MERCHANDISE REPLENISHMENT PROCEDURES

• Rate of sale

In some countries, this is known as "stocks on hand" and is measured in weeks. The average rate of weekly sales will give you an indication of the flow of goods required. If sales fluctuate during certain periods, recourse must be made to the records as well as alterations to the pre-planned projections. In other words, planned stocks must either be reduced or increased, depending on the sales strength or the lack thereof. A successful promotion may have had some spillover, generating unusual increases in the rate of sale of a particular basic item. For example, let's say your company determines that your weekly rate of sales in the menswear division should be 4 and, at the time you check your rate of sales, you have an inventory of $10,000 in business shirts, and your total sales for the previous six weeks amount to $18,000. The average weekly rate of sales is calculated by dividing total sales ($18,000) by the number of weeks (six), giving a figure of $3,000. The inventory ($10,000) is then divided by $3,000, to give a rate of sale of 3.3. This should tell you that if you don't re-order quickly, you will be very understocked.

• Delivery period

Estimate delivery schedules conservatively, from the time of ordering to the time the order hits your shelves. This should take account of the time it takes to place the order and the time the vendor takes to process it (existing stocks will normally take a few days, but if goods need to be produced, then a much longer time-frame is needed). Your estimate should also include the time it takes to price tag and/or EAS tag the goods, which can be done by the vendor, at your warehouse or at store level.

Let's say, for example, you are expecting goods to the value of $2,000, but these are late and the vendor cannot give you a firm delivery date. Your budget has an inventory of $10,000, and total sales of $15,000, or $2,500 per week, to cover a six-week sales period. Your ideal stock cover is 4. However, with the delay, your start-up inventory is only $8,000, which gives you just 3.2 weeks' cover ($8,000 ÷ $2,500), which represents just 80% of your ideal (3.2 ÷ 4). This would be a good time to negotiate a discount on the late delivery (if you still want the goods, that is).

- **Re-orders**

If a buyer has a high level of basic or staple goods that requires constant re-ordering, it is advisable to stagger the updating of these items. Say, for example, there are 1,000 SKUs on the basic stock-replenishment list, it is best to group them in lots of ten or 100 to be counted each day. These are then processed on a rolling basis.

- **Reserves**

To have sufficient reserves to meet planned sales, you need to compute the amount of stocks to be provided at each re-order. The need to prevent basic or staple goods from running out is more important than being temporarily overstocked.

- **Provisions**

The "provision" is calculated as the sum of projected sales for the re-order period, the sales for the delivery period and the reserves.

The quantities to be made available at any re-ordering point must be sufficient to cover expected sales during the lead time, as well as catering for the eventuality of additional sales during that period.

- **Open-to-buy (OTB)**

When goods-on-hand and on-order consist of a provision already made, their amounts should be subtracted from the calculated provision. The quantity that remains is the amount that should then be placed as a new order.

- **Tips**

Avoid scattering your buys: shallow and wide leads to high inventory that is quickly fragmented. Avoid styles or brands that duplicate each other. Concentrate on key items (historical best sellers). Eliminate lines or ranges that have contributed little to your sales.

Buy more frequently in smaller lots and with fewer styles

but in comprehensive size ratios. Carry small back-up stocks on key items (you don't want to run out of best-selling items in mid season). Get rid of slow-selling merchandise.

Remember: more merchandise does not mean more sales! Too much may confuse the customer, cause poor visual merchandising, be a heavy investment where mark-down dollars are at risk and cause duplication of styles or types of merchandise on the selling floor.

For the most part, retail buying involves a certain amount of creative thinking: whether it is in creating new ranges, dreaming up marketing campaigns or co-creating new business partnerships. Managing your numbers is a basic requirement, but imagination and creativity in merchandising is what makes many retail stores exciting to shop.

case study

Killing the merchandise with exaggerated mark-ups

This case is about a buyer who just didn't think things through.

A novice buyer, who was managing a small portfolio under the supervision of the division's merchandise manager, placed an order on a range of fabulous knits that our Italian agent had secured. The range was deemed sellable as the prices were very reasonable for that level of quality and styling. The merchandise came in as planned but the sell-through proved disappointing. The problem we found was ultimately linked to a local buy.

Here is what happened. During the same month that the Italian goods arrived, the buyer had accepted some promotional items from a local vendor at below budgeted margins to create a departmental promotion. Sales were strong, which meant that the more promotional goods he sold, the more the overall margins took a hit. Reading the performance report for that month, I noticed that while sales were 4% above budget, the month-end margin was down by 5%. Looking into the matter, I discovered that the source of the problem lay in the calculation of the overall margin.

The buyer's budgeted margin for the month was 38% and his sales were $58,000. By introducing the price promotion, he was confident that he could achieve his budgeted sales, and by lifting the retail price on his outright purchase of the Italian knits, he would be able to cover the low margins on the promotional items and reach his budgeted profit margins for the month. His calculations were as follows:

The landed cost of the 168 Italian knits was $105 per item (total cost being $17,640) and these were priced to sell at $199, a mark-up of $94, or 89.5%. This gave a total retail value of $33,432 and a total dollar mark-up of $15,792.

The buyer then changed the retail price on the Italian knits to give himself additional departmental margins to cover his price promotion. He increased the retail price to $299, giving him a mark-up on a cost of $194, or 185%. The total retail value was now $50,232 and the dollar mark-up was $32,592.

The initial gross profit margin was 47.24% ($94 ÷ $199 x 100%). With the introduction of the higher price, this increased to 64.88% ($194 ÷ $299 x 100%), an increase of 17.64% over the initial margin.

The buyer thought that by raising the margin on the Italian goods, it would more than cover the lower margin on the promotional items, which were bought in at a cost of $27.10 and sold at $39, a mark-up of 11.90, or 43.9%. However, the margin calculations showed that the actual margin of 30.5% (11.90 ÷ $39) was 7.5% below the budgeted margin of 38%.

The total number of units sold during the promotion was 734, giving a total retail value of $28,626 and a total mark-up of $8,734.60.

The budgeted sales for the month were $58,000 at a margin of 38%, giving a profit of $22,040. Actual sales were posted to be $60,320, or 4% above budget, and actual profits $20,938, or 5% less than budget. As the promotion was successful, it represented 49.3% of total month's sales and 40.03% of actual total profits. The problem was that the buyer did not sell sufficient merchandise at the high margin to make up the difference.

This also led to a related problem the following month when, as a result of the price increase for the Italian knits, the department's OTB (at time of price adjustment) was increased by $16,800. The merchandise proved to be slow selling and had to be marked down to clear.

The lesson to be learnt from all this is that without good judgment, it is difficult to make it as a buyer. Buyers are constantly making complex decisions in every aspect of their job. As they gain experience, many aspects become routine and creativity is part of buying and developing. However, logical thinking should prevail in all decision-making.

In this case the buyer created the problem by accepting promotional goods at a lower-than-budgeted margin in the hope of securing the top line—sales.

BUYERS' PLANNING

Whatever the forms of planning that buyers and merchandisers adopt, these can only ever be estimates and practical assumptions. They learn to work with uncertainty; with the "likelihood" of sales that could "possibly" yield increased business.

When buyers and MM/DMM do not agree on a plan, something is wrong somewhere, so each must state their points of view and come to a consensus.

In general, buyers are in a better position to appraise past mistakes and correct them. This normally leads to plans that demonstrate an improved performance. It could be, for example, that the buyer realizes that she ran out of girls' cotton blouses the previous season because her OTB allocation in this class was lower than actual demand. She would then allow for an increase in sales in that class to meet future demand.

These reflections should be backed up with strong presentations that are based on sound judgment, and on specific classifications only. If a buyer forecasts an increase in sales in a given department, she must then specify the class within this department which will yield the increase.

Experience has taught me over the years that success is not permanent, yet neither is failure fatal. However, failure to plan is failure, period! It is essential, therefore, to develop and achieve planned goals and budget targets in the following areas:

- Sales
- Mark-ups
- Mark-downs
- Shortages and shrinkage
- Improved return per square foot
- Improved stock turn
- Improved gross profit margins
- Any controllable elements affecting net profits.

BUDGETS AND FORECASTS

Sales forecasting is the most important part of retail planning. This is where the buyer can review lost opportunities, and look at potential opportunities and market trends. These plans consolidate all the possible components and influential factors that will have a bearing on your business.

Plans should first be prepared in draft form and amended as necessary in light of further consideration given to such things as resources, activities, market trends or market shifts, which have the potential to influence the business, and thus, must be taken into account.

Budgets also have to follow the cyclical nature of the business, allowing for holiday periods or seasonal trends which will determine when you will need to reduce or increase inventories.

BUDGET COMPONENTS

Outlined below are some of the components that are factored into budget planning.

- **Sales:** gross sales income from all sources, less allowances, rebates and returns

- **Cost of sales:** the cost of materials consumed to produce or support the sales. It customarily represents the opening stocks, materials purchased and consumed, less closing stocks

- **Gross profits:** the difference between sales and cost of sales

- **Variable expenses:** expenses created because of sales (examples might include gifts with purchase, free deliveries or, in some cases, rental of mall space outside the store for a specific launch or event)

- **Fixed expenses:** tied-down expenses which must be paid regardless of sales

- **Total expenses:** the sum of variable and fixed expenses

- **Pre-tax profits:** the difference between gross profit and total expenses.

BUDGETING EXAMPLES

The budgeting scenarios outlined in this section illustrate the different ways in which budget planning can be approached. The stores used in the examples are entirely fictitious and have no relation to businesses bearing similar names.

The company in question is a retail chain with five children's stores. For the coming quarter, management has forecast a sales budget of $225,000, which will be distributed amongst the five stores.

Budgets can be constructed in two ways: top-down or bottom-up. A top-down budget plan is when a total sales forecast is handed-down by management and where the buyer then allocates this into segments. These segments can be by store or by divisions within the store, and distributed according to the weight each division has within the department or store.

A bottom-up forecast is where a buyer analyzes the individual business segments, and draws up a plan according to the potential each has. Management may have given the general guidelines, expressed as a percentage increase in business or as a total sales amount to be achieved, but the buyer will plan increases/decreases according to the strengths and weaknesses of the business, usually by store, by division, and by merchandise class.

There are several ways in which the company can go about the budget-allocation process:

- **Plan A**

This is a generic top-down plan that distributes the $225,000 between the stores, on the basis of their respective historical performance. City Plaza, being the strongest performer, receives the highest budget; Mid Valley, being the weakest, receives the lowest.

Store			Total (%)	Total ($)
Plan A	A	Mid Valley	16%	$36,000
	B	Sunset Way	20%	$45,000
	C	Hong Li Mall	18%	$40,500
	D	City Plaza	26%	$58,500
	E	Orchard Link	20%	$45,000
		5	100%	$225,000

- **Plan B**

In Plan B, the $225,000 is distributed between the departments across the five stores. Again, this is a generic top-down application, based on historical data of the expected contribution of each department.

Store			Total (%)	Total ($)
Plan B	1	Girls & Teens	30%	$67,500
	2	Infants	50%	$112,500
	3	Little Boys	20%	$45,000
		Total	100%	$225,000

- **Plan C**

In Plan C, which uses a bottom-up approach, each outlet has been studied for its potential sales and the forecast is entered. The total buyer's forecast is estimated to be 4% more than management expectations and comes to $234,000, $9,000 more than the top-down plan given.

This is because in Plan C sales potential is factored in. In this case, a greater share of the budget increase has been allocated to Mid Valley, as there may be some historical data supporting a bigger growth in that store. The variation between Plan A and Plan C is shown in the last column.

Store			Original Distribution in Plan A		New Projection (%) 4% above management expectation	New Total Distribution	Variations
Plan C	A	Mid Valley	16%	$36,000	20.5%	$46,125	+10,125
	B	Sunset Way	20%	$45,000	19%	$42,750	-2,250
	C	Hong Li Mall	18%	$40,500	18.5%	$41,625	+1,125
	D	City Plaza	26%	$58,500	26%	$58,500	Same
	E	Orchard Link	20%	$45,000	20%	$45,000	Same
		5	100%	$225,000	**104%**	**$234,000**	**+$9,000**

Plan A expressed management's expectations of $225,000 according to each store's percentage of total business. In Plan C, the buyer has forecast better-than-expected results for two stores, Mid Valley and Hong Li Mall, which she believes can yield better growth.

- **Plan D**

Plan D, which is also a bottom-up plan, is based on forecasts of potential growth by department and merchandise classifications. This plan is, in my opinion, the best, as it gives the buyer the opportunity to evaluate each merchandise classification separately.

Here, the forecast is for higher growth in the Girls & Teens department, with an increase against the original plan of $10,500. Infants and Little Boys have been reduced by 3% and 0.5% respectively. In this plan, the buyer is signaling that Infants business will be stagnant and more purchasing power should be allocated to Girls & Teens, where the growth is expected.

Store			Total (%)	Total ($)
Plan D	1	Girls & Teens	33.5%	$78,000
	2	Infants	47%	$110,000
	3	Little Boys	19.5%	$46,000
		Total	100%	**$234,000**

- **Plan E**

Plan E is related to Plan A. It picks up the total budget for the Sunset Way store and re-distributes the allocated $45,000 to the three departments, in line with their respective historical contributions. In this scenario, the forecasters believe that the proportion of sales in all three departments will remain as forecast in the generic Plan B.

Sunset Way			Total (%)	Total ($)
Plan E	1	Girls & Teens	30%	$13,500
	2	Infants	50%	$22,500
	3	Little Boys	20%	$9,000
		Total	100%	**$45,000**
		Note: All departments follow the generic percentage allocations of Plan B		

- **Plan F**

Plan F is a build-up plan by department, mapping growth potential or variances in each department. In this case, for Mid Valley, it is estimated that the store will achieve an additional $3,000 above the original $45,000 (top-down) allocation. This re-assessment could be based on the view that it has the potential for increased sales due to better assortments and promotion plans.

Mid Valley			Total (%)	Total ($)
Plan F	1	Girls & Teens	33.3%	$16,000
	2	Infants	48%	$23,000
	3	Little Boys	18.7%	$9,000
		Total	100%	**$48,000**
		Each department is analyzed individually and estimates are planned according to potential		

DEPARTMENT STORE BUDGETS

In a department store, divisions or departments would have different criteria for their budgets. Typically, the children's department would carry wider ranges and assortments, and these would be planned by class and sub-classes in proportion to their respective sales strength. The same criteria on estimations and projections would apply. The graph below reflects a generic children's department, where there is no specific emphasis on boys or girls. Most stores would have separate departments based on gender, though the categories within each may be the same.

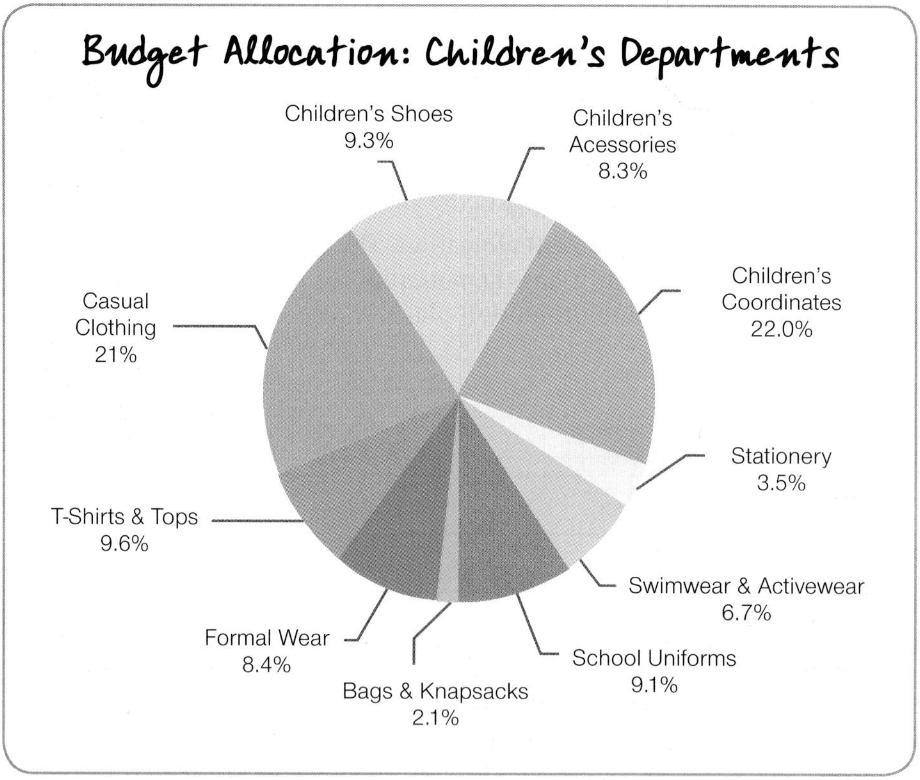

FAMILY-TREE PLANNER

A family-tree planner is a planning tool used to break down and allocate departmental OTB by class, brand, country of origin, price range or buying model. This is useful because it earmarks specific OTB for the major business models which may be operating in a particular department. For many retailers, buying in for a sale or a promotion can represent big business; this planner enables money to be segregated from the normal OTB by class and given its own OTB budget. This ensures that money is spent according to the planned business activities.

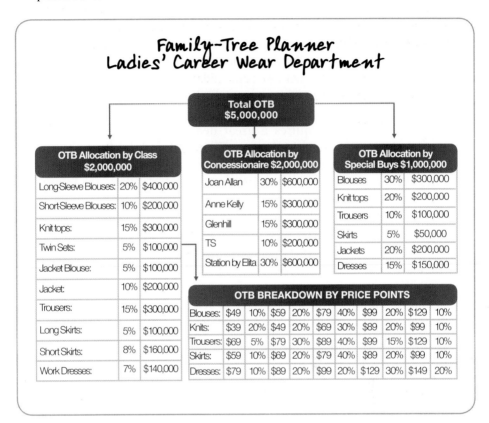

Family-Tree Planner
Ladies' Career Wear Department

Total OTB $5,000,000

OTB Allocation by Class $2,000,000		
Long-Sleeve Blouses:	20%	$400,000
Short-Sleeve Blouses:	10%	$200,000
Knit tops:	15%	$300,000
Twin Sets:	5%	$100,000
Jacket Blouse:	5%	$100,000
Jacket:	10%	$200,000
Trousers:	15%	$300,000
Long Skirts:	5%	$100,000
Short Skirts:	8%	$160,000
Work Dresses:	7%	$140,000

OTB Allocation by Concessionaire $2,000,000		
Joan Allan	30%	$600,000
Anne Kelly	15%	$300,000
Glenhill	15%	$300,000
TS	10%	$200,000
Station by Elita	30%	$600,000

OTB Allocation by Special Buys $1,000,000		
Blouses	30%	$300,000
Knit tops	20%	$200,000
Trousers	10%	$100,000
Skirts	5%	$50,000
Jackets	20%	$200,000
Dresses	15%	$150,000

OTB BREAKDOWN BY PRICE POINTS										
Blouses:	$49	10%	$59	20%	$79	40%	$99	20%	$129	10%
Knits:	$39	20%	$49	20%	$69	30%	$89	20%	$99	10%
Trousers:	$69	5%	$79	30%	$89	40%	$99	15%	$129	10%
Skirts:	$59	10%	$69	20%	$79	40%	$89	20%	$99	10%
Dresses:	$79	10%	$89	20%	$99	20%	$129	30%	$149	20%

This tool is also useful for departments or divisions where the emphasis is on private brands. In such cases, each brand is dealt with by individual range components and brand image.

Note, for example, on the chart below, that there's no OTB allocated for Claudia Massetti. This is because the brand identity and brand image of Claudia Massetti is high and thus not suitable for engineered-for-sale products. Engineered-for-sale products are lines or items bought at a lower-than-normal cost for the purposes of a specific sale or promotion. These can be stock-lot items bought from the usual source and, in the case of private-label fashion items, the cost saving is usually found in discounted fabrics that is then used to manufacture the promotional garments. In private-label manufacturing, the cut-make-trim (CMT) cost in producing the garments is fairly fixed. The savings are found in sourcing a lower-cost fabric that can be made into a garment that can retail at a lower price.

The chart below illustrates some brands with an OTB for both regular and promotional business, and other brands that are excluded for strategic reasons from partaking in discount-driven activities. Some brands, such as Claudia Massetti, have decided to retail at full regular price only, with season-end oddments to clear during the store's year-end sales; others occupy both segments of the business.

Retail business involving the creation of goods for specific promotions or sales requires a great deal of negotiation with the vendors. In some cases, the buyer will negotiate buying stock lots of merchandise at a discounted cost, or ask the vendor to produce "sales" ranges for an event, for which the vendor will source lower-priced fabrics or materials.

To illustrate this, let's say that the buyer plans a sale event for which she needs 1,000 blouses at 50% less than the normal price of \$79. She wants to buy these blouses to retail at no less than \$39.50 with a 30% mark-up and approaches one of her key vendors with this proposition, which he accepts. The vendor in turn approaches his fabric supplier and asks to see a selection of assorted fabrics suitable for blouses at under \$7 a meter. Depending on the styles, the amount of fabric required will vary (for example, a long-sleeve blouse will take up more fabric than a sleeveless blouse); however, with a lower fabric cost, the blouses can be produced at a profit and offered to the buyer at an acceptable cost price. The buyer selects the proposed styles and matches them to the fabrics and colors offered. The number of styles she chooses will be determined largely by the number of outlets or stores she is buying for: the more stores, the fewer styles, so that each style has sufficient quantities to sell.

Making opportunity buys in this way has a lot to do with the relationship the buyer has with her vendor, and he with his fabric supplier/manufacturer. Margins for both are usually lower than for regular ranges, so the true beneficiaries of these "best buys" are the customers.

Family-Tree Planner
Ladies Career Wear Department

Total OTB $5,000,000

OTB Allocation for Private Label Regular $4,000,000		
MLM	50%	$2,000,000
Gina Rossi	30%	$1,200,000
Claudia Massetti	20%	$800,000

OTB Allocation for Private Label Promotion $1,000,000		
MLM	50%	$500,000
Gina Rossi	50%	$500,000
Claudia Massetti	0%	$0

OTB Allocation by Class Regular $2,000,000	MLM 50%	G.R 30%	C.M. 20%	OTB Allocation by Class Promotional $1,000,000	MLM 60%	G.R 40%	C.M.
Long-Sleeve Blouses:	20%	10%	20%	Long-Sleeve Blouses:	20%	30%	0
Short-Sleeve Blouses:	10%	20%	10%	Short-Sleeve Blouses:	10%	20%	0
Knit tops:	15%	20%	0	Knit tops:	20%	30%	0
Twin Sets:	5%	0	0	Twin Sets:	10%	0	0
Jacket Blouse:	5%	0	0	Jacket Blouse:	0%	0	0
Jackets:	10%	0	20%	Jackets:	10%	0	0
Trousers:	15%	30%	20%	Trousers:	20%	0	0
Long Skirts:	5%	0	0	Long Skirts:	0%	0	0
Short skirts:	8%	20%	10%	Short skirts:	10%	0	0
Work Dresses:	7%	0	20%	Jacket Blouse:	0%	20%	0

SEASONAL PLANNING

For some retailers, the "season" is expressed as a spring–summer seasonal budget, which ranges from January to June, and an autumn–winter season, which ranges from July to December. Others follow the corporate calendar rather than the seasons and these are usually broken down into quarterly periods.

The next example showns the autumn–winter season budget for MLM Sports, which has three stores located in three different malls: Centrepoint, Suntec City and Raffles City. The month of July is included to indicate the beginning-of-month (BOM) stocks for August. The stock-holding of $550,000 determines how much the buyer will need to buy each month to generate the planned sales for all three stores.

Starting with the month of August, the chart explains how a buyer derives her OTB based on the sales she is planning, her stock levels throughout the season, the stock turn she expects to have and the mark-downs (MKD) she expects to need throughout the season.

As illustrated, the stores have planned a stock turn (see Chapter 4) of 3.0, and mark-downs of 0.5% against sales. This stock turn

Sales Budget Autumn-Winter 2008

Dept.7 - MLM Sports	Department Margin: 55%				Stock Turn: 3.0		MKD against Sales: 0.5%			
Season 2 - August - January	July	Aug	Sep	Oct	Nov	Dec	Jan	Feb	Total Season	
Sales % distribution by month		10%	15%	10%	15%	30%	20%		$2,200.0	
MKD % distribution by month		15%	10%	10%	10%	20%	35%		$110.0	
Centrepoint	% of Total Sales: 50%				Index 105					
Sales $		110	165	110	165	330	220	Average	$1,100.0	
MKD $		8.25	5.5	5.5	5.5	11	19.25	Stk	$55.0	
Purchases (OTB) $		180	150	150	200	280	200		$1,160.0	
BOM Stocks $	300	361.75	341.25	375.75	405.25	344.25	305.0	355.5	$2,100.0	3.1
Suntec City	% of Total Sales: 20%				Index 101					
Sales $		44	66	44	66	132	88	Average	$440.0	
MKD $		3.3	2.2	2.2	2.2	4.4	7.7	Stk	$22.0	
Purchases (OTB) $		80	80	50	100	100	80		$490.0	
BOM Stocks $	100	132.7	144.5	148.3	180.1	143.7	128.0	146.2	$877.3	3.0
Raffles City	% of Total Sales: 30%				Index 103					
Sales $		66	99	66	99	198	132	Average	$660.0	
MKD $		5.0	3.3	3.3	3.3	6.6	11.5	Stk	$33.0	
Purchases (OTB) $		100	80	120	200	165	80		$745.0	
BOM Stocks $	150	179.0	156.7	207.4	305.1	265.5	202.0	219.2	$1,315.7	3.0
TOTAL	% of Total Sales: 100%				Index 103					
Sales $		220	330	220	330	660	440		$2,200.0	
MKD $		16.55	11	11	11	22	38.45		$110.0	
Purchases (OTB) $		360	310	320	500	545	360		$2,225.0	
BOM Stocks $	550	673.45	642.45	731.45	890.45	753.45	635.0	721.0	$4,326.25	3.0

Note: Stock Figures expressed in $000s

may have been planned in line with management guidelines, based on historical data, or by the nature of the components bought in for these stores. A stock turn of 3.0 indicates a fairly high level of outright purchases involved.

Should a store operate with high levels of consignment or concessionaire business, the stock turn would be expected to be much higher. This is because the stocks are not reflected on the books as they belong to the vendor consigning the goods. Only the sales are planned and reflected in the budget.

Some retailers express a variance as an index derived from dividing the planned sales target by the previous year's figure—for example, sales target $103,000 ÷ previous year's sales $100,000 = index of 103. The other way of expressing the variance is to take the previous year's sales and multiply this by the planned percentage increase: $100,000 x 3% = $3,000 + $100,000 = $103,000. Likewise, when recording a decrease, the index would look like this: actual $100,000 ÷ target $103,000 = index of 0.97 or, as a percentage, this would be ($103,000 – $100,000 = $3,000 ÷ $100,000 = 0.03%) or –3%.

Sales Budget Autumn-Winter 2008

Dept.7 - MLM Sports	Department Margin: 55%				Stock Turn: 3.0		MKD against Sales: 0.5%		
Season 2 - August - January	July	Aug	Sep	Oct	Nov	Dec	Jan	Feb	Total Season
Sales % distribution by month		10%	15%	10%	15%	30%	20%		$2,200.0
MKD % distribution by month		15%	10%	10%	10%	20%	35%	Feb	$110.0

SALES PROJECTION

Sales are projected to have an index of 103 or a planned increase in sales of 3% over the previous year, for a total of $2,200,000. Multiplying $2,200,000 by 0.97% would give last year's figure at $2,134,000, indicating an increase of $66,000 for the current year.

TOTAL	% of Total Sales: 100%				Index 103					
Sales $		220	330	220	330	660	440	Average	$2,200.0	
MKD $		16.55	11	11	11	22	38.45		$110.0	
Purchases (OTB) $		360	310	320	500	545	360		$2,225.0	
BOM Stocks $	550	673.45	642.45	731.45	890.45	753.45	635.0	721.0	$4,326.25	3.0

STOCK TURN

When buying merchandise outright, it is important to also budget for the level of stocks on hand, which is expressed as a total stock turn for the season.

If a stock turn is planned to be 3 this would be calculated as follows: take the total month-end stocks ($4,326,250) and divide by six, which gives an average monthly stock turn of around $721,000. The total sales figure for all three stores ($2,200,000) is then divided by $721,000 to give a stock turn of 3.

Retailers want to know how many times their stocks turn as this has a relationship to their return on investment. Remember: in most cases, retailers rent their premises, and thus their primary investment will be in stocks—the merchandise they buy for re-sale at a profit.

MARK-DOWNS

The sales and mark-downs are allocated in monthly proportion and are expressed as a percentage of the total. These percentages also follow a historical sales curve; December and January have the highest percentage of sales, reflecting Christmas and year-end sales. (Obviously, the festive seasons vary in different parts of the world. In Indonesia, for example, Ramadan or Hari Raya is the most celebrated season; in Singapore, both Christmas and Chinese New Year are big months; in India, Deepavali (Diwali) generates the highest turnover in the year, and so on.)

Dept.7 - MLM Sports	Department Margin: 55%				Stock Turn: 3.0		MKD against Sales: 0.5%		
Season 2 - August - January	July	Aug	Sep	Oct	Nov	Dec	Jan	Feb	Total Season
Sales % distribution by month		10%	15%	10%	15%	30%	20%		$2,200.0
MKD % distribution by Month		15%	10%	10%	10%	20%	35%	Feb	$110.0

The sales and mark-downs are divided between three stores, Centrepoint receiving 50%, Raffles City 30%, and Suntec City 20% of the total budget. Each store is also given a percentage allocation for sales and mark-downs each month (10% of total sales for August, 15% for September, 10% for October, and so on).

Dept.7 - MLM Sports	Department Margin: 55%				Stock Turn: 3.0		MKD against Sales: 0.5%			
Season 2 - August - January	July	Aug	Sep	Oct	Nov	Dec	Jan	Feb	Total Season	
Sales % distribution by month		10%	15%	10%	15%	30%	20%		$2,200.0	
MKD % distribution by month		15%	10%	10%	10%	20%	35%		$110.0	
Centrepoint	% of Total Sales: 50%				Index 105					
Sales $		110	165	110	165	330	220	Average	$1,100.0	
MKD $		8.25	5.5	5.5	5.5	11	19.25	Stk	$55.0	
Purchases (OTB) $		180	150	150	200	280	200		$1,160.0	
BOM Stocks $	300	361.75	341.25	375.75	405.25	344.25	305.0	355.5	$2,100.0	3.1
Suntec City	% of Total Sales: 20%				Index 101					
Sales $		44	66	44	66	132	88	Average	$440.0	
MKD $		3.3	2.2	2.2	2.2	4.4	7.7	Stk	$22.0	
Purchases (OTB) $		80	80	50	100	100	80		$490.0	
BOM Stocks $	100	132.7	144.5	148.3	180.1	143.7	128.0	146.2	$877.3	3.0
Raffles City	% of Total Sales: 30%				Index 103					
Sales $		66	99	66	99	198	132	Average	$660.0	
MKD $		5.0	3.3	3.3	3.3	6.6	11.5	Stk	$22.0	
Purchases (OTB) $		100	80	120	200	165	80		$490.0	
BOM Stocks $	150	179.0	156.7	207.4	305.1	265.5	202.0	219.2	$1315.7	3.0

OPEN-TO-BUY (OTB) PLAN

The OTB or purchases are linked to the desired month-end planned stocks, ensuring sufficient stocks to generate the next month's planned sales. Let's take the month of October for Centrepoint as an example. Here, the month-end stocks are $375,750 to cover November's planned sales of $165,000 and mark-downs of $5,500.

Dept.7 - MLM Sports	Department Margin: 55%				Stock Turn: 3.0		MKD against Sales: 0.5%		
Season 2 - August - January	July	Aug	Sep	Oct	Nov	Dec	Jan	Feb	Total Season
Sales % distribution by month		10%	15%	10%	15%	30%	20%		$2,200.0
MKD % distribution by month		15%	10%	10%	10%	20%	35%	Feb	$110.0
Centrepoint	% of Total Sales: 50%				Index 105				
Sales $		110	165	110	165	330	220	Average	$1,100.0
MKD $		8.25	5.5	5.5	5.5	11	19.25	Stk	$55.0
Purchases (OTB) $		180	150	150	200	280	200		$1,160.0
BOM Stocks $	100	361.75	341.25	375.75	405.25	344.25	305.0	355.5	$2,100.0 3.1

As the following chart shows, the OTB for the month of November is, on average, higher than the previous months. This is because more goods need to be planned and delivered in preparation for December's sales of $300,000. Buying $200,000 in November gives the store a beginning-of-month (BOM) stock holding of $405,250 to generate planned sales of $330,000.

Dept.7 - MLM Sports	Department Margin: 55%				Stock Turn: 3.0		MKD against Sales: 0.5%		
Season 2 - August - January	July	Aug	Sep	Oct	Nov	Dec	Jan	Feb	Total Season
Sales % distribution by month		10%	15%	10%	15%	30%	20%		$2,200.0
MKD % distribution by month		15%	10%	10%	10%	20%	35%		$110.0
Centrepoint	% of Total Sales: 50%				Index 105				
Sales $		110	165	110	165	330	220	Average	$1,100.0
MKD $		8.25	5.5	5.5	5.5	11	19.25	Stk	$55.0
Purchases (OTB) $		180	150	150	200	280	200		$1,160.0
BOM Stocks $	300	361.75	341.25	375.75	405.25	344.25	305.0	355.5	$2,100.0 3.1

To re-cap, then: for the Centrepoint store, the total plan begins with the month of August and goes as follows:

Opening Stocks (month-end stocks July)	$300,000
Planned Sales (August)	$110,000
Planned Mark-downs	$8,250
Planned OTB	$180,000
Month-end stocks	$361,750

The month-end stocks for August automatically become the BOM stocks on hand for September. The same applies when all three stores are combined:

Month-end stocks July $550,000 = August opening stocks – Sales $220,000 – Mark-downs $16,550 + Planned purchases $360,000 = September's BOM $673,450.

Sales Budget Autumn-Winter 2008

Dept.7 - MLM Sports	Department Margin: 55%				Stock Turn: 3.0		MKD against Sales: 0.5%			
Season 2 - August - January	July	Aug	Sep	Oct	Nov	Dec	Jan	Feb	Total Season	
Sales % distribution by month		10%	15%	10%	15%	30%	20%		$2,200.0	
MKD % distribution by month		15%	10%	10%	10%	20%	35%		$110.0	
Centrepoint	% of Total Sales: 50%				Index 105					
Sales $		110	165	110	165	330	220	Average	$1,100.0	
MKD $		8.25	5.5	5.5	5.5	11	19.25	Stk	$55.0	
Purchases (OTB) $		180	150	150	200	280	200		$1,160.0	
BOM Stocks $	300	361.75	341.25	375.75	405.25	344.25	305.0	355.5	$2,100.0	3.1
Suntec City	% of Total Sales: 20%				Index 101					
Sales $		44	66	44	66	132	88	Average	$440.0	
MKD $		3.3	2.2	2.2	2.2	4.4	7.7	Stk	$22.0	
Purchases (OTB) $		80	80	50	100	100	80		$490.0	
BOM Stocks $	100	132.7	144.5	148.3	180.1	143.7	128.0	146.2	$877.3	3.0
Raffles City	% of Total Sales: 30%				Index 103					
Sales $		66	99	66	99	198	132	Average	$660.0	
MKD $		5.0	3.3	3.3	3.3	6.6	11.5	Stk	$22.0	
Purchases (OTB) $		100	80	120	200	165	80		$490.0	
BOM Stocks $	150	179.0	156.7	207.4	305.1	265.5	202.0	219.2	$1315.7	3.0
TOTAL	% of Total Sales: 100%				Index 103					
Sales $		220	330	220	330	660	440		$2,200.0	
MKD $		16.55	11	11	11	22	38.45		$110.0	
Purchases (OTB) $		360	310	320	500	545	360		$2,225.0	
BOM Stocks $	550	673.45	642.45	731.45	890.45	753.45	635.0	721.0	$4,326.25	3.0

OPEN-TO-BUY

As the season wears on, the plan is activated with actual data. Let's have a look at the month of September for Centrepoint.

Month – September	Original Plan	Revised (future plan)	
Opening Stocks	$361,750	$361,750	
Sales	$165,000	$160,000	(–$5,000)
Planned MKD	$5,500	$5,500	
Purchases	$150,000	$140,000	(–$10,000)
Month-end stocks	$341,250	$336,250	(–$5,000)

When the actual sales show that the department is $5,000 below plan, the first thing the buyer must do is to review the purchases. If the OTB for that month had, for example, orders worth $135,000 already, it then means that with the revised actual sales, the buyer is left with an OTB balance of only $5,000 for the month.

If the actual sales are further reduced by an additional $5,000, to $155,000, and the buyer had placed orders worth $135,000 before month end, this will mean that the OTB is overbought (by $5,000). In the simulation shown above, the sales are projected to be below original plan, to $160,000, and the purchases are adjusted down from $150,000 to $140,000, projecting month-end stocks of $336,250. Had the buyer not adjusted her purchases in this way, the month-end stocks would have been $346,250, or $5,000 over the planned figure. If this pattern had continued throughout the season, the department would have been overstocked, showing a lower-than-planned stock turn, with a possibility of incurring additional mark-downs to get rid of slow-selling goods, all of which depletes profits.

It is therefore strongly advisable that you *always* keep OTB reserves as a buffer in the eventuality of lower-than-planned sales; maintaining a healthy stock-holding is key.

When your OTB is "off", action is needed. As mentioned earlier, budgets and plans are based on suppositions, on educated guesses. Your OTB can be critically off for a number of reasons, including wrong forecasting or planning errors; overly optimistic forecasting; unseemly distribution by class, resulting in wrong merchandise mix; buying mistakes (wrong styles, colors, size specs, design, price); unsuccessful promotions; unexpected successful promotions (customer demand greater than planned); or a failure to place timely purchase orders. It could be any one or a combination of these factors, or it could be the result of late deliveries (see the case study at the end of this chapter).

- **Action in response to late shipments**

There comes a time when buyers need to make decisions on whether to accept or reject late deliveries. Advertised merchandise should have much earlier delivery dates to counter any eventuality of late shipments. If goods are late, even with such provisions in place, the penalty should be severe, and the validity of such suppliers questioned.

As a rule of thumb, you should view each delay as having a cost. One week's delay means one week fewer in which to sell the goods, and in such circumstances, it may be reasonable to charge the vendor for the delay on a sliding scale: say, one week late = 5% discount on the invoice; two weeks, 10%; three weeks, 20%; and so on.

In fact, any delay later than this should lead to a cancellation of the order; unless your business is desperate for the goods, in which case, you may wish to do one of the following:

• Reduce initial quantities to reflect the reduced selling period

• Negotiate a reduction in the cost of the goods

• Ask for a mark-down on goods not sold within an agreed time period.

Negotiate from a position of strength. The more meaningful your business is with these vendors, the more likely it is you will be able to negotiate a decent deal that will at least cover some of your potential losses arising from late shipment.

I would also caution buyers to be careful to not succumb to time pressure. Your vendor may offer you substitute styles or merchandise just to avoid a penalty or to fulfill your order. Unless these substitutes are just as good or better, I would not advise taking that route. It is a compromise which, once taken, you will have to live with and with no restitution should these goods not sell as well as expected.

If your OTB is over plan, but under plan in a critical classification, seek approval from your MM/DMM to override the plan.

OTB Buffer

In advising my buyers to keep enough OTB reserves, I used to say: "Always keep OTB money aside. You never know when someone will show up with a lamb with five legs!" What I meant by this was a situation where a supplier offers a fantastic buy but the buyer is unable to do anything about it because the OTB has been used up or, worse still, the buyer is overbought.

To my surprise, flying from Indonesia in 2006, I came across an in-flight magazine illustrating the world's first example of a lamb with five legs. I was thrilled when I saw it: after all those years of using a made-up metaphor, it now actually exists...his name is Jordan. So from now on, I can say: "Always keep OTB money aside. You never know when someone shows up with a Jordan!"

case study

Late deliveries

One December morning, I happened to be walking through the buyers' office. I could not help but overhear that one of the buyers was having an agitated telephone conversation with one of her suppliers.

I hand-signaled to her: What's going on? She cupped the phone and briefly told me that the promotional Christmas gowns from the vendor were going to be delayed by two weeks. I asked her to pass me the phone and said the following: "What do you mean the goods will be late by another two weeks?! Who needs Christmas trees after Christmas?! Ship by this week or don't ship at all."

A burst of laughter could be heard throughout the office. The buyers just loved it. The goods did arrive on time, but only just.

I bumped into that vendor a few months later. He apologized and admitted that he had been busy juggling many customers' orders at the time, and had mistakenly disregarded the information stated on the PO about this particular order being intended for a Christmas promotion. He confessed that he had learnt a valuable lesson.

The Art of Retail Buying

7 ASSORTMENT PLANNING

ASSORTMENT PLANNING

Implementing an effective assortment-planning process may be the key to offering the right products to the right customers.

The traditional notion of having the right product, in the right place, at the right time, in the right quality and at the right price, still holds true in today's retail marketplace, but with one important change. Retailers—whether traditional or not—must have a compelling selection of merchandise for the right customer as well.

To determine the best course of action for reaching the right customers, it is important to examine one of the most important factors in the merchandising process: **assortment planning**. This involves asking questions: Which product? How much of it? What colors? What sizes? Where to place it? Who is the target customer? The answers to all of these will influence product selection, price, timing and micro-merchandising.

Extinguishing delivery fires and meeting marketing and financial planning obligations use up valuable time, forcing companies to take the easy approach to merchandising by repeating assortment breadth and depth from previous seasons, creating store assortments based on store volume and ranking items by sales volume alone.

Yet, to attract the right customer in today's increasingly competitive environment, assortment planning must focus on creating appropriate product breadth and depth based on the customer's desires and shopping patterns, taking into account lifestyles, climates and trends.

Furthermore, assortment planning must present a compelling mix of products to illustrate the company's strategic vision.

- **Product attributes**

This set of parameters helps the retailer relate to the customer, by factoring into the plan such things as brand, vendor, fabric, silhouette, shapes, price points, and themes.

These parameters enable the planner to tailor the assortment and build the proper relationships among the various components. For example, the planner can determine the right percentage of brands, the right quantity of each brand, and similar calculations.

- **Store structure and characteristics**

Before product assortments can be defined, the planner must take the critical step of categorizing stores according to size, volume, type, climate and customer type. The store characteristics are pivotal in micro-marketing and they also support distribution to the stores.

- **Time dimension/product seasonality**

The time dimension for an assortment plan considers the usual week, month and season definition, along with product transition and crossover between seasons.

Assortment planning also needs smaller time periods or mini-seasons such as back-to-school, holiday, or season-end clearance. These overlapping time periods consider events and/or time periods that help define the product characteristics needed to address customer demand.

PLANNING BY PRODUCT

- **Space dimensions/space utilization**

As the assortment plan develops, it allocates available space based on the product definition. Factors such as the number of styles and the quantities of each style will affect space utilization.

Product dimensions, product density, product display requirements, store structure, store layout, store "look" and visual merchandising all affect the space plan and, consequently, the assortment plan as well.

Remember: product planning has to work back to your space plan and space allocation, which in turn affects–positively *or* negatively–your sales and profit per square foot.

PLANNING WITH SYSTEMS

- **Managing the volume of detail**

To handle all of the calculations in these key areas, assortment planning systems that go beyond simple spread-sheets are becoming available for retailers. Built in to these are the "what-if?" scenarios necessary in today's assortment planning process. As these systems can churn through the calculations in all of these areas, retailers are better able to develop a good assortment plan.

Treat these systems as your best friend: no one thing will support you as well or with as much accurate information as your computerized data.

TEN STEPS TO ASSORTMENT PLANNING: APPLICABLE TO FASHION GARMENTS AND ACCESSORIES, HOUSEHOLD, BED LINEN AND HOME

- **Classification and type**

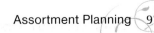

Planning by classification–for example, business wear, sportswear, career wear; or household goods, bowls, stemware–requires fewer changes than classifying according to individual styles.

Analyzing past sales by classification helps in planning future sales as a generic designation, where type has a more specific selection factor within the class.

In the "business shirt" class, for example, you may find sub-categories or types such as "formal—button-down" or "formal—spread collar." The buyers may find that more button-downs were sold and may use this information in planning the assortments, using, say, 70% button-downs and 30% spread collars in their planning. However, analysis is required here since actual sales of regular collars may not reflect potential demand. It may be that sales of this type of shirt remained low because fewer were carried in stock. Repeating this plan may cause lost sales. The same is applicable for an array of merchandise throughout retail assortments.

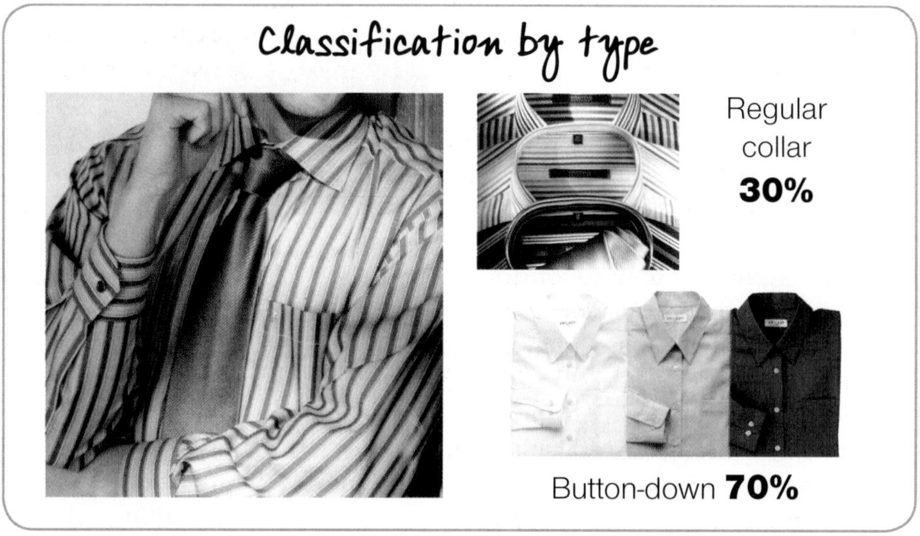

- **Planning by brand**

When planning for a brand, all items within it should be summarized to enable an analysis of the brand as a whole. It is impossible to carry all brands, so be selective and try to stick to these plans.

There will be many reasons why buyers are tempted to add in more than planned brands. It could be, for example, that a buyer is approached to carry an additional brand because it has a product that is going to be supported by heavy national advertising, generating potentially high customer demands. Though tempting, this could create several problems for a zealous buyer focusing on stimulating additional sales alone. Unless pre-planned, this can lead to space-availability problems, slower-than-planned sales on existing merchandise and a pile-up of slow-selling odds and ends this new brand may incur.

Determine which brands are best suited for your store and, within each, which product types and which price points sell best. You may also determine how many you want to carry—you don't necessarily need them all.

Designer names or luxury brands as part of your assortment

Designer names are the "rich relatives" of branded goods and serve as an effective point of reference that lends prestige to the store. While they may have a loyal following, unless your store is positioned in the high end, it would be advisable to do some market research into how commercial they are before committing to them because such operations are expensive and affordable only to the makers or stores that can generate enough sales to realize the inherent profits.

Consequently, a store's prestige derives partly from the number of such lines it can assemble and maintain, as Selfridges in London clearly demonstrates.

- **Assortments by price range**

Price is a stable selection factor and sales analysis provides good guidelines for planning. Increases or decreases resulting from outside pressures can cause havoc in your planning. Such pressures can come from new production technology driving costs, and therefore consumer prices, downwards, personal computers being a good example of this. But the opposite happens when special items or items in demand become scarce.

One word of advice: Never let your calculator determine the selling price. It's what the market can or cannot take and/or the value of the item which should be the sole determinants of price.

What many buyers do is to ask for the cost of the item and apply a pre-determined factor—which may include shipping, agent's fees or currency fluctuations, and their desired margin—to arrive at a retail price. This is the wrong way to go about it. Rather, what you should do is ask yourself how much your customers would be willing to pay for this item if your planned mark-up needs to be 40%.

For the sake of illustration, let's say that you estimate that the price of the item you are considering would have a perceived price of $39.90

With this price in mind, you then ask the supplier for the cost and, after applying your factor, the price lands at $53. (This factor includes your margin, freight costs, agent fees in case of any or any other additional costs attaching to a retail price.)

You then ask yourself whether that price would be competitive and if your customers would be willing to pay that much. The answer will most likely be no, because setting a retail price at $13.10 above the value you first judged the item to be worth is a path that can lead to slow-moving goods and potential future mark-downs.

In this instance, you may want to negotiate a better cost, bringing you closer to the ideal retail price of $39.90, but keeping to your planned margin.

If this is not possible, you should try to find a vendor selling a similar item at a cost which, with a mark-up of 40%, gives you your ideal price point of $39.90. This is calculated using the formula: Cost = Retail – Mark-up. Your ideal retail price is $39.90 with a mark-up of 40%, giving you a cost of $23.94 and a mark-up of $15.96.

The first cost price quoted by the vendor equates to a retail price of $53 ($31.80 cost price + $21.20 mark-up), which you deem too high for this item. The cost in this instance is $7.86 more than you are willing to pay. (Buyers may also use a factor which includes their ideal mark-up for quick calculations. The factor is calculated by dividing the retail price by the cost of goods. In this case, the factor is 1.667). Cost of goods: $31.80 x 1.667 = $53.01 or cost of goods $23.94 x 1.667 = $39.90. Within the factor of 1.667 lies a gross margin of 40%.

Should you want to increase the margin on a given item to, say, 50% or more then, the calculation is as follows: $49 – $23.94 ÷ $49 = 51.1% margin. In this case, your calculation factor will be 2 ($49 ÷ $23.94 = 2).

On the other side of the scale, using the same methodology of evaluating the item's worth, you may find that, after allowing for the supplier's cost and applying your factor, the item comes in cheaper than the $39.90 you had deemed your customers would be prepared to pay. In such cases, and again assuming that you know your customer profile well, my advice would be to price it at $39.90 and enjoy a better margin.

Let's say in this instance, the item costs $14.99. If you decide to sell it at $39.90, rather than the first calculated $25, your mark-up would be $24.91 ($39.90 – $14.99), or 62.43% ($24.91 ÷ $39.90)—22.43% higher than planned:

Depending on how your internal systems are set up, I am a great advocate of using what I call the checkbook system, which works through a balancing process through which mark-ups are used to offset necessary mark-downs within a department, as illustrated below.

Mark-up

Description	Article No.	SKU	Quantity	Unit Price	Mark-up	Variance	Total
Cotton Blouse	13970	150221369	54 pcs	$25.00	$39.00	$14.00	$756
Total MU							**$756**

Mark-down

Description	Article No.	SKU	Quantity	Unit Price	Mark-up	Variance	Total
Knit Tops	99-365	150225963	30 pcs	$29.00	$15.00	$14.00	$420
Jeans	12074/13	150223100	16 pcs	$59.00	$39.00	$20.00	$320
Total MKD							**$740**

We establish that an item bought at $25 is meeting the budgeted margin for the department. The goods came in at a retail price of $25 per unit, and we marked them up to retail at $39 (which was determined to be a good price for this item), giving an overall mark-up value of $756. Within the same week, however, there are some slow-moving items which are marked down, to a value of $740, to enable the stocks to be cleared. Here, the mark-up annuls the mark-down.

This seems to me to be a sensible way of going about things but, depending on their systems and procedures, many retail stores treat mark-downs separately and measure total used mark-downs against turnover. However, by utilizing mark-ups in the way I suggest, you do not erode your planned mark-down reserves and get to clear poor-performing merchandise, and either ease up your OTB or gain a better-than-budgeted margin.

The other instance where the checkbook system is used is when buyers engineer sales or promotional buys. In many Asian countries, for a product to be sold with a "before and now" price, the merchandise must have been on the shelves for at least a month or two before this can happen.

So, let's say that a buyer buys an assortment of "sales" merchandise from one of her regular suppliers. The intended retail price for the planned sales is $19. The items bought had a regular value of between $39 and $59. This provides a chance to engineer these goods at the regular price during this pre-sale period.

For the sake of this illustration, we assume that the buyer bought 300 pieces that can be split into three price groups: 100 at $39, 100 at $49 and 100 at $59. The buyer can opt to engineer the entire consignment to the full price, enjoying a mark-up value of $9,000

(100 x $20 + 100 x $30 + 100 x $40 = $9,000), but by doing this, she will have to mark down the balance of the unsold merchandise before the sales. I do not recommend this, for a couple of reasons.

The buyer may show a higher-than-budgeted margin during the month of the mark-up, followed by a lower margin the following month, where the mark-down is necessary, creating a margin "spike" for the following year's budgeted margin plan. Secondly, by marking up the full consignment, you don't know how much money you really have available for mark-downs. Are you going to sell 30%, 40% or 50% at full price? We need to anticipate that in most cases, only a portion will be sold at the high price and the balance will have to go back to the intended $19, using mark-downs.

The other way of going about things would be for the buyer to mark up only the number of pieces she is confident of selling during the pre-sale period. If she feels she can sell 30 pieces per price group, then she would enjoy a mark-up of $2,700 (30 x $20 + 30 x $30 + 30 x $40 = $2,700), and these extra dollars can be better managed to conduct mark-downs on problem stocks or, optionally, to enjoy a better margin, although not forgetting the spike this will create.

The third option is to do nothing at all, acquiring the sales goods at the intended $19 just in time for the event. This way, there are no problems but there is no gain either.

When determining your price ranges for regular products, it is important to take the store's pricing policies and positioning into consideration. A Marks & Spencer store will work on price parameters different from a Debenham's in the U.K., or a Tangs store will be different from a John Little's in Singapore. This is determined by the ranges or brands the stores carry. Having well-known brands commands a certain price level, and you may confuse your customers if you also carry budget price points at the same time (outside sales periods, that is).

Everyday discounting

Your store's clear positioning is important. Unless it is a hypermarket, frequently discounting your regular goods can put the store's "integrity" in jeopardy. The number of discounting events during the year must be managed. A branded store may opt to have two season-end sales per year; but a department store would have more. As we saw in Chapter 6, most stores operate with a spring-summer and an autumn-winter season and, for stores selling fashion goods, merchandise from one season will be cleared to make way for the next one. In addition, they may opt to create two mid-season price promotions. These could be category driven, such as a "white sale" to sell discounted bed linen, and/or, for the bigger department stores, card-member events or a credit card event for holders of Visa, Master or Amex cards. These would normally offer a store-wide discount of 10% to 20%.

A hypermarket would typically have monthly price reductions, which are not necessarily advertised as a matter of course, and a small shop may have yearly sales, with some special offers to boost sales of a range or item in mid year.

In Asia, it is common for small shops to be open to negotiation, with possible price cuts varying from 10% to as much as 30%. It has to be remembered, though, that while the discount sounds great, the pre-negotiation price is also many times higher than it should be. In most cases, both the retailer and the customer enjoy the bargaining as part of the shopping experience.

Application of loss leaders

Loss leaders are basic items with high sales rates that can be used by almost any kind of retail format as a vehicle to bring in the crowds.

Recently, I saw a newspaper ad for inexpensive flat-screen TVs. It also offered a $200 trade-in for the customer's old TV, irrespective of brand or condition. I went along expecting to come away with a great bargain but left paying more. Why? Because the picture on the advertised TV paled by comparison with the more-expensive, high-resolution models next to it, and the shop offered only a six-month guarantee. Though the price we paid for ours was decent, it was not what got us into the store in the first place. The loss-leader in this case did not have the quality expected.

One of the more successful practices that we had in our stores was to generate a "buildup" on the first morning of our sales by using loss leaders we called "9:30 Specials." The store opened an hour earlier than usual, allowing the early birds to rush in for these super bargains. Each main department would have at least one super-special and all goods had to be sold within a couple of hours for the event to be considered successful.

Our 9:30 Specials—a mix of bought-in merchandise and slow-moving overstocked items were offered at steep discounts, generally below cost, in order to attract a rush to the store. The intent of this pricing strategy is not just to have the customer buy the loss-leader items, but also to purchase other products that are not as heavily discounted.

Creating a rush generated by loss leaders is one sure way of getting customers into the store. Our sales would normally start on a Thursday and last for a six-week period; as much as 45% of our revenues for these events would be generated during the first four days.

Sales and price events are an integral part of running a retail business. Some retailers use them simply to clear season-end oddments; others both clear their oddments and mark-down items as well as buy in for the event. Stores that carry high levels of consignment goods would also encourage these brands to participate, to broaden the range of goods on offer, and make the sale more interesting and worthwhile for shoppers.

Prices are also determined by the gross profit margins that you, as a buyer, are responsible for. So, while working out the cost-to-retail prices, look at the figure you arrive at and evaluate if it is right for the specific item or product.

Instead of compromising on a price-fit, you should look at reducing the cost. Negotiate a better cost price to fit an ideal retail price.

Price endings (the last digit of the price) are also important and should be revised frequently. Keeping competition in mind, it is a waste of mark-up to price an item at $5.95 when you could just as well price it at $5.99 and sell just as effectively. You will be surprised: these small differences are more significant to the store than to its customers.

• Assortment planning by material/fabrics

Some buyers structure their planning around materials or fabrics in accordance with customer demand and according to the season (summer/winter). Materials may be categorized as:

• silk, wool, cotton, linen, micro fiber, polyester blends, denims, and so on

• lightweight, medium weight, heavy weight, soft, medium stiff, and so on

• dull, bright, shiny, plain, small patterns, checks, smooth, textured, and so on.

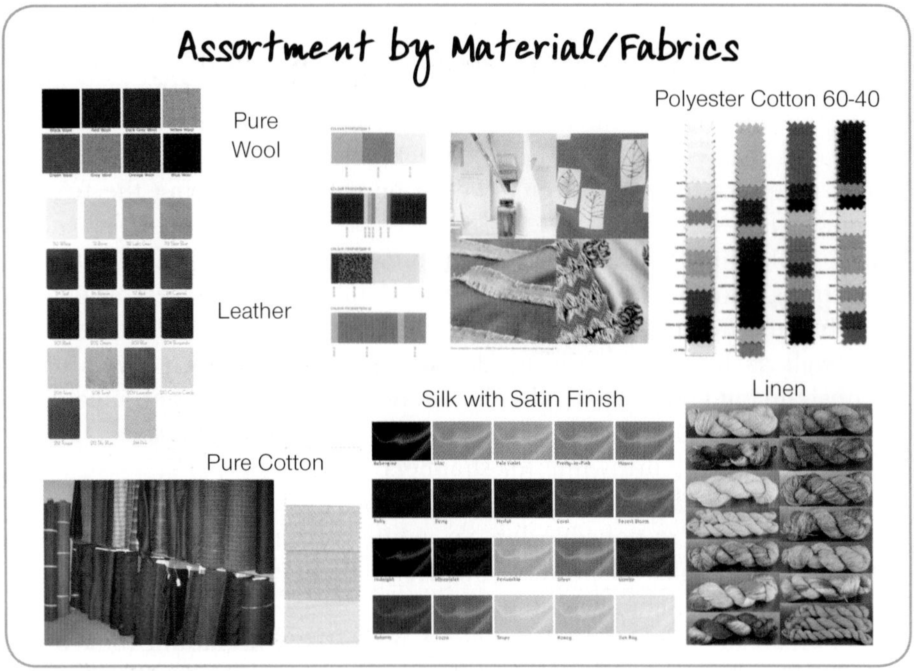

Depending on the market, some customers may prioritize fabric content where others look more at fabric effects.

- **Assortment planning by color**

When working out your color assortments, divide them into three groups: Basic; Seasonal; and Fashion—as illustrated below.

Autumn Pallet Assortment could, for example, be:

Basic: Black, Charcoal, Brown
Seasonal Classics: Wine, Dark Green, Purple
Fashion: Ice Blue, Frosted White, Deep Turquoise

Where the basic colors and, to some extent, some seasonal shades may be repeatable, fashion colors are not as easy to predict and plan. You may have had success with a "Frosty Shades" theme the previous year, but the chances of having the same high returns from the same colors again this year are very slim.

Fashion buyers need to research color trends well in advance of their buying season. This can be done through an Internet search

Assortment Planning by Color

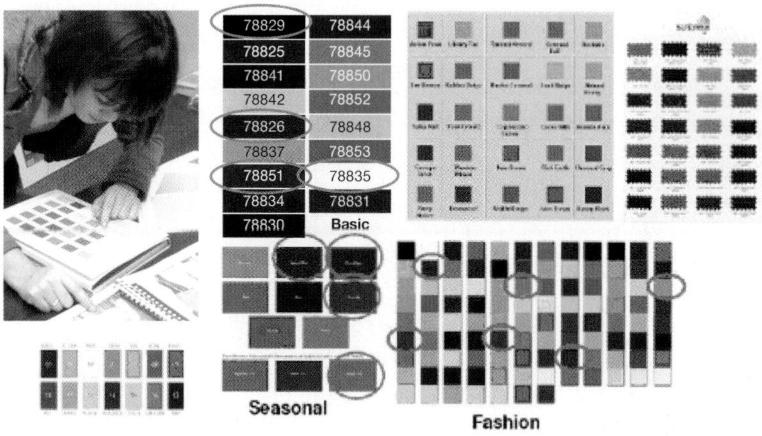

or by going through professional trend, style and color books. The important thing is to have a clear idea of which direction you want to take.

Early season color tests

Most buyers will place their basic color assortments well in advance. In some cases, this can be done for seasonal colors too, based on predictable popular demand. However, fashion colors and trendy shades are trickier.

Testing out a number of color shades being sponsored by manufacturers and fashion publications can be beneficial, especially when launched early in the season. Color testing is used for outright buys, line buys or product development.

The suppliers who are agreeable to the idea of supplying test runs or sample orders are usually suppliers who manage their own productions or fabric dyeing. This is rarely the case with line buys, unless these suppliers keep stocks and are able to repeat orders in mid season.

Color testing has many advantages. By monitoring the customer's response, it is then possible to catch and stock up on the season's newest color fads. Early shoppers differ from later shoppers. One is a "trend setter," always looking for the latest; the other waits to see if the trend is here to stay for the season.

Fashion Cycle

The **testing period** is when buyers need to move fast to repeat the "hot-sellers" so that they can be part of the take-off, and peak in more important units, and thus make greater profits

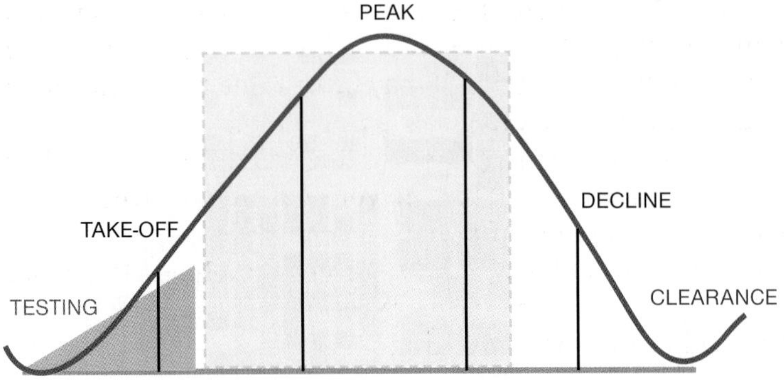

It is within this grid that retailers are able to make full profits on their merchandise

Source: Joseph B. Siegel

Hardgoods Cycle

There is a big contrast when looking at a hardgoods merchandise lifecycle. The norm or the peak usually coincides with peak festive seasons or during promotional events.

A testing period in a hardgoods department may be of a new brand, a new product (as in kitchenware and kitchen appliances), or introduction of a new category. The other peak that can be experienced is when a brand is given a promotional area to launch a new product with some brand promoters.

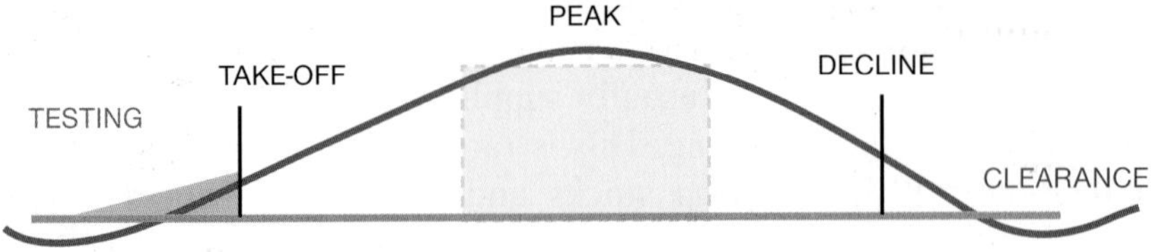

It is within this grid that retailers are able to make full profits on their merchandise

Source: Joseph B. Siegel

When considering repeat orders on trendy styles and colors, be aware that these must be monitored closely. Trends can become saturated. I have seen many good buys repeated once too often and have to be discounted later because demand slowed down and the surplus did not move.

In the case where the company is dealing mainly with international brands, where the principals dictate colors, themes, silhouettes, styles and fabrics, it may be of value to do some research on trends and colors before placing your orders.

You should have an opinion on the trend forecasts and which colors you deem most suitable for your customers. It will help you in your selection at time of purchase.

Not all your brands will have the same levels of choice, but the more choices you have; and the more you are prepared, the more confident you will be in choosing your fashion direction within your brand.

Color forecast and fashion trends

The latest color trends (as illustrated below) can be found simply by typing in the words "fashion trends 2008–2009" on Google or one of the other search engines. The important thing to remember is that each time you decide on the color direction, styles or looks, you should ensure that it is done with your customers in mind, the public mood (how buoyant the economy is), influences from celebrity trendsetters, foreign fashion influences and fashion cycles.

Color Trends & Directions Forecast Book

Trend & Fashion Forecast Books for product development

There are several online research portals to which retailers can subscribe that offer extensive information on fashion trends, fashion reviews, cat walks, retail articles and more, but these are also quite expensive and best suited to larger retail organizations, where the membership can be shared amongst many buyers.

In my experience, and especially for people involved in fashion design, product development, private labels or merchandise planning, trend books such as the ones produced and sold by Leng Peng Singapore have the greatest value (see www.lengpeng.com).

What I like about them and find most useful is that they are very focused. Each Trend & Fashion Forecast book focuses on certain styles and looks, represented by a selective collection of pictures from the runway fashion shows of renowned designers. They are very inspirational and some books have back-page sections highlighting details, shapes and forms, as well as prints and color combinations. Other books specialize in specific merchandise categories such as shirts, dresses, pants or jackets and, of course, there are the color and fabric books, where users can touch and feel the fabric swatches. These highly specialized books are hot favorites with retail professionals as they help reduce guesswork to a great extent, and condense essential information for product design and development as well as range building.

Men's Business Assortment

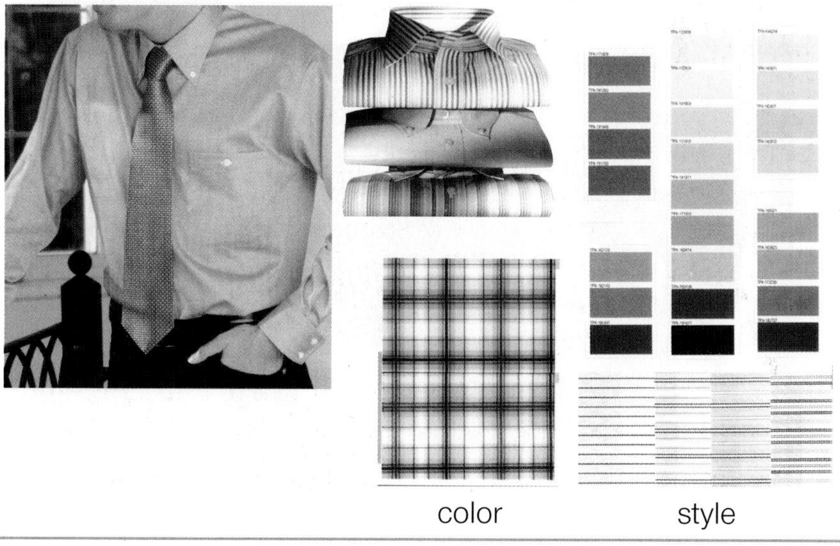

Fashion Clothing – By Categories

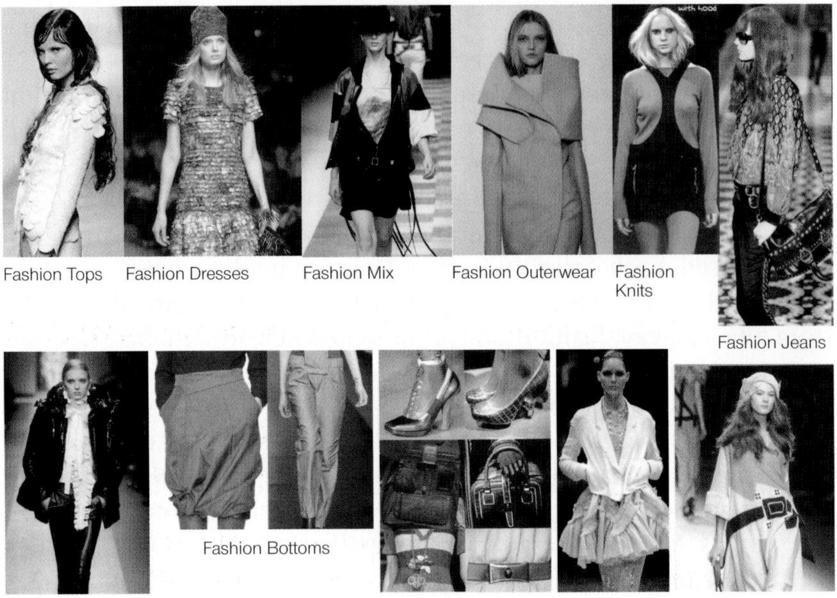

Fashion Tops
Fashion Dresses
Fashion Mix
Fashion Outerwear
Fashion Knits
Fashion Jeans
Fashion Leathers
Fashion Bottoms
Fashion Accessories
Occasion Wear
Fashion Dresses

Fashion Defined

• **Assortment planning by styles**

A garment often has a lifespan of at least one year and perhaps several. By analyzing sellthrough on certain shapes, styles and colors, customer demand can be anticipated.

Styles and silhouettes may have slight variations but, on the whole, they fall into the following predictable categories:

- Hemlines–slim fit or flare
- Waist lines and belt lines
- Necklines
- Sleeve length and types

Some of these specific factors can be summed up as a type and sales can be analyzed accordingly. Depending on the type of store involved, planning may be done according to specific categories or styles: for example, tops, bottoms or woven knits. In other cases, stores may opt to plan by type of range, such as a career wear or a contemporary office range. The secret here is to be consistent: changing your assortment parameters too often will wreak havoc in your sell-through analysis and you may lose some historical data.

Planning by styles can also be applicable in other areas of the business. Take Home, for example, where a style could also be determined as Country (floral and frilly with a French or Old English twist), Oriental (from Chinese, Thai Indonesian/Balinese ...) or Modern Minimalist (clean-cut no-fuss ranges in solid colors, which can also be further interpreted as a more defined look like ZEN or an interpretation of East-meets-West).

• **Planning by range**

When planning by range, the focus will be in the balance of the components within the range.

For fashion, a range can comprise blouses-knits-skirts-pants-jackets-dresses. To be considered a range, these components must match or at least complement each other. Jackets complement and can be coordinated with the bottoms or, in this case, the shift dress. Here the buyer would exercise a top-to-bottom ratio of 3 to 1 or 4 to 1, depending on her customer profile. Some retailers will sell as many as four tops (blouses, T-shirts, knits etc) to one bottom (pants, skirt, bermuda etc).

Basic-Classic Career Wear

Top-Bottom Ratio

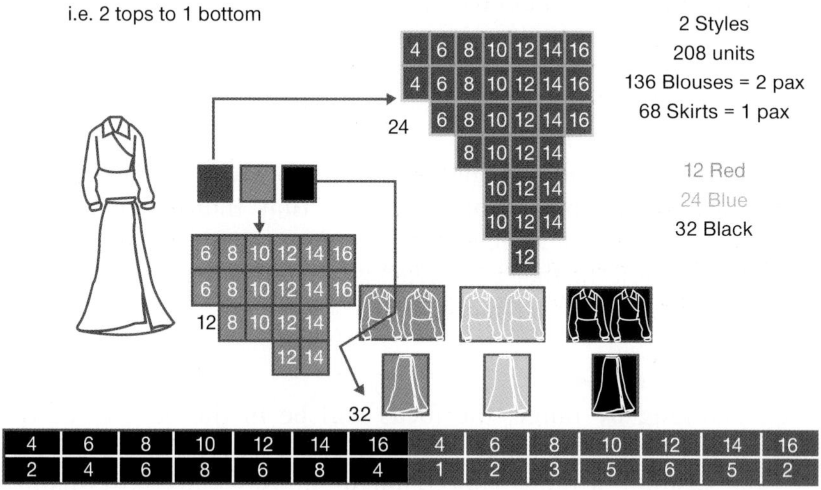

- **Assortment planning by consumer type**

Before we look at what makes a fashion assortment, we need to understand the consumer types, of which there are four categories:

1. Innovators
2. Early Adopters/Early Majority
3. Majority
4. Late Majority/Laggards

When planning merchandise assortments, the ranges will be divided into segments that match the store's customer profile.

Innovators, also known as the trendsetters, are those who will purchase an item first. For the Innovators, the buyer would seek to have the latest fast-forward fashion merchandise early in the season. The assortments are usually shallow in the beginning and are often considered test-lines. If these prove to be a hit, the buyer will place more substantial re-orders to meet demand coming from the next group of Early Adopters, and then from the Majority. Remember that by the time the Early Adopters are buying these styles, the Innovators would already be on their way to something different and newer.

Early Adopters can easily adapt to change and will follow the fashion publications for guidance. Assortments bought for the Early Adopters will be a spillover from the ranges bought for the Innovators. The ranges would have some fast-forward fashion styles, new colors and trims, but combined with easy-to-wear items; in other words, they are not as "pure" as the first ranges launched.

Production Life & Sales Cycle

Five stages

- Product development—Sales are zero and investment costs are high
- Introduction—Profits do not exist and product introduction is expensive
- Growth—Rapid market acceptance and increasing profits
- Maturity—Slowdown in sales growth. Profits level-off. Increase outlay to compete
- Decline—Sales fall off and profits drop

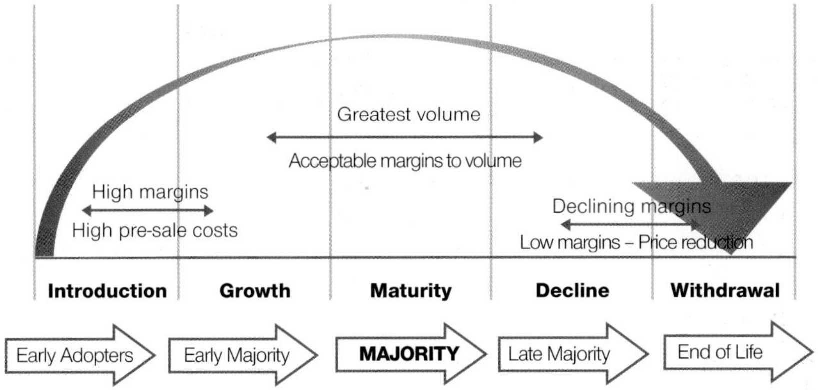

The Majority will change, but only after some pressure or when they see people wearing the goods on the streets. The assortments are very similar to the ones brought in for the Early Adopters; the only difference is that more people are buying them. This is also called "commercialized fashion" for the wider masses. The point at which the Majority buys is also when your range or product lifecycle is at its peak. The buyer is advised to exercise caution because after the peak comes the decline in interest.

Late Majority/Laggards resist change to varying degrees, perhaps as a result of personal style preferences, regardless of what the fashion magazines dictate. They also tend to buy during season-end sales. This is an important segment for retailers. The assortments bought for this customer group are usually basics and, in many cases, quality conscious. This customer segment is especially important to department stores, which traditionally carry high inventories of fashion goods that need to be cleared each season, and where garments are more a utility than a fashion statement–which suits Late Majority/Laggards just fine.

Fashion Lifecycle

A	Begin receiving new season
B	Fashion presentation before this point
C	No re-order of this season's merchandise past this point
D	Begin season mark-downs at this point

Date				Action	Season
February	1		A	Sell	Late Cruise - Early Spring
	2		B	Clear-out introductions	
	3		C	Sell	
	4		D	Clear-out introductions	
March	1		A	Sell	
	2		B	Clear-out introductions	
	3		C	Sell	Spring
	4		D	Clear-out introductions	
	5		A	Sell	
April	1		B	Clear-out introductions	
	2		C	Sell	
	3		D	Clear-out introductions	
	4		A	Sell	Early Summer
May	1		B	Clear-out introductions	
	2		C	Sell	
	3		D	Clear-out introductions	
	4		A	Sell	Sales
	5		B	Mix of regular & Sales	
June			C	Season-end Sales	Sales

Source: Joseph B. Siegel

- **Assortment planning by vendor**

Another factor that plays an important part in assortment planning is forecasting by vendor or manufacturer. Analyzing the best-selling styles, range sellthrough and the profit generated from each of the vendors enables the buyer to choose vendors more selectively, to set benchmarks for future performance, and thus enhance the chances of maintaining success.

- **Assortment planning by size**

Probably the most complex assortment planning is the size ratio. Conflicts may arise in deciding the sizes, width or depth of the range of clothing and (especially) shoes the buyer should bring in. Feedback from the selling floor may indicate a need for smaller or bigger sizes, and the buyer will have to make a judgment call based on this information. Remember: if you don't carry it, your sales data will not be helpful.

While the human form has a boundless diversity of measurements, elements of stability and clustering make the problem more manageable. An analysis of sellthrough by size will show that the popular sizes vary little within the same geographic area. The question the retailer may want to ask is: Should I carry the full range of sizes, 6 to 16, or concentrate on the popular ones, 8 to 12?

A common mistake I have often observed in Asia is the perception the retailer has of its customers. If a retailer is targeting a young customer profile, the chances are that the size ratio will be limited

Garment Size Ratio

Ladies' Garments	Local		4	6	8	10	12	14	16	Total
	European		32	34	36	38	40	42	46	
Units Allocated	% of total		6%	10%	23%	25%	21%	15%	optional	100%
Men's Shirts	14	14.5	15	15.5	16	16.5	17	17.5	18	
Units Allocated	4%	7%	10%	23%	23%	20%	5%	55%	3%	100%
Ladies' Shoes	5	5.5	6	6.5	7	7.5	8	8.5	9	
Units Allocated	3%	8%	15%	20%	22%	14%	10%	5%	3%	100%

The above is just a general guide. Size ratio will vary from country to country. The important factor here is to determine your triangle size ratio or the 2–3 sizes that are the most sellable in your store [departments].

to smaller sizes, thus limiting potential sales. Young girls are taller and bigger than their counterparts of a decade ago, and middle-aged women are more youthful and active, and definitely much younger in mind than their counterparts half a century ago.

"Mind age" is the big thing right now. The baby-boomers of the 1960s are buying fashionable clothing which was not initially designed for them but is appealing to them nonetheless. They want the looks and styles that are in now but, in many cases, the sizes they want are not available. If you don't carry the right sizes, the customers will find a retailer that does.

Size also becomes a consideration depending on the type of store and the type of merchandise the retailer has to offer. For men's business shirts, for example, there are variations in collar sizes, and sleeve lengths within each size ratio. Men's suits also come in a range of sizes: short, regular, long and extra-long. In men's shoes, the buyer may see the need to expand on the number and range of shoes within each width grading.

When planning size ratio allocations, it has to be remembered that the "odd" sizes also follow demand from "odd" customers. Such customers become loyal customers if they can find their sizes each time they shop with you, and you become a niche market, specializing in a wide assortment of sizes as the word spreads.

Size definition

Each country has its own numbering system for clothing sizes. It is important to keep in mind that these are basic guidelines, and that they may differ slightly by range or brand. Basically, U.K. clothing is marked about one size larger than U.S. clothes (a U.S. 4 is a U.K. 6) and Australia is about two sizes larger (a U.S. 4 is an Australian 8).

To understand sizes properly, one needs to understand the number code used in key geographic areas.

Sizes XS-S-M-L-XL are used for loose-fitting garments such as T-shirts, drawstring pants or loose fitted dresses. So, customers who are a U.S. size 8 or 10 would fit a T-shirt in a size M (medium). A customer who is a size 8 in the U.S. would be looking for a size 10 in the U.K., size 12 in Australia, a size 39 in France and, though not mentioned in the chart, a size 38 in northern Europe. With the exception of France, all sizes are given in even numbers. A full size ratio in the U.K. would range from a size 6 to a size 18. (Size 20 and above are considered plus-sizes.)

Size Conversion Chart

	U.S.	U.K.	Australia	France
XS	2-4	4-6	6-8	35-36
S	4-6	6-8	8-10	37-38
M	8-10	10-12	12-14	39-40
L	12-14	14-16	16-18	42-43
XL	14-16	16-18	18-20	43-44
1X	16-18	18-20	20-22	44-46
2X	18-20	20-22	22-24	
3X	22-24	24-26	26-28	

A full size ratio in Germany would range from size 34 to size 46. In the U.S., this would start from a size 2 and go up to a size 14. (Sizes 16 and above would be considered plus-sizes.)

Standard sizes, also called "missy" sizes, are those that are commonly carried in standard women's clothing stores. Generally, this size range runs from a 2 to a 14. Many people refer to this size range as "normal" or "regular" sizes.

In fashion and clothing, **petite sizes** are standard clothing sizes designed to fit women of shorter height, typically 5'3" (approx. 160 cm) or less.

Traditionally, **plus-size** garments have a much looser silhouette than regular-size clothes and are less form-fitting. Often, even the smallest sizes in a plus-size store will have an allowance for a large chest. Plus-size fashion is evolving, and many brands are becoming more stylish and body conscious, but most of the mass-merchandise plus-clothing is still a little bit on the loose side. Plus-size clothing is usually not sold alongside missy sizes. Generally, brands sell one or the other (for example, Bebe, a regular-size store, only goes up to a size 12, and Lane Bryant, a plus-size store, only starts at 14).

ASSORTMENT PLANNING: GENERAL MERCHANDISE

- **Classification and type**

Analysis of past sales by classification helps in generic planning for future sales. In bed linen, for example, buyers may find that in a given period, more Queen-size sheets were sold and may thus follow the same pattern, ordering, say, 50% Queen-size, 30% Single and 20% King-size. Once again, however, further analysis is required here because the previous sales may merely reflect what was in stock. It may be that sales of King-size remained low because fewer were carried in stock and repeating this plan may lead to lost sales.

Kitchenware planning can be organized under the category of pots and pans. The assortments can be by type; as in stainless steel, aluminum, copper, porcelain, titanium, cast-iron or non-stick; by price range; and by brand, as in Biro, WMF, Gordon Ramsay Royal Doulton, Viking, and so on.

Classification by Type, Price & Brand

Some stores also buy their assortments by quality. A good example of this is the Gordon Ramsay Royal Doulton Range, a collection of professional-quality cookware illustrated on the following page. The pieces feature heavy-duty, tri-ply technology for durability and cooking efficiency. Heavy-gauge aluminum core is bonded between a polished 18/10 stainless steel or copper exterior and brushed stainless interior cooking surface.

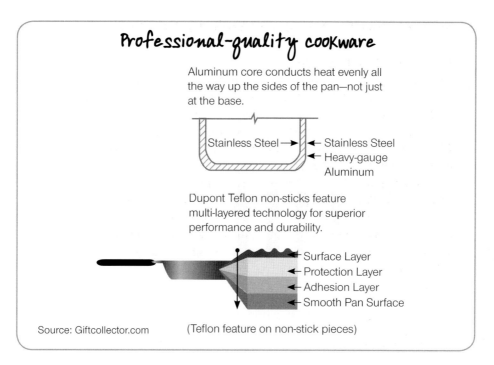

Professional-quality cookware

Aluminum core conducts heat evenly all the way up the sides of the pan—not just at the base.

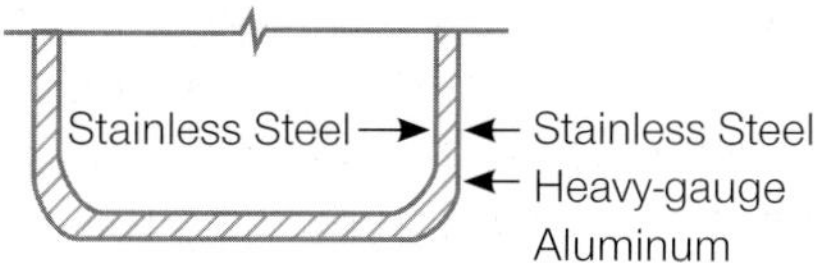

Dupont Teflon non-sticks feature multi-layered technology for superior performance and durability.

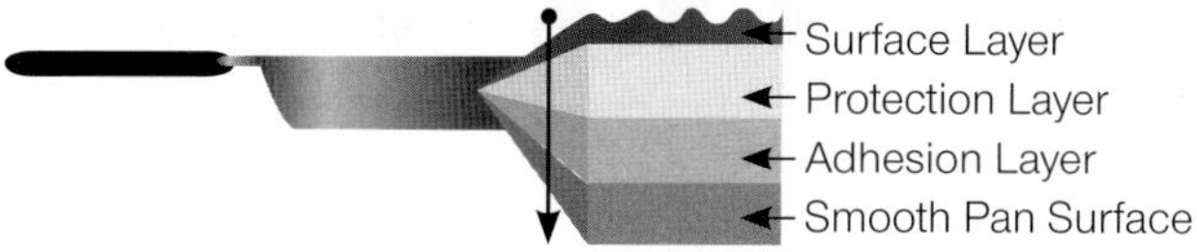

Source: Giftcollector.com

(Teflon feature on non-stick pieces)

- **By theme**

In working out assortments according to themes, it pays to define the groups into specific classes or categories: basic–basic white or solid colors; modern–Zen, Retro, Fusion or Minimalist; and traditional–local or European (say, French Provencal or Old English).

Where an assortment (tableware, glassware or cutlery in sets, for example) can be re-ordered, it is important to determine whether some single components can be bought. For example, customers may be enticed to buy a tableware set, only to find out later that a broken tea cup or dinner plate cannot be replaced. The entire purchase has suddenly lost its appeal.

- **By type**

Using the picture on the next page as an example, depending on the availability of store space, the customer profile and sellthrough, some stores may opt to buy a selection from within an assortment, rather than the complete assortment, or of one style rather than equal numbers in all styles. For example, a buyer may buy only three forks to complete the assortment, but may buy half-a-dozen or more of the chef's or bread knife. So, the quantities will follow the customer demand or the sellthrough for each type.

• **Assortments by color**

Color also plays a part in categories other than fashion, a good example of this being very iconic Crocs shoes. In this case, the colors reflect the owner's personal lifestyle and mood.

Assortments by color

Other examples in which color matters are bedding, home accessories, tableware, plasticware, gifts, and more.

COMMON SENSE COUPLED WITH INNOVATION

Whatever the merchandise, a high degree of flair and imagination is used in the buying process. Buyers will always require a combination of good business sense (the numbers), creativity and a knack for picking the right trends for their respective markets. They also need a sense of innovation, without which retailers become stagnant.

Retail is a great industry for people who are imaginative in creating new reasons for consumers to shop. Innovation may be linked to performance and growth through improvements in products, quality, productivity, competitive positioning and market share. It can and will involve aspects of the business other than merchandising.

While retailers are looking for ways to improve and grow the business, innovation also involves change and, to some degree, risk. Some of these changes may have greater organizational consequences, the additional value the innovation brings being weighed against any additional operational cost. *As a buyer, I hope I have, and keep, an imaginative and creative spirit. Let the accountants figure out the rest.*

As Teresa Amabile of the Harvard Business School expresses it: "All innovation begins with creative ideas...We define innovation as the successful implementation of creative ideas within an organization. In this view, creativity by individuals and teams is a starting point for innovation; the first is a necessary but not sufficient condition for the second."*

The Innovation Triangle

Any form of innovation begins with creative ideas... We define innovation as the successful implementation of creative ideas that we hope will translate into a demand that subsequently transforms into profits.

Source: Teresa Amabile

---

* Quoted in William Andrews Sahlman et al., *The Entrepreneurial Venture*, Harvard Business School Press, 1999, p.521.

case study

Finding the X factor in merchandise

What makes a store? The merchandise makes a store. What makes a great store? Great merchandise makes a great store. It's all about finding merchandise that has the "X Factor."

During a CPD Fashion Fair in Düsseldorf, we came across a brand called *She* and knew immediately that this was meant for our stores. The problem here was that the people at the stand did not allow non-clients to view the collection and, in addition, they did not need new customers. So, prior to the next CPD Fair, I contacted the owner and arranged a meeting. After some persuasion, he agreed to let us look at the range but, before we did, he asked what kind of OTB we had planned for his range. To that, I answered: "We have no OTB. The range will determine how much we believe we can sell." We had prepared our numbers, but I was not prepared to divulge them at that point. The range consisted of 10 programs, eight of which were very suitable for our market. We worked the styles, units, costs and average retail prices, and the overall total came close to what we anticipated the brand would need.

We told the owner (whom we nicknamed Mr BB) that we were quite sure of the brand's success in Singapore, and that we were planning to dedicate a proper counter to the brand, and organizing a big launch complete with press ads, Orchard Road window displays and a press conference for him. His response: "How could my people have kept you away from my collection!" He was impressed and, naturally, flattered.

The launch was a great success. Mr BB's collection received some fantastic reviews and gave rise to a memorable quote. "Why call the brand *She*?" asked the *Straits Times* journalist.

"Ah! My lovely lady! This is because I love everything about women! A woman is my passion; it is my universe!!!"

Now, who could resist such a line? The brand, like its owner, had the X factor.

We had many good years selling the brand until Mr BB decided to retire. Once this happened, the collection started to lose its appeal and, along with it, its X factor.

case study

The case of the purple shoes

One of the biggest sales successes we have enjoyed arose from good-quality job lots we were able to obtain from our European vendors. We were able to buy season-end goods at up to 50% off, savings which we were able to pass on to our customers during the sales. Our customers loved it, especially the Italian shoes and handbags.

On that particular trip, I wasn't able to accompany my Shoes & Accessories buyer as I had other commitments. We went through the Trip Planners, OTB Planners, the units to be bought and the price she should be bidding on. In other words, she was ready for the trip to Italy. At that time, when buyers bought assorted job lots, the POs were organized by units and price points, without a full description of the items. This saved time in the creation of the POs and when clearing goods at customs.

It was also customary that when job-lot goods arrived, the buyers would go to the warehouse and establish the usual price (UP), based on the styles and quality from that particular vendor. I happened to be at the warehouse that day as we had a great deal of sales merchandise coming in from all over, and most of my buyers were there working on their price points. It was also fun opening the cartons and admiring the goods, and the buyers were naturally eager to show me their goodies.

I approached my Shoes & Accessories buyer and asked to see what she had bought. We opened the first box, and there were purple shoes; we opened the second box; more purple shoes; we opened the third box and, again, more purple shoes! “Good grief!” I said, “What’s with all the purple shoes?”

“Well,” she said, “I did what you told me. I found the best styles, in as much of a full size assortment as possible, and at the right price.”

This was in 1994, where funny-colored shoes were not the “in” thing. Our customers were very conservative; the shoes they bought were elegant, classic, styles best sold in black and, with a bit of goodwill, brown. But purple!!!

Needless to say, the shoes did not sell. The UP for this brand was S$239 and our intended price for the sale was S$99. We adjusted the price and labeled them at S$59, a steal for such quality, but no, customers did not even try them. We reduced them further to S$29 and sold some but, with only a week left until the sales ended, we still had a substantial stock in hand.

So, we finally resorted to a “Final Reduction: Buy-1-get-1-free” ploy, in which customers were invited to “buy any shoes and get these fashion colored shoes free.” Eventually—painfully—we managed to get rid of them and it proved to be a very costly lesson.

When buying regular or promotional lines, keep this in mind: The right styles in the right colors in the right sizes at the right price—not one or the other.

8 ANTICIPATING CONSUMER TRENDS

What do you know about your customers? As you will have gathered by now, I see spending time on the selling floor as a prerequisite for every buyer. In fact, it's not negotiable. Meet the customers, serve them, understand their needs, listen to their criticism, and listen to what they would like to buy from you ... if only you carried it. Observe how they accept or reject the merchandise on the floor, and understand why.

A SUCCESS STORY

As most of you may know, the Nordstrom department store in the United States is well known for its outstanding merchandise selection, which ranges from fashion to home lifestyle, and for its fantastic customer service. Its success is built on an organizational structure that is quite different from most in the retail industry, as can be seen in the illustrations below.

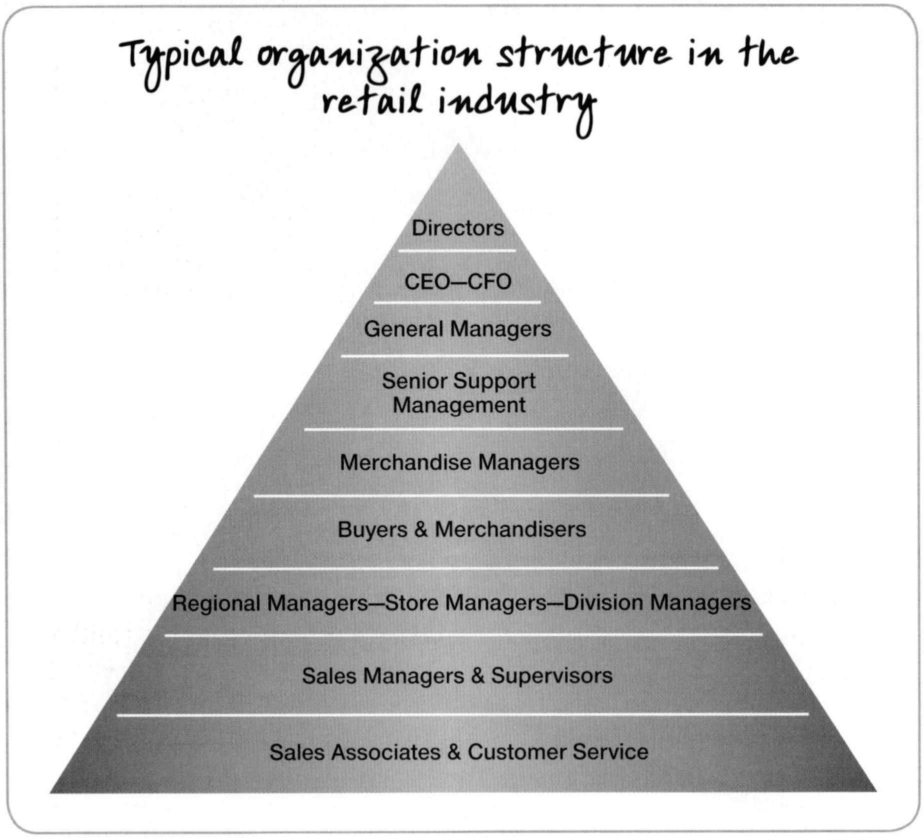

Nordstrom's business philosophy has always been to value its sales people as the most important people in the organization. This is because its sales associates render outstanding customer service, and give feedback to the buyers on what customers are looking for. This is the fundamental Nordstrom culture. The secret of its success is, and will always be, its outstanding customer service.

Nordstrom chooses its buyers from the selling floor. In the Nordstrom organizational pyramid, the sales assistants take first place. Everyone is required to start from the selling floor because the company recognizes that without the insight into what customers are ready to buy, it is impossible to buy the right merchandise.

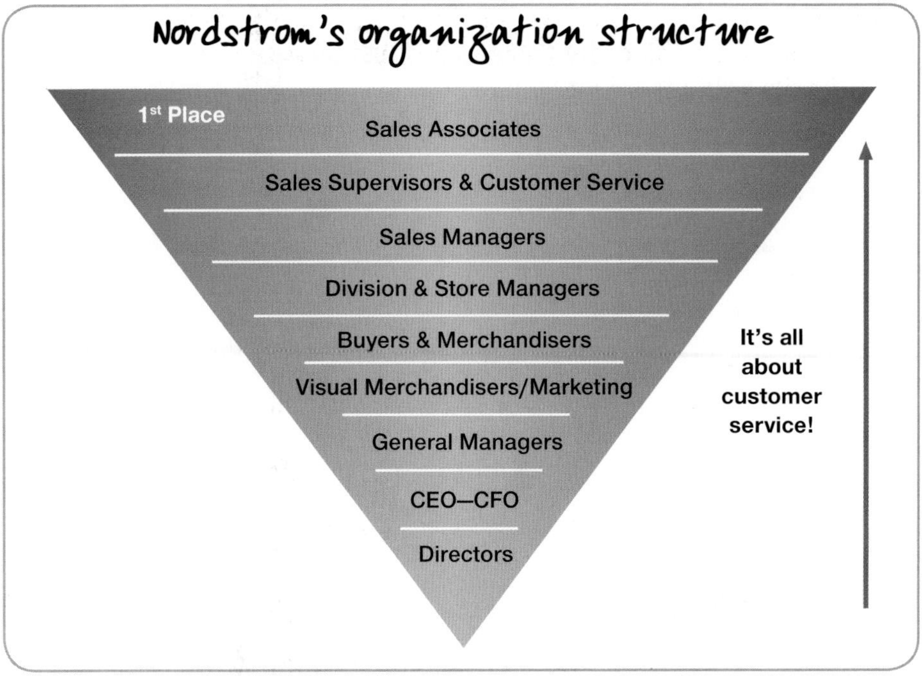

THE BATTLE OF THE CAMPS

Anyone with any experience of working in retail will be familiar with the clash between buyers and operations. This is a sensitive area, with each blaming the other if merchandise does not sell. The buyers blame the operations staff for not selling the goods; the operations staff blame the buyers for buying merchandise that the customers don't want. So, who is right? Who wins the argument? The answer is that if the fight is simply about making a point, no one wins.

The point is that if the buyers don't buy the right stuff, sales people will not be able to sell it. In most cases, the operations people are right and the buyer would benefit from listening to the sales people and buying-in according to customer demands.

Such infighting does nobody any good. Instead of arguing with operations staff, buyers should team up with them, supporting them with merchandising information. In turn, sales staff should support the buyers with customer information. Together, they can find new ways of enchanting the customer who, after all, is the source of your most potent advertising: word of mouth. Excellent customer service coupled with terrific merchandise will get you just that!

The battle of two camps

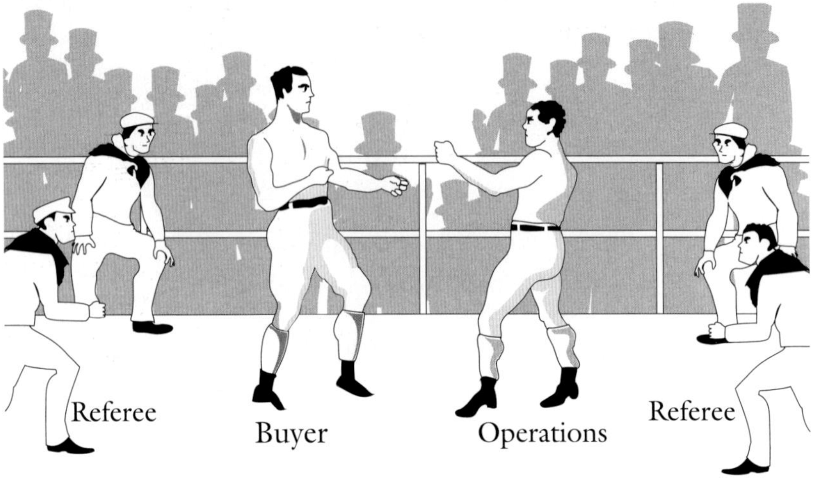

Merchandising vs. Operations

Buyers
Sales are down because you're not selling my merchandise!
Operations
The merchandise is not selling because our customers don't want it!

CREATING A WINNING CULTURE

With buyers and operations staff working together, every retail organization can build an internal culture that will breed success. Much of this will come from the buyers spending time on the selling floor, taking time to understand the customers, their spending power and their behavior. Through this, buyers will also come to realize that there are some merchandise segments that are slow sellers and can take immediate action to start clearing these items.

Great buys are easy to sell; in fact, they are known to sell themselves. So if the operations team is saying that a particular range is not selling, this is most likely to be because the customers have rejected it or that there are too many duplications (similar styles at different price points) on offer, confusing the customer and making choice difficult.

The more the buyers work closely with their selling team, the higher the chances of developing a great team culture, one that leads towards a common goal: purchasing the right merchandise to satisfy customer demands.

Conducting market surveys with your competitors will also give you an indication of who their customers are and what you need to do to make your offer even more appealing.

It's worth saying one more time: Spend time on the selling floor. If you don't, you haven't a clue who you are buying for!

CONSUMERS AND THEIR BUYING POWER

• Anticipating consumer demands

While no two customers will have exactly the same likes, dislikes, requirements, demands, lifestyle or buying power, stores should aim to please groups of customers with similar tastes in, say, price points, fashion quality classics or modern contemporary styles.

Understanding and responding to consumer trends is more important than ever before. A retailer's capacity for developing and implementing a sound strategy is determined by its ability to identify and understand its customers. Only then can it identify its specific target market, and the customer it aims to satisfy.

The prime objective of the buying function is to anticipate the needs and wants of customers, even before the consumers are consciously aware of their desires. For this to happen, a great deal needs to be known about them.

Demographic profile

To understand your consumers, you need to build a composite picture showing you who and where they are; how old they are; their educational level; their occupations and incomes; their social and marital status; their family and their lifestyles.

Motivation

People's actions are motivated by wishes, desires, needs and likes, and driven primarily by the survival instinct to overcome such things as hunger and thirst, and by the need to reproduce and the need for shelter. But there is a secondary category of motivation which has more to do with the elements of identification, acquisition, recognition and exhibition, and it is in this area that the retail buyer operates.

If people bought only what they needed and could afford, there would be no such thing as retail therapy. People buy emotionally and justify logically.

Behavior

This is an area in which people's reasons for, and patterns of, buying are analyzed closely, in an effort to understand the underlying motivations, be they rational or emotional. It looks at how much time they are prepared to spend shopping and how they react to prices and quality.

It would, I think, be an interesting and revealing exercise for you at this stage to list the numerous factors that prompt consumer behavior. Perhaps, too, you could list the types of consumer who frequent your store (taking into consideration factors such as age and income), checking your ideas with some of your store's sales staff.

Social motives

Individual customers are just that—individuals. Each has a unique set of drives and a set of priorities for satisfying those drives. Neither drives nor priorities are stable or necessarily logical or rational. A powerful influence on consumers' purchasing decisions is *predisposition*, a built-up attitude towards the product and the seller. This is also known as **patronage**. For patronage to be sustainable, retailers needs to anticipate the changing needs of their markets and the new markets they decide to court.

Perception

Basic perception is a process whereby people select, organize and interpret a sensory stimulation into a meaningful and coherent picture. It is determined by motivations, needs and values. Perception is selective and interpretative, which enables both rejection and distortion. It is vital, therefore, to endeavor always to see all products and all promotions through the customers' eyes. What the customers perceive as the total benefit of a proposed purchase may transcend the merely physical attributes or the obvious characteristics of a product.

DEMOGRAPHIC ANALYSIS

By examining the various demographic components, retailers can make decisions on where to locate a store and tailor their products to the needs of those within these market boundaries. Some retailers analyze their potential customer segmentation by zip-codes or classification of residential neighborhoods.

These can clarify differences in social rank, household composition, mobility, ethnicity, population density and housing information—all of which are important to appropriate merchandise purchases.

For standalone stores, it is important to understand the consumers' shopping patterns. A suburban dweller would more than likely buy more casual clothing than his city counterparts, who would be inclined to buy more formal businesswear. Likewise, a person living in the suburbs may buy more home décor and household items while a city dweller may use more of his disposable income in restaurants. Buyers buying for chain stores need to carry merchandise that is suited to the demographics of the particular areas in which the individual stores are situated.

CONSUMER CLASSIFICATIONS

• Age

Age today has little to do with the number of years you have experienced. More than ever before, people are looking younger, feeling younger and acting younger. Age perception can be deceptive though. With anti-aging drives from cosmetics brands, nip & tuck TV programs, fitness workout programs and eat-well literature, there is a lot of pressure for people to look younger. However, there will always be differences between a young body shape and an older one and, to a certain extent, what an older woman can get away with as far as garment silhouettes and fashion styles are concerned.

Some retailers classify customers into four age categories:

1. Baby Boomers (those born between 1945 and 1959)
2. Generation X (those in their twenties)
3. Generation Y (those in their teens).

The fourth category is the mature market for those above 65 years of age. It is estimated that the mature market in Asia will grow by at least 13% in the next decade. By 2020, there will be twice as many elderly people as teenagers. They are better off financially than the younger group, currently enjoying some $200 billion in Asia alone. They are too often considered as a homogenous market, which is incorrect: there are as many segments in this category as in any other.

• Occupation

The type of career a person has plays a significant role in the planning of their purchases, particularly of clothes.

A lawyer and a plant manager may have similar incomes but their apparel needs would be quite different. The growing trend towards people working from home also requires buyers to re-think their merchandise mix. Continuous re-evaluation of occupations and the place of employment will give the buyer a head start in purchase planning.

- **Income**

It should go without saying that consumers' spending is, to a large extent, determined by their respective incomes. If a store traditionally caters to a moderate-income family and believes a higher-priced merchandise assortment should be introduced, it must be certain that a portion of its clientele can afford it.

The fact that people would like to have higher-priced merchandise doesn't guarantee that they have sufficient disposable income to satisfy these desires.

- **Education**

Education will determine the types of jobs consumers are likely to have and, thus, their clothing requirements. But a higher education also means that these consumers are likely to take a greater interest in what they are buying. A better-educated consumer, even though mindful of price, would want to know the quality standards and value of the items to justify the purchase.

- **Children**

This is a very important group to cater to, as young families are big consumers of all items ranging from baby products, children's wear, toys and books to furniture, appliances, tableware, cookware, home products, and so on. In affluent Asia, children are very pampered. Considering the high number of children being born into two-income families, it would appear that the future of children's wear retailing is indeed bright.

- **Working women**

As the number of working women continuously increases, time in which to pursue leisure activities is a luxury that these consumers are looking for. Convenience and time-saving services are thus rising in value.

SPOILT FOR CHOICE

Consumers are being exposed to so many products at such an incredibly fast speed that making a buying decision becomes complex. Take toothpaste, for example: in Asia five years ago, there might have been three or four major brands available; today, there are more than 80. Toothpaste is no longer just about fighting cavities. Consumers are bombarded by brands boasting miracle stain removers, anti-bacterial agents and fluoride anti-cavity protection, in an array of colors and flavors.

In planning their buys, buyers would do well to keep this in mind. Too much choice can confuse customers or, at least, create uncertainty as to which product or brand to buy. In retail, less sometimes means more.

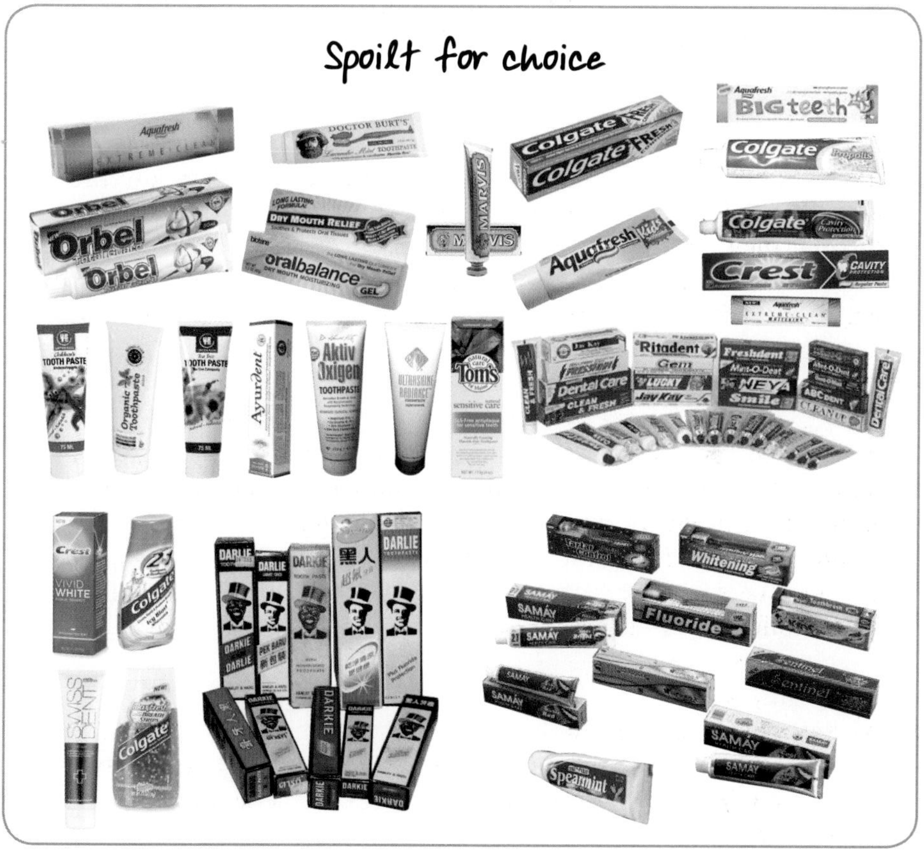

The Art of **Retail** Buying

9

FORECASTING CUSTOMER DEMANDS

In today's retail world, consumers are clearly better informed than before. They are less likely to be dictated to, increasingly demanding and increasingly unpredictable.

Retailers that can identify and understand the complexity of consumer dynamics are also capable of developing and implementing sound and profitable strategies. However, this is no easy task.

In today's globalized world, consumers are more diverse than ever before. People travel 10 times more today than a decade ago. The Internet has become the heart, soul and engine of information and people are seeking individuality mixed with a touch of global culture. These lifestyles have a huge influence on consumers and their motivations to buy.

ANTICIPATING CONSUMER DEMAND

As we have seen already, to understand consumer demand, you must first understand who the consumers are, what their attitudes and lifestyles are and what their needs are.

Within the industry, it is generally accepted that lifestyle factors can be split into eight profiles and characteristics:

1. **Actualizers:** People with high self-esteem and abundant resources who are successful, sophisticated, active, and take charge.

2. **Fulfilled:** Mature, satisfied, comfortable and reflective people who value order, knowledge and responsibility.

3. **Achievers:** Successful career- and work-oriented people who like to feel in control of their lives.

4. **Experiencers:** Young, vital, enthusiastic, impulsive and rebellious people who seek variety and excitement.

5. **Believers:** Conservative and conventional people with concrete beliefs based on traditional and established codes: family, religion, community and nation.

6. **Strivers:** Those who seek motivation, self-definition, a secure place in life, and approval from the world around them.

7. **Makers:** Practical and traditionally inclined people who have constructive skills and value self-sufficiency.

8. **Strugglers:** Chronically poor, ill-educated and low-skilled people without social bonds—elderly, passive and concerned about health.

While it is interesting to have a general demographic profile of your customers ("She is between 25 and 35 years old, well-educated, married with one child, has a good job, lives in a condo in an upscale neighborhood, travels abroad at least twice a year..." or "She is in her mid thirties, the privileged wife of a rich husband and doesn't need to work, has more than one home, sends her children to the best schools..."), it is of great value to understand their behavior-based personalities and activities, as these also influence their relationship to your products and services.

- **Behavioral profile**

Make it your business to know your customers' behaviors and, where possible, fit them into one of the eight categories listed above. This helps to make it possible for you to anticipate their buying decisions based on their social activities, and thus, to be able to make your buying decisions accordingly.

- **Lifecycle stages**

Understanding your customers incorporates knowing their respective lifecycle stages, which have a substantial influence over their shopping interests.

There's the bachelor stage or the singles leaving the family nest. These customers generally have fewer financial burdens, have a high interest in fashion and the latest gadgets, have high levels of activity and prioritize their leisure time. They would most likely buy very basic home appliances, furniture or cars, but would spend a great deal of time and money on things that mesh with the mating game.

The next stage in the lifecycle could be described as "the young couple" stage. These pre-baby customers have frequent social gatherings, are avid travelers, have the highest rate of purchase and, as they are at the nest-creating stage, the highest average rate of purchasing durables.

This gives way to the baby stage, where investing in a home is of great importance. Cash flow is low but the interest in new products is high. Interest in advertising is also at its highest. Value for money is the main theme for durables such as washers, dryers, general home appliances, TVs and DVD players, baby products, baby food and vitamins, and toys. Activities surround the baby's growth and development, and other baby playmates.

Next comes the schooling stage. Finances are better but the main emphasis is on the children's education and on extra-curricular activities (sports, dancing and music). This stage is characterized by having less time to shop and to be less influenced by advertising. Items are bought in family packs or multi-unit deals: this includes family-friendly vacations and outings. Less attention is paid to fashion and more emphasis is placed on healthy lifestyles.

When the children are ready to leave the nest, the cycle starts again. While the children are at the beginning of the cycle, the parents have reached the comfort stage. This is probably the biggest and most interesting group for retailers, because disposable income is high for luxury items, better vacation destinations, home improvements and spending related to health improvement.

Understanding behavior has everything to do with matching products with customers and choosing the best segments for your store to target.

CONSUMERS' MINDSETS

Studying consumers can help retail organizations improve their marketing strategies by giving them an insight into psychological issues which can influence purchasing behavior. Having an understanding of the psychology behind how consumers think, feel, reason, and select from different alternatives (brands, products, quality, price); how environmental factors (culture, family, social status, signs, media, location, parking, public transport, time, queuing) all exert an influence on consumer behavior; how limitations in consumer knowledge or information-processing abilities influence decision-making; how consumer motivation and decision strategies differ from one product to another and influence buying patterns—all these can lead to astute marketing strategies and promotions to reach the consumer more effectively.

Understanding these issues helps retailers adapt their strategies by always taking the consumer into consideration and enables them to pinpoint the different messages that will compete more successfully for the attention potential customers. In doing so, retailers can save a great deal of money by being more effective in their communication with consumers who, at times,

will be persuaded more by logical arguments and, at others, by emotional or symbolic appeals.

By understanding your consumer, you will be able to make a more informed decision as to what types of merchandise to buy and which strategy to employ.

THE STRATEGY CLOCK

Given the high degree of competitiveness among retailers in a marketplace, how does one retailer gain competitive advantage over the others? When there are only a limited number of unique products and services out there, how do different organizations sell basically the same things at different prices and with different degrees of success?

It has been established and proven that there are only three fundamental strategies: cost leadership, product differentiation and market segmentation.

Bowman's Strategy Clock, illustrated below, is based on the competitive and strategic options businesses have. These consider the competitive advantages in relation to cost or differentiation advantages and are organized into eight core strategic options:

Option 1: Low cost and low value–segment-specific

Option 2: Low price–risk of price wars–need to be cost-effective

Option 3: Hybrid (mixed or cross-breed)–low cost
Low prices but with some differentiation

Option 4: Differentiation–no price premium–perceived added value by users–market share benefits; or has a premium price–perceived added value high enough to command a higher price

Option 5: Focused differentiation–perceived added value to a specific segment, warranting a premium price

Option 6: Increased price standards–higher margins–higher prices–perceived high value

Bowman's Strategy Clock

The first chart illustrates the eight competitive positions.

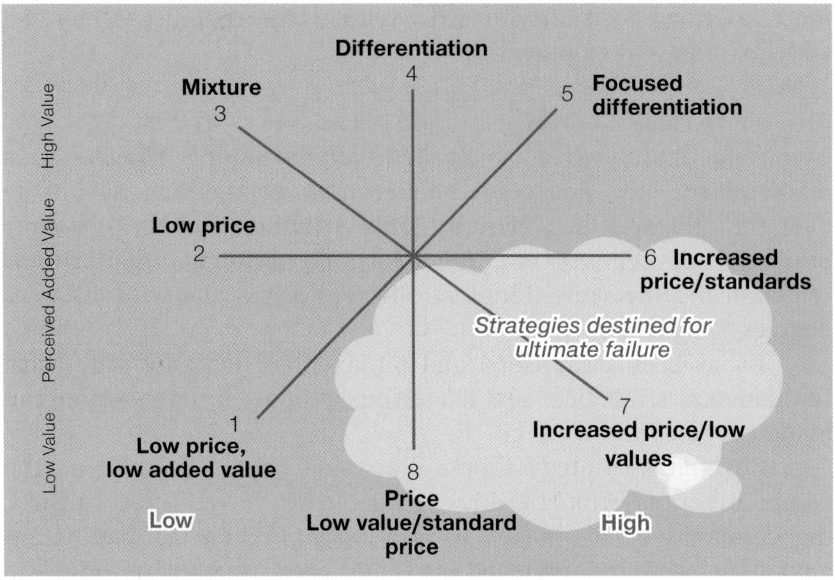

The second chart illustrates the fate of positions 6, 7 and 8.

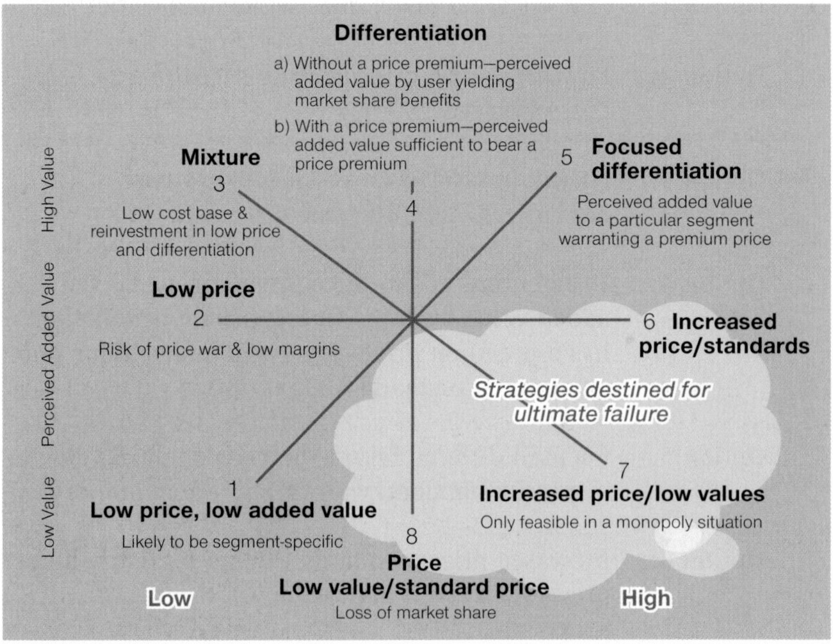

Source: www.marketingteacher.com/Lessons/lesson_bowman.htm

Option 7:	Increased prices–low value–OK if you're a monopoly
Option 8:	Low value–standard prices–loss of market share.

COMPETITIVE ADVANTAGE

This matrix examines the benefits of obtaining a competitive advantage through cost leadership and/or differentiation, as highlighted in Bowman's Strategy Clock.

Even though it may not be possible for you to become a cost leader, you can continue to thrive by maintaining significant differences from the offerings of your competition. This can be through the depth in your assortments (evergreen, always available), the width in your assortments (lots of choice), the newness in your assortments (novelty items exclusive to your store), and special assortments (hard-to-find items).

STRATEGIC GAP ANALYSIS

Once the general expectation of performance in the industry is understood, it is possible to compare that expectation with the level of performance at which the company currently functions. This comparison becomes the gap analysis, which can be performed at the strategic or operational level of an organization.

Gap analysis is an assessment tool applicable to any type of business. It enables a company to compare its actual performance with its potential performance. If an organization is under-utilizing its resources or is forgoing investment in capital or technology, then it may be producing or performing at a level below its potential. As its name suggests, the goal of gap analysis is to identify the gap between the *optimized* allocation and the *current* level of allocation, and thus to pinpoint areas that have room for improvement.

The analysis process, which flows naturally from benchmarking and other performance assessments, involves determining, documenting and approving the variance between business requirements and current capabilities.

Gap analysis is a formal study of what a business is doing currently and where it wants to go in the future, and may focus on different aspects of the business: organizational (for example, human resources); direction (for example, expansion or starting a private-label program); processes (for example, buying processes or

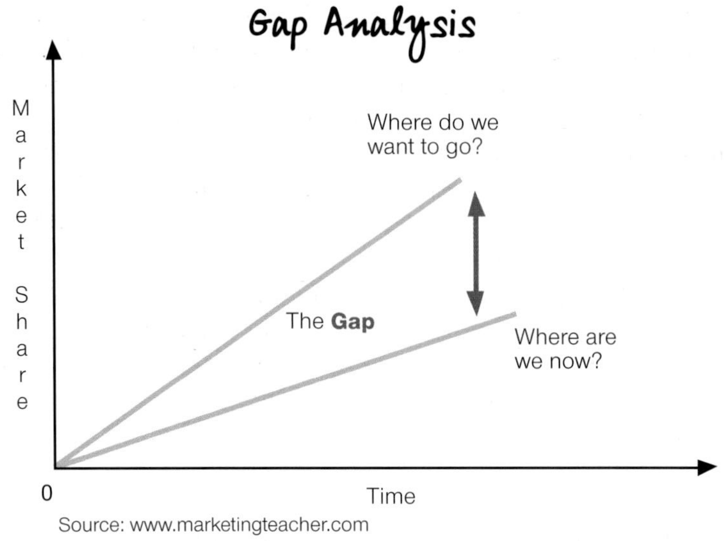

loss-prevention solutions); or information technology (for example, CRM or revamp of POS systems).

Such analyses provide a foundation for measuring the investment of time, money and human resources required to achieve a particular outcome, and there are good reasons why these should be undertaken periodically. If, for example, your sales are beginning to stagnate, there may be more than one reason for this. It may be a problem with your merchandise or because the competition is becoming more aggressive and gaining the edge. A gap analysis allows you to look at your business in an objective way, reveal the cause and lead you towards finding a remedy for the situation.

In undertaking a strategic gap analysis, the first step is to gather information about the business processes and infrastructure based on the company's vision. These should be specifically defined and documented.

Documentation is critical because this forces an explicit definition of the problems to be resolved; the benefits to be gained; the players involved; and a step-by-step definition of the business processes integral to your solution.

You can close the gap by using tactical approaches, effectively modifying the marketing mix so that you get to where you want to be. The "marketing mix" is probably the most famous phrase in marketing and comprises the "four Ps": price, place, product, and promotion. The concept is simple. Think of it as a kind of cake mix. All cakes contain varying degrees of eggs, milk, flour, and sugar. The shape and taste of the cake can be determined by altering the amounts of each of these elements. It is the same with the marketing mix. The offer you make to your customer can be altered by varying the mix of elements. So, for a high-profile brand, this might mean an increased focus on promotion and desensitizing the weight given to price.

GAP ANALYSIS AS A MARKETING TOOL

Strategic gap analysis is also used as a marketing tool that helps you analyze and deploy specific business plans. The analysis can consist of all four elements as set out in the following diagram, or individual segments from it.

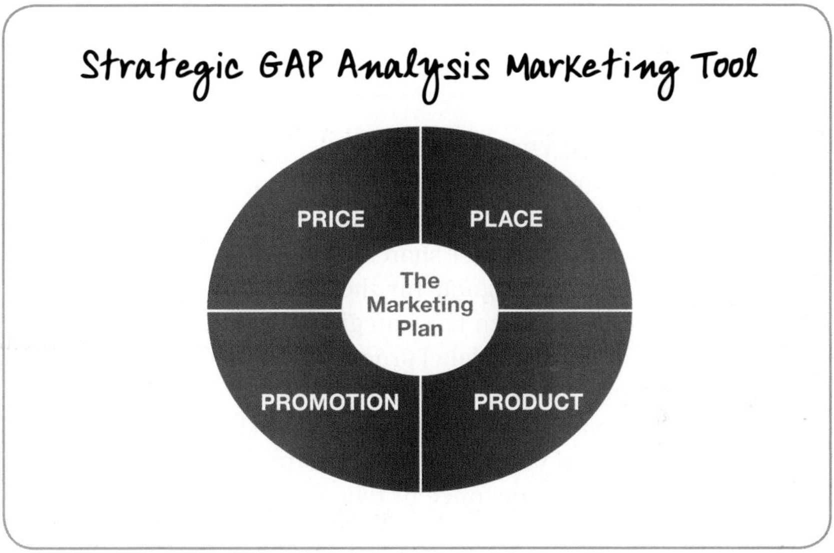

Retailers may opt to start with, say, market development, and have an internal focus group come up with suggestions of how to develop the market further through, perhaps, developing new business in a new suburban area. It may be that the retailer wishes to penetrate a new selective market (as happens when a department store opens a standalone specialty store with exclusive brands). It is also possible that the retailer needs to widen his points of differentiation vis-à-vis the competition by developing new product ranges, in-house brands, and labels.

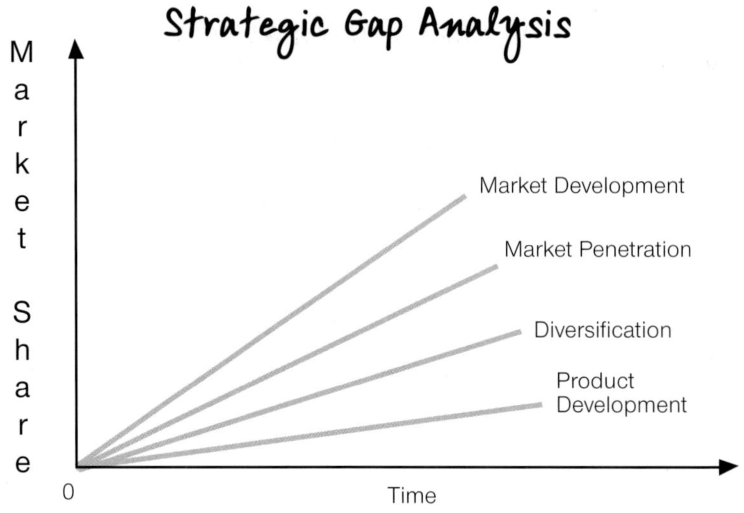

TACTICAL GAP ANALYSIS

Tactical gap analysis is used in the same manner as the strategic analysis, but focuses on specifics and the influence each component has on gaining a bigger market share.

This analysis is quite good for the retail industry as it covers all key points necessary when re-strategizing your business, opening new stores, starting a private-label program or undertaking any major changes in your processes.

In fact, the analysis in itself is one that should be conducted periodically to gauge if you are on the right track with your company goals. For some, this is done once or twice a year during the budget-planning process, when they are revised and adjusted in accordance with market trends and expected future performances.

The analysis is focused on the following elements (known as "the seven Ps"):

- **Price**

Decisions may be taken to increase prices by a certain percentage to cover increased operational costs. Increasing the gross margins can be achieved by obtaining greater trade discounts from suppliers but, more often than not, both reducing the cost of goods and increasing retail pricing is necessary to ensure adequate impact.

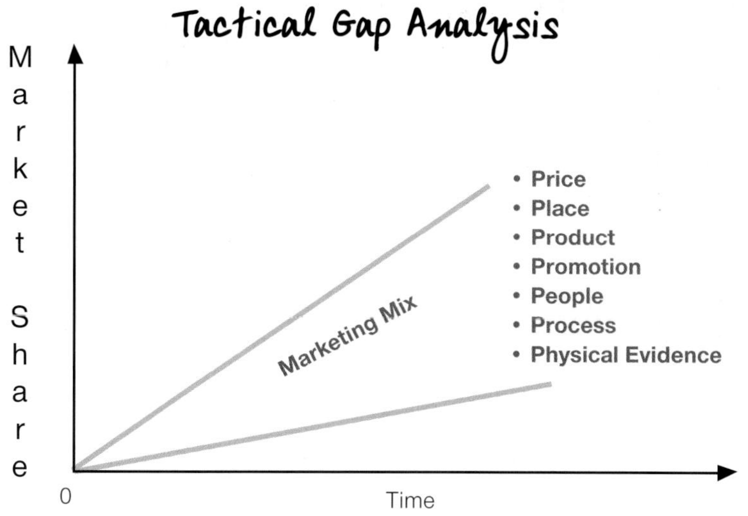

Source: www.marketingteacher.com

- **Place**

Reviewing the location of your retail outlets is a crucial part of the analysis. You may consider opening a store in a new retail mall or expanding within an existing mall where, for example, the mall operators offer existing tenants additional space.

- **Product**

As products are the backbone of the retail industry, this is an area that warrants quarterly, half-yearly, and yearly revisions. The same questions are asked each time: Is our product offering the right merchandise at the right price, in the right quality, at the right time? Are we carrying the right quantities and in the right balance to cater to consumer demands? Are the products in the right location on the selling floor? Do we have the right balance between regional brands and exclusive brands?

- **Promotions**

Promotions are also planned well in advance. These are typically the half-yearly sales, price promotions, VIP-card member events, festive-season promotions and activities, fashion launches, or in-store demonstrations. They can include launches for new stores or brand or warehouse sales.

- **People**

Next is the budgeting of head counts by division, by department, by store. In the planning, revisions are made on additional needs for selling staff, positions that need to be filled in various functions or requests for specialized talent in certain areas of the business.

Reviewing individual staff performance is also important. These reviews are usually conducted annually by heads of divisions.

- **Processes**

A review of processes is an integral part of any analysis. Internal service functions may be revised and cost efficiencies and/or reductions may be introduced. Increasingly, retailers are investing in automated IT functions and processes such as ERP to streamline their internal processes.

- **Physical evidence**

This incorporates a summary of all components—the facts and figures, the bottom line, the fiscal year-end results—tangible evidence that the thousands of decisions made during the course of the year were good ones.

Analyses such as this are designed to reveal deficiencies. As a buyer, the more you strive to achieve merchandising excellence, the greater the impact you will have in reducing these gaps.

SWOT ANALYSIS

SWOT analysis is a potent technique for understanding your strengths and weaknesses, and for looking at the opportunities and threats you face. Used in a business context, it helps you carve a sustainable niche in your market. Used in a personal context, it helps you develop your career in a way that takes best advantage of your talents, abilities and opportunities. What makes SWOT particularly potent is that, with a little thought, it can help you uncover opportunities that you are well placed to take advantage of. By understanding the weaknesses of your business, you can manage and eliminate threats that would otherwise catch you unawares.

- **Strengths**

In looking at your strengths, ask the following questions: What advantages does your company have? What do you do better than anyone else? What unique or lowest-cost resources do you have access to? What do people in your market see as your strengths?

Consider these from an internal perspective, and from the point of view of your customers and people in your market. If you experience any difficulty with this, try writing down a list of your characteristics. Think about these in relation to your competitors. For example, if all your competitors provide high-quality products combined with excellent service, a high-quality production and service process is not a strength in the market, it is a necessity.

- **Weaknesses**

Questions to ask in this regard include: What could you improve? What should you avoid? What are people in your market likely to see as weaknesses?

Again, consider this from an internal and external perspective. Do other people seem to perceive weaknesses that you do not see? Are your competitors doing any better than you? It is best to be realistic now, and face any unpleasant truths as soon as possible.

- **Opportunities**

Here, you need to ask the following: Where are the good opportunities facing you? What are the interesting trends you are aware of? Useful opportunities can come from such things as changes in technology and markets on both a broad and narrow scale; changes in government policy related to your field; changes in social patterns, population profiles and lifestyles; and from local events.

A useful approach to looking at opportunities is to look at your strengths and ask yourself whether these open up any opportunities. Alternatively, look at your weaknesses and ask yourself whether you could open up opportunities by eliminating them.

- **Threats**

Pertinent questions here include: What obstacles do you face? What is your competition doing? Are the required specifications for your job, products or services changing? Is changing technology threatening your position? Do you have bad-debt or cash-flow problems? Could any of your weaknesses seriously threaten your business?

Carrying out this analysis will often be illuminating, both in pointing out what needs to be done, and in putting problems into perspective.

Strengths and weaknesses often come from within the organization. Opportunities and threats often relate to external factors. For this reason, the SWOT analysis is sometimes called Internal-External

SWOT Analysis for Your business

Strengths	Weaknesses
Opportunities	**Threats**

SWOT your brand

With your brand in mind, use this map to answer the six key points according to Ries & Trout. Move the Price line and Quality line to fit your current positioning. Then decide where you want to be!

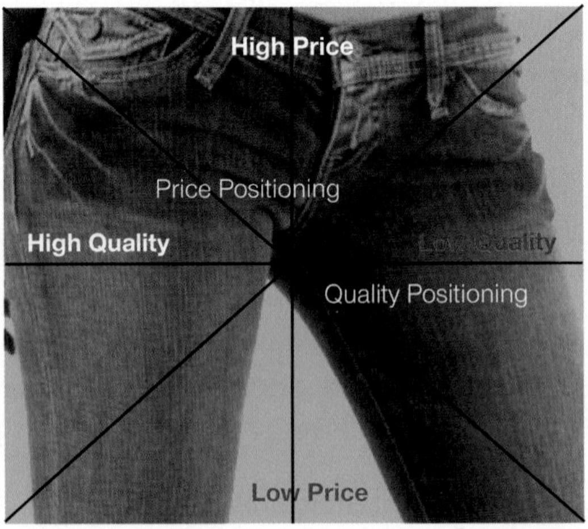

1. What position do you currently own?
2. What position do you want to own?
3. Who do you have to defeat to own the position you want?
4. Do you have the resources to do it?
5. Can you persist until you get there?
6. Are your tactics supporting the positioning objective you set?

Source: *Positioning: The Battle For Your Mind*, Al Ries & Jack Trout, McGraw Hill Professionals, 2001

Analysis and the SWOT Matrix is sometimes called an IE Matrix Analysis Tool.

You can also apply SWOT analysis to your competitors. As you do this, you'll start to see how and where you should compete against them. It can also be used specifically on product ranges, especially in a market where quality, brand and prices are very competitive.

MENTAL PREPARATION

Prior to the buying season, buyers should conduct meetings with their department sales manager and review in detail the sales performance, the lessons learnt, the stock analysis of under-bought and overbought items, slow-moving ranges, mark-downs and the reasons for them, and mark-up opportunities.

They should listen to what the sales staff have to say on such things as customer feedback, lost opportunities (such as being out of stock), reactions to colors or styles, price points, and so on.

They should read publications that are applicable to their buying portfolio in order to be aware and prepared for new market trends. They should re-evaluate their consumer classifications and be prepared to make appropriate changes in light of changing trends and demands as and when necessary.

> "There are two kinds of people. Those who do the work and those who take the credits." Try to be in the first group; there is less completition there.
>
> **Indira Gandhi**

case study

Creating a concept

I was looking for a promotion that would lift our sales in August, a slow month. We had just finished with the "Great Singapore Sales" and it was a bit too early for the new autumn arrivals, so I decided to do something special for our National Day (August 9).

The orchid is Singapore's national flower, so why not do a promotion based on orchids in conjunction with our National Day celebrations? We started to conceptualize both ladies' and men's ranges. Our linens would be sourced from Hong Kong and our batik and hand-paints from Bali.

The concept took many months and the ranges were shaping beautifully, especially the ladies' resort-wear range. We found a new vendor who had had experience in designing silk jacquards, and created a beautiful jacquard based on the orchid "Vanda Lamellata."

The catch, however, was that we were required to take high minimum quantities per color in each style. We did not feel comfortable with this. The price, the vendor maintained, was a really good deal for this quality of silk. It was still a lot of units as these were meant for men's casual shirts; but I felt we needed those items to complete the range, so we bought them. The result of this promotion gave us a lot of publicity; we had Orchard Road windows to back the theme up, and a 12-page spread in a popular magazine called *Her World*.

The sellthrough was brilliant on all counts except for the silk jacquard range. As anticipated, the units were too much for us to absorb and we didn't make a profit on this buy. The concept in itself completely covered the intended styles, colors and fabrications. It was fresh, new and appealing. However, this "completeness" had one flaw. The concept required the silk jacquards but the compromise on the high units cost mark-downs. Lesson learnt: even the boss can make mistakes. If it feels bad, it probably is bad.

It is not the strongest of the species that survives, nor the most intelligent, but the one most responsive to change.
- Charles Darwin

10 CENTRAL BUYING

BUYING FOR BRANCHES

In the past, when department stores and specialty stores expanded their businesses, they tended to treat these additional units as offshoots.

The same buyers were made responsible for purchasing for these offshoots, even though they may have had quite different customer segmentations. They were also expected to make frequent visits to these stores. This was not ideal in the long term and new solutions were developed.

From buying for "flagship stores" with similar ranges for the branches, many retailers saw the need for central buying with the aid of computer technology.

Data analysis enables buyers to manage the purchases, though on-site assistance from branch managers may be needed. This leads to some flexibility in the individual outlets to cater more accurately to localized requirements. These must be planned for as sub-categories in the OTB Planners.

- **Data gathering**

Since central buyers do not have the advantage of interacting with customers and learning their needs first hand, they need input from the selling locations, in addition to computer-generated data.

Some of the larger chains have integrated CCTV systems into their stores, allowing buyers to do virtual tours of their outlets.

- **Local tastes and local demands**

Although general assortments may be applicable across a range of stores, variations do exist in certain communities. Some may require larger or smaller sizes. Color, design, fabrication or fabric preferences may also vary in some stores. Seasonal timing of deliveries may also vary, which can be an advantage in that staggered deliveries enable some product testing in stores with faster demands.

- **Selling functions**

As the buyer's selling functions and interactions with customers diminish greatly when buying is done centrally, detailed information on the selling features of the goods bought is necessary. Logging merchandise information on the company's intranet system has many advantages in this regard.

- **Planning and control functions**

The planning and control functions are more vital to multi-store retailers than single-store operators. In most cases, the techniques are more sophisticated and are likely to be performed by staff specialists. Buyers are then able to concentrate on their procurement functions.

VISUAL MERCHANDISE CATALOGS (VMC)

Visual merchandise catalogs (VMC) are pictorial stock controls and are an efficient way to control, review, and revise season-end action to be taken on stock obsolescence.

VMC (as illustrated opposite) can be shared with your MM/DMM, buying offices, vendors and sales department managers. They also help in evaluating sellthrough on each item and in determining the success or otherwise of particular items.

They are also practical when conducting product-knowledge sessions with your selling staff, particularly when samples are not on hand.

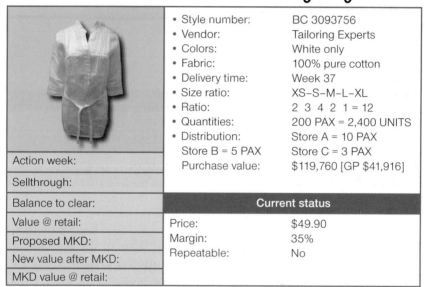

Visual Merchandise Cataloguing

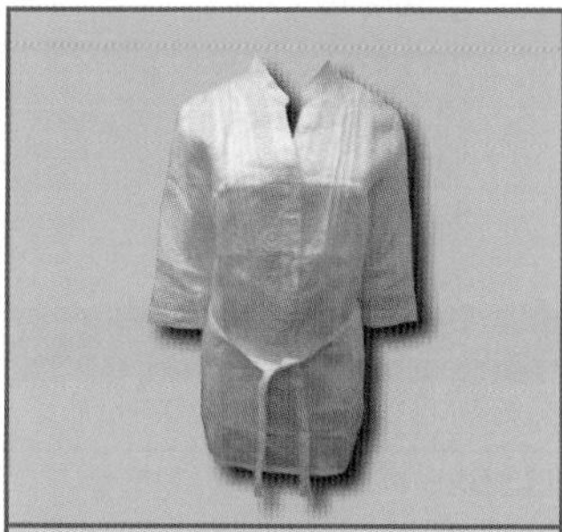

- Style number: BC 3093756
- Vendor: Tailoring Experts
- Colors: White only
- Fabric: 100% pure cotton
- Delivery time: Week 37
- Size ratio: XS–S–M–L–XL
- Ratio: 2 3 4 2 1 = 12
- Quantities: 200 PAX = 2,400 UNITS
- Distribution: Store A = 10 PAX
  Store B = 5 PAX Store C = 3 PAX
  Purchase value: $119,760 [GP $41,916]

Action week:	
Sellthrough:	
Balance to clear:	
Value @ retail:	
Proposed MKD:	
New value after MKD:	
MKD value @ retail:	

Current status

Price:	$49.90
Margin:	35%
Repeatable:	No

- **Sales performance and evaluation**

At first glance, you may consider an 85% sellthrough (as illustrated in the VMC below) acceptable; but when you analyze the value of the balance, the picture is not so rosy.

In this case, the 15% balance represents 360 units at $49.90 each, giving a value of stock to be cleared of $17,964.

The cost of goods before mark-down was $11,676. By selling the goods at 50% off, these stocks now have a retail value of only $8,982, bringing you a margin of –0.23%. The goods are basically sold below the initial cost, at a loss of $2,694.

This calculation does not include the cost of selling these goods, which involves, among other things, the cost of the extra

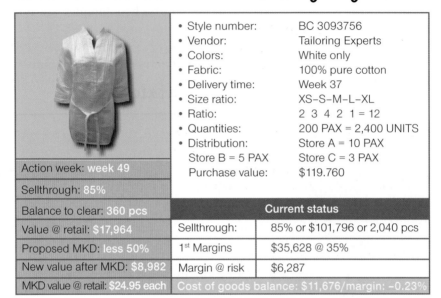

Visual Merchandise Cataloguing

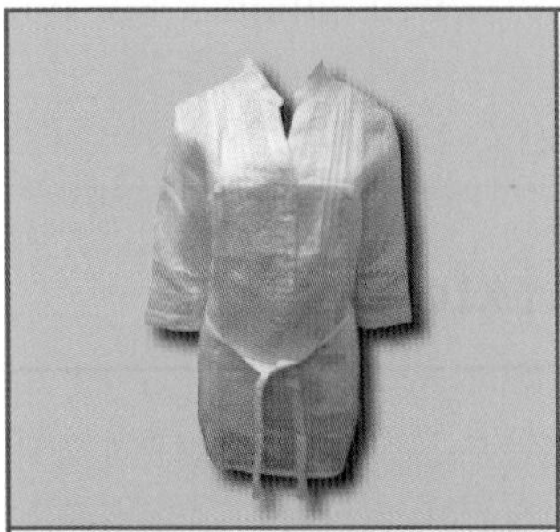

- Style number: BC 3093756
- Vendor: Tailoring Experts
- Colors: White only
- Fabric: 100% pure cotton
- Delivery time: Week 37
- Size ratio: XS–S–M–L–XL
- Ratio: 2 3 4 2 1 = 12
- Quantities: 200 PAX = 2,400 UNITS
- Distribution: Store A = 10 PAX

  Store B = 5 PAX Store C = 3 PAX

  Purchase value: $119.760

Action week:	week 49
Sellthrough:	85%
Balance to clear:	360 pcs
Value @ retail:	$17,964
Proposed MKD:	less 50%
New value after MKD:	$8,982
MKD value @ retail:	$24.95 each

Current status	
Sellthrough:	85% or $101,796 or 2,040 pcs
1st Margins	$35,628 @ 35%
Margin @ risk	$6,287
Cost of goods balance: $11,676/margin: −0.23%	

handling of the merchandise from the shop floor to the warehouse; the changing of the price tags; the promotional efforts needed to sell the goods; and the additional signage required in advertising the changes.

Granted, the same information that is registered on the VMC can be captured from the company's computerized data analysis, but VMC tracking enables you to monitor the particular style (or, to use the industry jargon, "KIV (keep in view) the product").

With the handling of so many SKUs, it is difficult for the buyer to remember all buys. VMC is practical when tracing outright purchases, product developments, and basic repeatable stocks.

CENTRAL BUYING SYSTEMS

For the store-level replenishment of basic stocks, systems are now available to capture point-of-sale data that diminishes the use of branch-store or chain-store computer system organizers. For smaller retailers, however, the manual method may still be viable and the only means to replenish basic stock.

Following are different types of systems or procedures used by smaller retailers. They have different functions but are set up to facilitate merchandise replenishment or distribution from the outlets.

- **Warehouse and requisitions**

This manual check-list requires that stores compare their stocks on hand against stocks at warehouse. It requires monitoring to ensure that stock levels in store can carry them through to the next stock check.

The requisitions for re-orders are planned by the central buyers, leaving little control over the composition of assortments to the operational department managers. Department managers do, however, control the depth of these at the warehouse, allowing requisition fill-ins or replenishments. They can be for basic items or staple foods for which there is steady demand, and which require width in assortments.

- **Approved resource systems**

Some smaller retailers allow replenishment from pre-approved vendor listings, which enables store managers to order directly from the suppliers. These listings, comprising specific SKUs and cost and retail price details, are provided by the central buyers to the store managers.

Opening-stock distribution plan

This requisition plan allows the department manager or store managers control over opening stock for each basic item/or re-order. These can be bought directly from a specified vendor. However, ordering new styles or new items is the responsibility of the central buyers.

Auto open-to-buy

Auto-OTB is linked to the opening-stock distribution plan. Allocations are planned for each department for new merchandise to be received during the season. These are controlled by the central buyers and after opening stocks have been completed.

Distribution point function

A distribution point is different from a warehouse in that it does not hold or store goods. Goods are shipped from the vendor to the distribution point (DP), where goods are subjected to quality-control checks. Price tagging and EAS tagging is also performed here, which saves time and is less expensive than if done at store level.

The quantities distributed to each outlet are based on current inventory needs at the time of delivery, and may differ from the planned allocation at time of purchase.

The central planner will also check sales information from each store to determine just where additional supply is needed.

Direct shipment

Some retailers find it too costly to have a DP, and arrange for the vendors to ship directly to the individual stores, which then carry out the quality-control function. Increasingly, vendors are agreeing to keep some back-up stocks ready for quick replenishments.

Warehouse distribution

In addition to the usual warehouse functions, some home-furnishings retailers use the warehouse to conduct deliveries of customers' purchases. The departments "selling from warehouse" have very high per-square-foot returns, as not all retailers bill departments directly for warehouse costs.

Another delivery method commonly used by stores selling bulky furniture is to have the supplier/vendor conduct the home deliveries. This has the practical advantage of having the supplier/vendor installing the purchased item at the customer's home. This service is negotiated, with the cost being reflected in a lower margin.

SYSTEMS AND PROCEDURES

• ERP

Enterprise Resource Planning (ERP) systems integrate (or attempt to integrate) all of an organization's data and processes into a single, unified, computerized system. A key ingredient of most ERP systems is the use of a single, unified database to store data for the various system modules.

The term "ERP" originally implied systems designed to plan the utilization of enterprise-wide resources, primarily in a manufacturing environment. Today, though, ERP systems have a much broader scope across a wide range of organizations, including bigger retailers.

To be considered an ERP system, a software package generally would only need to provide functionality in a single package that would normally be covered by two or more systems. Technically, a software package that provides both payroll and accounting functions (such as QuickBooks) would be considered an ERP software package.

However, the term is generally reserved for larger, more broadly based applications. The introduction of an ERP system to replace two or more independent applications eliminates the need for external interfaces previously required between systems, and provides additional benefits that range from standardization and lower maintenance (one system instead of two or more) to easier and/or greater reporting capabilities (as all data is typically kept in one database).

Examples of modules in an ERP which formerly would have been standalone applications include manufacturing, supply chain, financials, CRM, human resources, and warehouse management. ERP enables a company's information to be linked to one main database, enabling a high level of cross-interpretational analysis that was previously not automatically available.

Information Distribution

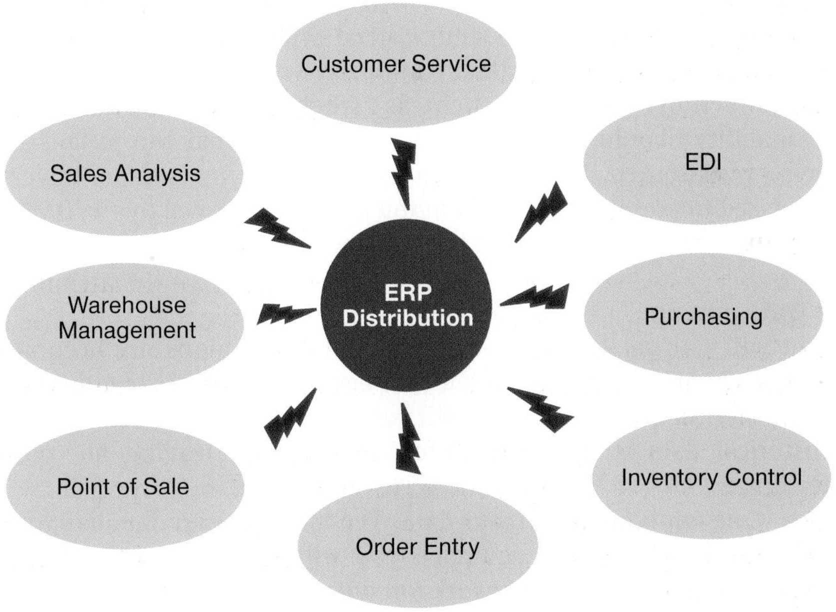

Source: www.openpro.com/erp.html

EDI = Electronic Data Interchange

In my experience, buyers are generally not keen on reading computerized reports. They may cope with the most obvious—sales and margin reports, stock reports and OTB reports—but there is much more information available which is seldom read, let alone used as a tool for better buying. I have also found that fear of not achieving sales targets goes away when the buyer is fully conversant with the data, and uses the data to make changes or better buying decisions that reflect current dynamics. As Ralph Waldo Emerson said: "Knowledge is the antidote for fear."

IMPACT OF COMPUTER TECHNOLOGY

Larger and more advanced retailers see the benefits of using advanced technology, whose function eliminates the need of some or all manual steps of merchandise planning. Some functions are totally automated while others are farmed out to the vendors. In both cases, the goal is to free store personnel to concentrate on selling.

Buyers should work with company systems in all aspects of the systems' capabilities.

• Data analysis

It is imperative that you fully utilize your company's data, especially if your role involves multi-store or multi-operating divisions. This analysis should be viewed and worked with on a daily basis for sales—by department, by classification, by vendor or by SKU.

Inventory controls such as stocks on hand and OTB availability should be constantly updated to avoid the pitfalls of being overstocked. In preparation for a new buying season, buyers are asked to present a detailed buying plan for approval by the DMM. This may need to be revisited in light of any prior buying trips.

• Data mining

You will gain a lot of respect if your buying plans are accurate and based on facts. It puts you in a better position to negotiate an expansion of a classification, SKU or a brand with a given vendor. Historical data is the premise for future plans, leaving no room for error.

Constantly monitor your data. The more you are familiar with the business, the better equipped you will be to take correct and timely action. Use the network or data to bridge branch stores, operating divisions or multiple departments. Make sure you evaluate your vendor performances. This can be on a monthly, six-monthly or yearly basis. Don't expect those under you to be as familiar with the details as you. Having this information will enable you to answer any questions your superiors may have on the previous day's sales, on which brands are performing, and whether a given promotion is meeting expectations.

If your position requires you to travel, never leave town without your detailed buying plans. These should include vendor sellthrough by article number, SKU and range type; OTB plan for possible new brands or product range; price-point range list; and stock, seasonal and mark-down lists. You should always have your activity planner with you to help in planning promotions or sales with your vendors. Also, be familiar with terminologies used when dealing with foreign vendors, some of which are set out below.

Useful international terminology

DPP	Direct product profitability	UPC	Universal product code
DSS	Decision-support systems	UVM	Universal vendor marking
EDI	Electronic data interchange	UVM/UPs	Universal vendor marking in UPC codes
E-Mail	Electronic mail	OTB	Open-to-buy
EDP	Electronic data processing	EAS	Electronic article surveillance
EPS	Electronic packing slip	RFID	Radio frequency identification
GP	Gross profit margin		**Local Buying Terms**
JIT	Just-in-time inventory ordering	S.O.R	Sale or return (Merchandise paid upfront but with returnable conditions on goods not sold)
MIS	Management info system	CON	Consignment (loaned goods paid only once goods are sold)
OCR	Optical character recognition	Conces.	Concessionaire. Contractual agreement between supplier and retailer on Sales & GP. Monthly payment on achieved sales.
PC	Personal computer		
PLU	Price look-up		
POS	Point of sale		
QR	Quick response		
QC	Quality control		
SKU	Stock-keeping unit		

While you may not use these terms daily or internally, they are handy for communicating with foreign vendors or buying offices.

THE BUYER–COMPUTER RELATIONSHIP

• Planning and forecasting

The advantage of computer technology is that it enables you to simulate the "What if?" scenarios: What if I trade down in this class? What if I trade up in another class? What if I change the weight of my merchandise mix? Such scenarios are particularly useful when retailers experience stiff competition in certain types of merchandise. The computer is able to provide answers in a matter of minutes.

When planning and forecasting your sales, gross profit margins, inventory, mark-downs and mark-ups, the system enables you to view the effects of any changes you may want to explore.

• Daily operations

Having appropriate computer programs relieves buyers of time-consuming day-to-day tasks such as inventory control, the receipt and distribution of goods and re-ordering basic stocks.

Some computer software can analyze historical data on sales of specific SKUs and determine the optimal level of inventory for each month or period. However automated the system, the buyer still needs to check these levels periodically.

• Out-of-stock (OOS) situations

In today's retail environment, having point-of-sale (POS) information will enable you to monitor stock levels by SKU. But what the data input and output will not tell you is if there are shortages due to shrinkage or spoilage.

Check with your operations people that the stock balance sheets tally with physical stocks on hand. Remember that the POS system can only show the balance of stock on hand, not how many goods are unaccounted for as a result of theft, for example. Only a physical stock count can do this.

> Approximately $20 billion in revenue is lost to the global consumer packaged goods (CPG) market each year and 76% of such losses are created at store level. Being out of stock can be the result of many factors. Your job as a buyer is to ensure that negligence on your part is not one of these factors.
>
> Each time this happens, you risk losing more than 30% of your customers, as the following chart indicates.

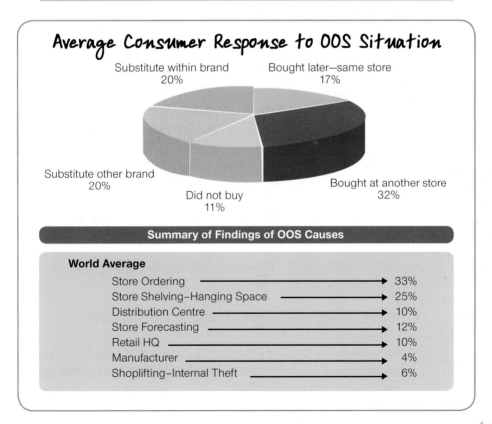

Average Consumer Response to OOS Situation

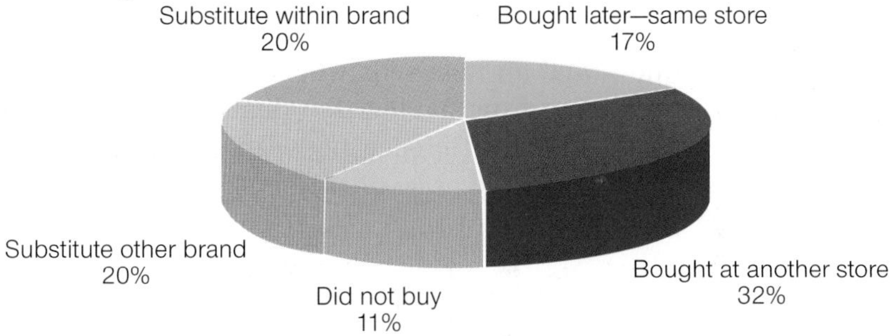

Summary of Findings of OOS Causes

World Average

Store Ordering →	33%
Store Shelving-Hanging Space →	25%
Distribution Centre →	10%
Store Forecasting →	12%
Retail HQ →	10%
Manufacturer →	4%
Shoplifting-Internal Theft →	6%

Shifts in consumer demand: Slow reaction to consumer demands, leaving too few stocks of popular items or specific brand preferences.

Promotional planning periods: A promotion is undervalued, resulting in lost sales when sales are better than expected and replenishment is slow.

Sophistication of the supply chain: A distribution system that requires that goods are sent to a central warehouse before they are distributed to the outlets can cause delays in having the goods on the selling floor.

Allocation of rack space to total units as opposed to sellable units: Shelf space is allocated to brands that don't sell well, reducing the space available to other fast-moving products.

Shoplifting and internal theft: This is a fact of retail life that is difficult to manage as there are no daily records indicating that the merchandise is missing.

DETERMINING OOS LOSSES

Using a point-of-sales (POS) system, which provides information on specific sales and how well an item sells when in stock, the retailer can calculate losses arising from having that item out of stock. The lost-sales opportunity is the difference between actual sales and expected sales, multiplied by the price of the item, multiplied by the number of days the item is out of stock.

POTENTIAL FIXES FOR OUT-OF-STOCK SITUATIONS

Having identified some of the culprits causing OOS, there are a number of approaches the retailer can take to combat the problem.

- Focus on the store; it's where the biggest opportunity for lower OOS exists.
- Adjust re-order quantities to suit the speed of sales.
- Re-adjust and localize planning to ensure that specific retail products are placed on retail shelves/displays in order to increase customer spending.

- De-list the "dogs," the slow-sellers taking up space, time and money. Stop ordering them.

- Evaluate adjacent categories. This is especially important for cross selling: ties next to shirts; shaving crème next to razors...

- Provide appropriate staff training in replenishment processes, ordering regular goods and, fast ordering of chronic OOS items.

Solving OOS problems is not merely an academic study. Once the immediate cause has been identified, put the resolutions into action. Measure current OOS levels and monitor improvements. Understand true consumer demand, by store, by SKU, by day, allowing some products more space to meet these demands. Develop a continuous OOS scorecard to be monitored by the store managers. Celebrate the high scores, as these are potential losses turned into sales. Create ongoing tactical actions that reduce lost opportunities and increase sales. Measure the results. It's about creating a continuous, systematic solution. It's about leveraging information and harnessing technology, not creating more inventory and labor. The chart below sets out what you may be looking at if you don't.

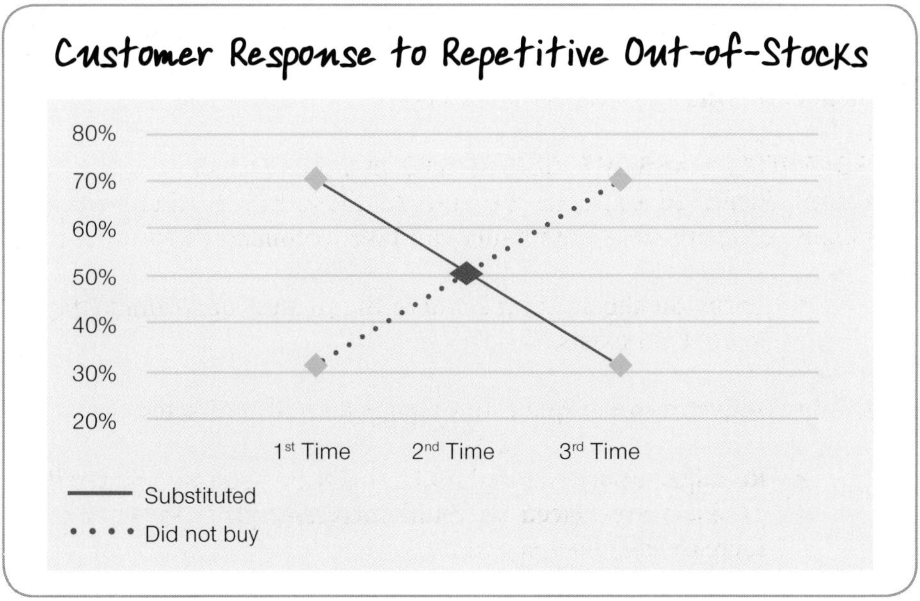

The graph indicates that when customers experience OOS on a product for the first time, 70% opt for a substitute. When this happens a second time, only 50% opt for a substitute. After a third unsuccessful attempt to get what they want, only 30% will settle for a substitute, which means that 70% walk away without buying a product. This leads ultimately to a rapid decrease in customer loyalty, not only to the products they expect to find in the store but also to the store itself.

The Art of Retail Buying

11 THE TRUE ESSENCE OF BUYING

Most department stores today recognize the need to reinvent themselves if they are to stay competitive. I have attended several round-table discussions with top retail executives and members of various international associations on this very key subject. Though all agree that changes to their business formats are necessary, few agree on a unified solution, let alone a joint buying strategy.

The main reason for the discrepancy is that each retail company regards its markets and customer profiles as unique, with unique requirements.

Interestingly, the need to change the way department stores do business is largely due to the invasion of new-age fashion brands like Zara, Mango and H&M, which have been enticing shoppers away from the department stores in most parts of the world.

The key element that will make shoppers stay loyal and spend with department stores is, as Zara, Mango and H&M have discovered, to ensure that they have a "glocal" appeal—one that is both global and yet appeals to local tastes and lifestyles. In other words, they have been able to understand and implement the concept of disposable branded fashion.

While these concepts are here to stay, we should recognize that they do not appeal to all customers. Buyers should continuously look for appealing merchandise that fulfills their customer requirements and not necessarily try to duplicate the formulas used by the global giants, who enjoy the benefits of economies of scale, making their production cheaper, bigger, wider and faster.

To sustain growth in most retail formats, stores have to decide the best basis on which they can retain customers, whether through having the majority of goods on consignment, on concession or on a sale-or-return basis. Each store has to ask itself whether it can increase its profits by having similar merchandise to the store down the road.

What retailers need to avoid is a customer perception of "The same old, same old": nothing new, nothing different, nothing special.

BUYING FOR YOUR CUSTOMERS

Buyers need to select merchandise based on their resources, insight into customer preferences and, to some extent, sixth sense. Selecting merchandise is very much a process of elimination: the right item is not likely to pop up and announce itself. The buyer needs to have a clear image of what is required, which makes it much easier to sort out the items that do not conform to all the set criteria.

Your starting point is to find merchandise that you feel will sell *in your store, to your customers.* Before you buy, try to visit a competitor or a store selling a similar product line. Browse the store's product selection and making a mental note of the brands carried, the products that seem to be selling well, the price points, and the items consigned to the clearance bin.

Choosing a product may very well be the most difficult decision you will need to make as a buyer. The choices are limitless and the task may be overwhelming at first: a fashion buyer may have 30 different dress styles to choose from in selecting just two; a food buyer may have to see 100 items before settling for a

Deciding what to buy

couple; and homeware buyers may have to view 1,000 items during a trade show to pick the best 50. There never seems enough time, space, data or money to accommodate the entire requirements of decision-making. Nevertheless, decisions have to be made, constantly and swiftly.

Not only should there be a demand for your products, but they must be profitable and something for which you feel there is a need. Let's face it, it won't matter what products you buy if your customers aren't buying.

If you are making the transition from high consignment trade to some outright purchases, you should start with product lines that are narrow and focused. This will give you the chance to try out lines and concepts. As your business grows, so can your product line and ranges, as long as you keep new products compatible with the type of business, your location and your market.

When it comes to selecting products to sell based on what's popular, timing is extremely important. New trends and products can be a great boost to your business but you'll need to be in at the beginning of the product lifecycle in order to be successful. Learning to pick a hot product before it becomes hot is a valuable skill that comes from knowing your market.

When deciding which products to sell in your store, ask yourself this question: Is this product something I would bring to my best friend? If the answer is "No", you may want to keep looking. Remember that your reputation is on the line.

In selecting products, you may like to keep the following questions in mind:

- Would you buy it and use it yourself? (Consider look, quality and price)
- Can you see yourself getting excited about this product?
- Would you sell it to someone you know?
- Is there a real need for the product in the market?
- Can you imagine yourself selling this item for the next several months/seasons/years?

The key to having success in the retail business is to believe in the product that you are selling. If you do not believe in the product yourself, then you probably won't be successful at selling it. Be persistent and you'll find a product or product line that meets both the needs of your target market and your own ability to locate, purchase and sell it.

BUYING CONSIDERATIONS

As a buyer, you are responsible for developing merchandising strategies for your department, section or store. If you work for a bigger organization, you would seek guidance from your merchandise manager (MM) or divisional merchandise manager (DMM). If you are running your own store, you have to rely on your own sound judgment; but the following checklist is applicable, whatever your store format.

First, you must take into consideration your company policies—quality standards, image, positioning and customer profile—and then each of the factors listed in the following chart.

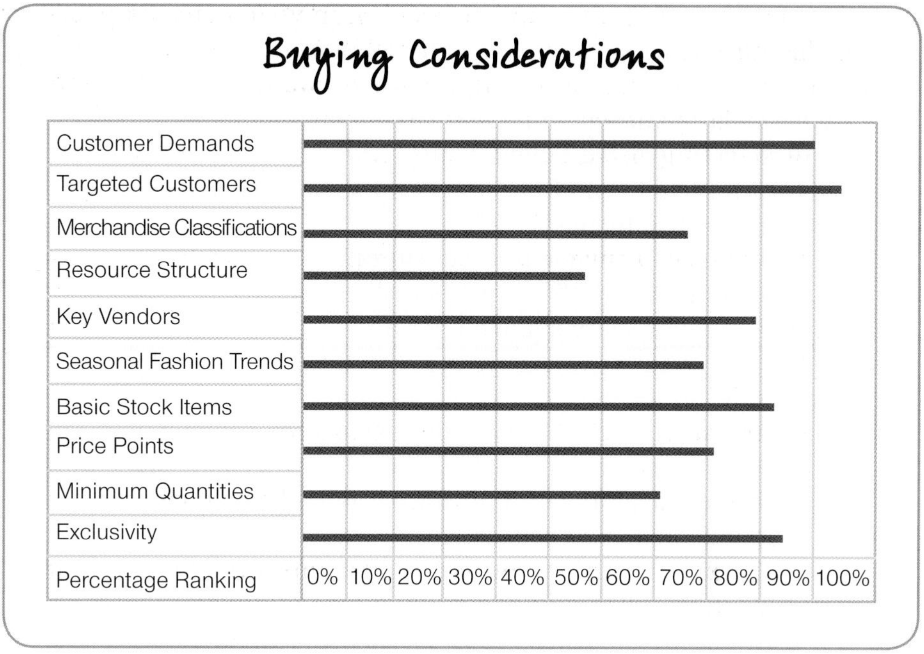

SHOPPING VENDOR LINES

Visiting vendors' showrooms and buying offices is a good way to view their prime lines or items, rather than expecting them to visit you (in which case, they are unlikely to bring everything they have prepared for the forthcoming season). Visiting their premises may also allow you to meet up with the principals and open a door to negotiate beneficial terms.

It is during the buying season that you need to communicate sellthough performances—what worked and what didn't—and the merchandise type that you wish to avoid in the coming season.

SELECTING NEW ITEMS

In selecting new items, buyers ought to have the following points in mind.

- **Features of the product**
  1. Will it have wide appeal? What is that appeal?
  2. Is it similar to anything else that has had proven success?
  3. Is it in line with current trends?
  4. Is it distinctive enough?

5. Will it provide total satisfaction in use?
6. Is the packaging suitable for the store and the customer?

- **Relationship to stock**
  1. Does it fit into the buying plan?
  2. Is it clearly different from current stocks on hand and on order?
  3. Can it be re-ordered?
  4. Is it already available in other stores?
  5. Is it a key item of the vendor's line?
  6. Is there floor space available for it?

- **Reconsiderations**
  1. Has the item (or items) been considered from different points of view? (For example, consider the case of a store that has a cosmetics department but not a toiletries department. In working on a planned expansion, the subject of having a toiletries department comes up for discussion. This is where gap analysis would be of value, leading to questions such as: Do we want it? Would it be profitable? Would we generate more traffic in the store if we had one?)
  2. Have the opinions of others been obtained?
  3. Can acceptance be tested in a small quantity before placing a more substantial order?

- **Promotions**
  1. What will be the best way to promote this item?
  2. What selling points should be passed on to the sales force?
  3. Will the seller provide advertising support and suitable display fixtures?
  4. Will the seller supply promoters to sell the items?

FACTORS INFLUENCING BUYING DECISIONS

Buyers consider vendor offerings that are appropriate in quality, pricing, style and consumer preference to their type of retail business. In addition to suitability, the buyer needs to question whether the items are sellable and, if so, in what quantities. When it comes to selecting fashion merchandise, buyers will require uniqueness, originality and, in some cases, a level of exclusivity. Design, innovation, novelty and even packaging are factors that will influence purchasing decisions.

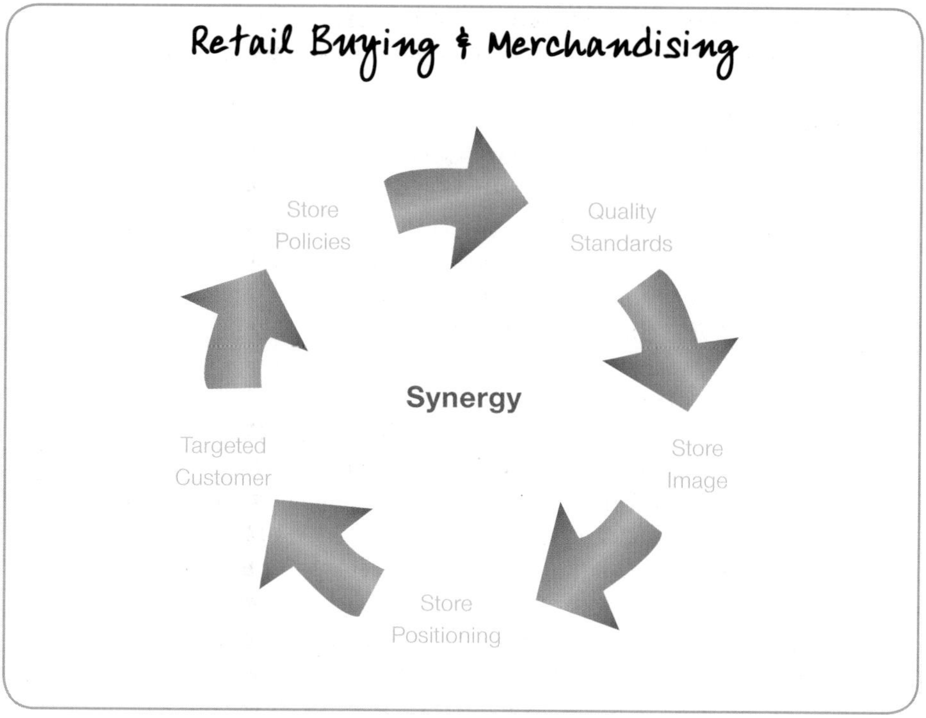

ON TIME, EVERY TIME

Getting your merchandise on time is also crucial. A great buy is only a great buy if it is available when it's needed on the selling floor. Empty shelves will only turn customers away to seek solace elsewhere; so dependability should be high on a buyer's vendor selection.

BACKING WINNERS

Another important aspect in selecting merchandise is to ensure that your vendors are flexible and adaptable enough to react to market trends and market demands. It is not uncommon to have great demand for merchandise when it is introduced at the beginning of the season and then to find that it is quickly out of stock and without any way of replenishing it to meet continuing demand. There has to be the ability to reproduce these winning lines on a timely basis, as and when required.

Finding the right level of cooperation with vendors is essential for any successful retailer but, in the end, it is the merchandise that is most important. Once the vendor has proven that its products are suitable and sellable in your stores, there is room to develop that relationship into a strong collaboration. Part of a buyer's responsibility is to take calculated risks in placing company money on merchandise they anticipate will sell. Of course, there is the possibility that not all merchandise will sell, but that's why retail calculations on mark-ups are there—to enable a profit to be made on a sales mix of items at full price, at reduced prices and at prices to clear.

TYPES OF SUPPLIERS

• Manufacturers

Some manufacturers sell their products at wholesale prices direct to the retailer. However, they may sell their products in too-large quantities or set a minimum quantity per item/color/style that is too high for the small retailer to absorb.

If there is a particular product you want to buy but not in the quantities the manufacturer requires, it may be better to approach the distributor(s) or dealer used by the manufacturer to obtain the product in the quantity you need.

• Importers

Globalization has made importing products much easier than it used to be. Retailers can purchase from importers or buy the products direct from a foreign company. However, it is important to understand all the aspects of the paperwork, shipping time, product life-cycle and all costs involved.

• Distributors

A distributor generally sells a large variety of a certain classification of products at a slightly higher price than if the item was purchased direct from the manufacturer. Retailers can buy lower quantities, which are not generally subject to a minimum order. Some distributors even offer free freight on orders over a certain amount.

• Other wholesalers and liquidators

Wholesalers often sell many kinds of products. Some will sell closeouts (items in which all remaining stock is disposed of, usually at greatly reduced prices), truckloads and pallets of merchandise and even damaged goods. Before buying from this type of supplier, be sure you completely understand the conditions, price and terms of the sale.

• Auctions

Retailers can find many bargains on eBay, the world's largest auction site, through browsing the appropriate Wholesale Lots category. Not all product prices on eBay are truly wholesale but, if you spend time watching the auctions and learn how to buy effectively, you're sure to find a deal.

CHOOSING A VENDOR

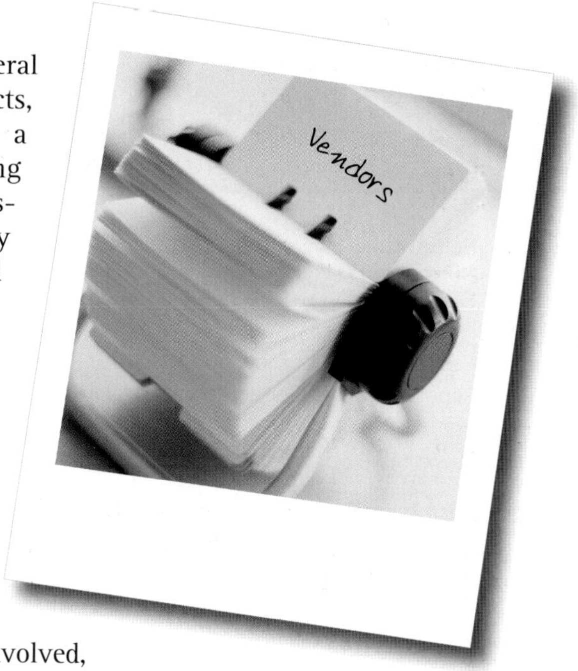

Once you've located several sources for your products, evaluate each vendor on a variety of factors, including quality, reliability and customer service. The necessary information can be gathered through references, marketing material or by simply asking the sales representative how the company conducts its business.

Other factors to consider would obviously include price and terms of sale, the vendor's location, the shipping options available, the costs involved, whether online purchasing is offered and its policy governing returned merchandise.

It may take some time and research to find the best merchandise to sell in your retail store but don't be discouraged; this is the name of the game in the retail industry.

OVERSEAS BUYING TRIPS

• Preparation

Planning for buying trips should begin at least a month prior to departure, and buyers should never leave without being thoroughly prepared. This preparation will include knowing the current position regarding stocks on hand and on order at the beginning of the new season; the new season's OTB budget, by class and by country; the styles and quantities required and the price lines; whether the merchandise is for regular business or a specific promotion; a list of vendors to visit and previous sellthrough details for those vendors. A typical planner may look like the one set out below.

Buying Trip Planner

Department/ XYZ
For period: X X X X
Total OTB: $000,000,00
Purchase destination: (Country)
% of total OTB reserved: (xxx%)
Total amount planned: ($000,000)

Departure date: Return date: Number of days in country: Flight details: Hotel details:	Average retail price per brand: $ Average retail price per unit: pcs Total purchase—regular: $ Proposed purchase—sales: $ Proposed total units—regular: pcs Proposed total units—sales: pcs
Planned OTB Allocation: $ 000,000	

Regular: $000	For delivery: xxx	Promotional: $000	For delivery: xxx
Brand type		Proposed units:	
Merchandise type		Proposed units:	

Brand	Type/Class	Regular	Sale/Promo	Total $
Xxx	Xxx			
Xxx	Xxx			
Xxx	Xxx			
Xxx	Xxx			

It should go without saying that whenever you travel, you should ensure that, in addition to your laptop and phone, you have a calculator and a camera with you. You should also ensure that you have a plentiful supply of name cards, copies of your company profile, and manual purchase order forms (if applicable).

Remember: you are representing the company, and wherever you are in the world, a smile works wonders.

- **Communicating with overseas buying agents**

Another essential part of your preparation should be to communicate relevant and necessary merchandising data to your foreign buying offices, key foreign vendors or major manufacturers producing your private labels. This will entail submitting preliminary buying plans; lists of the best- and worst-selling merchandise units from these sources; and a preliminary list of items you wish them to source for you.

This wish list would incorporate details on such things as product type, quantities per style or per color, fabrication details and fabric type, ideal price points, terms and conditions, delivery schedules, discounts, and transportation allowances. It is essential that any communication between buyer and buying office/vendor manufacturer must be clear and precise.

- **Trade shows**

Overseas buying trips often incorporate visits to trade shows during the January–April (for autumn buys) and June–September (for spring buys) buying seasons. The major shows for buyers looking to buy foreign merchandise are set out below.

Key trade shows

Prêt a Porter	Paris
Modamont	Paris
CPD	Düsseldorf
CIFF	Copenhagen
Bread & Butter	Barcelona
Moda Prima	Milan
PURE	London
MAGIC	Las Vegas
GDS	Düsseldorf
MICAM	Milan
MIPEL	Milan
Ambiente	Frankfurt
Hong Kong Houseware Fair	Hong Kong
Spring Fair	Birmingham
Macef	Milan
International Houseware Fair (BIG+BIH)	Bangkok
Maison & Objet	Paris
Canton Fair	Guangzhou

For more information on trade shows, see www.biztradeshows.com/trade-events/mega-macao.html

biz tradeshows

- **Working the fairs**

The venues for trade shows usually stretch over large areas and can be a bit intimidating for the inexperienced (see the CDP site map below, for example). Narrowing your search by listing the type, name and location of the exhibitors you wish to visit will make things less overwhelming.

Trade shows are usually big, so expect a lot of walking if you are scouting for new lines. Using the various catalogs and planners provided (as illustrated opposite) to list your priorities and plan your route around the various exhibition halls will save you a lot of time and a lot of walking.

Site Map of CPD Fair, Düsseldorf

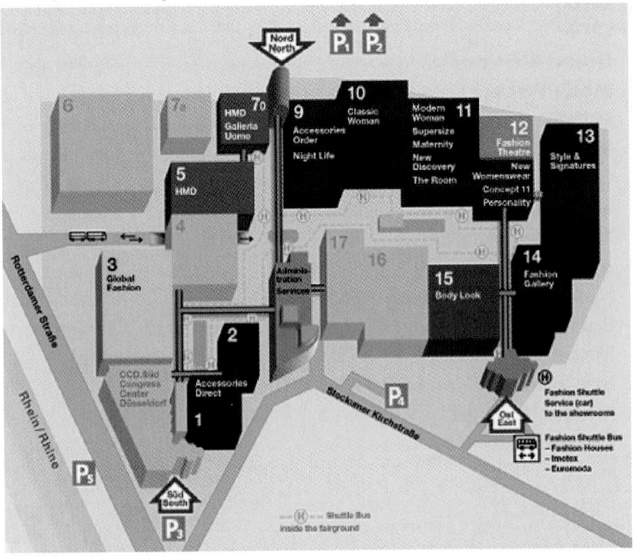

Trade Show Planner

Supplier	Hall	Booth	Date	Purchase

The same goes for showroom visits. Pre-planned vendor visits (see below) are the norm and part of any buyer's itinerary. In most cases, the fair or trade show visit will be combined with showroom visits.

Supplier Showroom Planner

Supplier	Location	Meeting with	Date	Purchase

BUYING AND SELECTION FACTORS

The following is a list of factors that the buyer needs to consider in selecting merchandise. The list is by no means exhaustive but provides an indication of the type of things that can influence customers' purchasing decisions.

- Basic or generic styles or silhouettes (single-breasted vs. double-breasted; Swedish glassware vs. Venetian)

- Decoration or trims, patterns, prints, weave or embellishment

- Material or fabrics (thickness, weight, texture, transparency, durability and finish; basic components such as yarns, threads, metal, wood, glass or chemical treatment)

- Packaging (for aesthetics or safety)

- Packs (singles, multiple or family-size packs)

- Product size (compact or larger, or as in fit; size ratios)

- Sensory factors (color, sound, texture and taste)

- Ease and cost of maintenance (washable, non-stick, crease-resistant)

- Health and safety (natural vs. synthetic, dietary and nutritional properties)

- Social considerations (eco-friendly, energy consumption, biodegradable, use of child-labor)

- Utility or versatility

- Brand (identification for products from a given maker under the retailer's label) or designer name (akin to brand but with a wider recognition)

- Fashion (vogue)

- Taste (fondness for specific aesthetic factors—good taste vs. bad)
- Quality of workmanship ("grade")
- Price (obvious but of varying significance).

NARROWING THE SEARCH

Sales and buying plans provide the framework that helps to narrow the number of items that must be compared during the selection process. They reflect customer demand by merchandise classification—type, price, and so on.

The buyer may scan through an entire range, eliminating all unsuitable items, before undertaking a more detailed evaluation of the remaining items. Those that survive this second stage are considered to have the potential for a buy. (It is at this point that negotiations on best terms begin.)

If the buyer cannot find certain items to fit the plan, the plan may be changed slightly to accommodate this. However, the buyer should always be wary of compromising too much in the selection of goods. Too much substitution can lead to too many buys that are a far cry from the original plan.

ASK QUESTIONS

Question which products are being ordered by other bigger retailers and look into the possibility of group buying. In many cases, local stores or department stores are not big enough to develop their own private labels, and it may pay to explore potential benefits to be derived from group buying.

For stores conducting product development, walking the fabric markets is essential. An assistant from your buying office may accompany you on these market surveys and help you negotiate prices on fabrics and accessories. In some cases, these fabrics can only be purchased on a cash basis, and will therefore require the assistance of your buying office to facilitate payment.

SEEKING NEW TRENDS ABROAD

Conducting meetings with department managers and sales people will give you the in-store information you will need for future buys and products that you can seek while on buying trips. Read trade publications to keep up to date with current trends.

Foreign buying trips are especially beneficial for staying in touch with what's hot and what's not. Explore new merchandise trends and new vendors. Don't be afraid of testing out items from the market: featuring them early in the season can give you an edge over your competitors and enable you to place timely re-orders.

Identify and maximize fast-selling items for re-ordering. These can be identical goods or identical shapes but in new colors. Part of maintaining your customers' interest is having new lines, fashion items and novelty items to discover when they visit your store.

For this reason, you should always keep enough monthly OTB available. Over-buying or buying up to the brim will rob you of opportunities that would otherwise create enormous success.

REPORTING ON BUYING TRIPS

It is standard procedure in many companies for buyers to create and deliver detailed reports of their buying trips to their managers or GMMs. The example shown below is a variation on the original Buying Trip Planner illustrated earlier. The form sets out the OTB

Buying Trip Report

Department/ XYZ
For period: X X X X
Total OTB: $000,000,00
Purchase destination: (Hong Kong)
% of total OTB reserved: (xxx%)
Total amount planned: ($000,000)

Part 1

Departure date: February 26, 2007 Return date: March 3, 2007 Number of days in country: 5 working days Flight details: MH 123 & MH 321 Hotel details: Hotel ABC Actual OTB Allocation: $ 000,000	Average retail price per brand: $ ← Average retail price per unit: pcs ← Total purchase—regular: $ ← Proposed purchase—sales: $ ← Proposed total units—regular: pcs ← Proposed total units—sales: pcs ←

Regular: $000	For delivery: month	Promotional: $000	For delivery: month
Brand type	XXXXX	Purchased units:	1234
Merchandise type	XXXXXXXXX	Purchased units:	1234

Brand	Type/Class	Regular	Sale/Promo	Total $
description	description	$000,000	$000,000	$000,000
description	description	$000,000		$000,000
description	description		$000,000	$000,000
description	description		$000,000	$000,000

spending, delivery timetables, names of brands/products bought and if they are meant for regular or promotional activities.

The reporting mechanism will often incorporate an assessment report (see below) which asks the buyer to evaluate the overall value of the trip and comment on such things as timing, product availability, price issues and local buying agents. This report will have a bearing on the way future buying trips are conducted.

Buying Trip Assessment Report

Department/ XYZ
For period: X X X X
Total OTB: $000,000,00
Purchase destination: (Hong Kong)
% of total OTB reserved: (xxx%)
Total amount planned: ($000,000)

Part 2

1	Overall assessment:
1a	Highlight your best buys:
2	Did you purchase what you had planned for?
3	If not, what is outstanding?
3a	Where do you propose finding the missing items/brands?
4	Was our buying agent helpful?
5	How can this buying trip be improved in the future?

It is important to review unfulfilled purchase orders on a regular basis and to take appropriate action. Part of the buyer's role is to identify problems and make suggestions that will help translate merchandise on hand into sales. To this end, when visiting the shop floor or branch, check assortments of merchandise and the way it is displayed. Ask yourself if these are helping or working against sales.

Shop and analyze competitors' stores to evaluate assortments, prices and merchandise presentations.

STOCK CONTROL

Maintaining a well-balanced stock-holding and merchandise assortment is essential. But this is an area where many buyers go wrong. It is not the dollar value of the stock that counts but the desirability of that stock; that is, having balanced size ratios, basic colors, and seasonally appropriate silhouettes and styles.

Not all of the buyer's merchandise will achieve equal success, and it is therefore critical to keep abreast of what is selling and what is not. Appropriate action should be taken to clear any slow-moving items as soon as they are identified to ensure that precious OTB funds are available to replenish items that are selling.

Remember; the first mark-down is always the cheapest. The wrong fit or wrong color has a zero value. So, get rid of it!

A perpetual inventory control system is a running record of stock on hand, in which stock on hand = beginning stocks + new arrivals.

A periodic inventory count system is a monthly check of the quantities of each item or unit. Here, stock on hand + new arrivals since last count – stock on hand at the time of the last count = sales for the period.

In today's retail environment, computer systems automatically update the specific SKUs and require close monitoring. Basic stock-control systems alert buyers when stocks reach critical levels and re-ordering becomes necessary.

The following information is needed to calculate how much stock should be on hand and how much should be on order *at each re-order.* This helps the buyer to calculate the OTB provisions required for each SKU.

- Determine the probable rate of sales for each SKU identified as a basic item.
- Determine the ideal delivery period of each, which should be in sync with your original planning.
- Establish the re-order periods or frequency needed. Your sellthough by class, by week, or, for most, by month will determine this.
- Establish levels of reserves needed to provide sales that exceed forecasts. As mentioned in a previous chapter, it is a good idea to pre-determine a percentage of the OTB

that is to remain untouched to allow for re-ordering, for purchasing new hot items, or for when sales are not meeting budgets.

- Calculate stocks currently on hand and on order. When re-ordering a basic item, unless your SKU is unique (by style, by size and by color), a visual/manual assessment of stock holdings is necessary before re-ordering. This will help ensure that only particular items that are running low are ordered.

Some stores operate their basic stocks on pre-orders or block orders for future weeks or months. The danger with this is that if the buyer is not vigilant, these block orders may have items that are not selling as fast as anticipated, subsequently creating a snowball effect. Whenever possible, the ideal would be to have the vendor check your basic stock requirements and have them do the replenishment based on a "no less than and no more than" basis, as both the buyer and the vendor benefit from avoiding OOS problems when the merchandise is required without tying up OTB unnecessarily.

case study

When certain concepts are better left alone

Buying the right merchandise has everything to do with knowing your customers, as the following example clearly shows.

This case involves a store that is in a prime location, has first-class floor layout, visual merchandising, and a good selection of exclusive home décor items. Its fashion goods, for both men and women, are considered avant garde and, while its imported (indent) brands are perhaps too expensive for the young clientele for which it caters, these pricing issues are balanced out by offering affordable private brands.

The store was ranked number one when it came to the "fashion in department store" category. Its in-house brands were featured in all the fashion magazines and newspapers, and people went out of their way to buy them.

Despite all of this, however, the store was not very profitable. I believe that the problems began with "the move."

A decision was made to expand into a brand new mall. The move entailed moving its in-house label standalone store to these new premises. The new concept store—big, beautiful and expensive-looking on a grand scale—was the talk of the town for a while but turned out to be a flop. The store, in all its beauty, aspired to appeal to the more affluent customer, causing it to lose its core middle-class customers. The store looked expensive, that was the way it was perceived by shoppers, even though this was not reflected in its prices.

In all of this, the store's private brands suffered. The new location weakened the concept. In the previous location, the in-house brand was handled very much like a boutique. It had a boutique atmosphere, with boutique clothes and accessories, and a brilliant shoe selection. The customers who shopped there were not shopping in a department store; they were shopping in a boutique that was associated with a department store. By moving this concept to be a part of the department store in the new location, it lost its special appeal, becoming just another clothing department in another department store.

The up-market concept in this case was a very expensive lesson, and a concept that should have been left alone. What's the point in striving to be different when "different" is not what your core customers are shopping for?

case study

Packaging an idea

In 2000, the store for which I was working was preparing its buys for a second outlet at Raffles City in Singapore. We decided to explore Spain as a new buying territory because we needed different and younger brands for the new store. We did manage to find some, and came back with a couple of interesting ideas too.

Visiting one fashion boutique in Madrid, we noticed that all of its tops were in bright, fresh colors—coral pinks, honey dew, pale turquoise, cornflower blue, misty blue, cadmium lemon, chartreuse.... It was powerful.

We decided to give our in-house brand the same treatment. The collection comprised eight different-styled knitted tops/twin-sets in 12 gorgeous colors. The next thing was to bring together the same or similar colors from the accessories departments and create "mood tables" by color blocks. The effect was convincing. The sellthrough, magic! As anticipated, customers bought two or three colors over several styles.

The other idea we brought home came from watching the launch of H&M (Hennes & Mauritz) in Madrid, its first store in Spain. It covered the entire building with one strong message: ***Hola Madrid! Hasta la vista 10 Noviembre!*** (Greetings Madrid! See you on 10th November!)

This was cheeky, because H&M was penetrating the home of Mango and Zara. According to my Spanish agent, the Spaniards did not know who or what H&M was; it could have been a music store for all they knew, so it was fun to see what happened when the store opened. As anticipated, the launch was crazy. There was a five-mile queue to get in and shoppers emerged with arms full of merchandise.

So what we adopted was the exclamation mark. It was different, eye-catching and captured our excitement with the new store.

We had opening specials for our Raffles City launch, and all the special prices and special buys had a swing ticket with this exclamation mark. Robinsons was finally at Raffles City! It turned out to be a good and commercially successful launch.

The lesson to be learnt from this is that traveling can produce more than good merchandise; so keep your eyes open for new concepts and new ideas!

case study

Leave it to the experts

The following case study was related to me by Mr Gianfranco Guidotti, the founder of Gianfranco Guidotti Buying Office in Florence. I asked him to share some stories that could be beneficial to readers on buyers working the Italian fashion market and the consequences of these buying decisions.

"If one takes an X-ray of the retail business in any of the so-called civilized countries, I think the picture will be more or less the same, with a lot of players on the scene, all trying to grow and erode competitors' ground. Very often, we get the feeling that branded goods are on top of the list and famous names like Prada, Gucci, Dolce & Gabbana, Cavalli, and Burberry are winning the battle, dominating the market and leaving no room for the smaller operators. This is only partially true. Famous brands are growing mainly due to a couple of factors: new customers in emerging markets and their second line, such as Just Cavalli, D&G, Versus, and so on.

If we leave the above niche alone, we find a very vibrant retail life with a lot of actors: Benetton's territory has now been invaded by other volume retailers—Zara, H&M and Mango, for example– and by many aggressive new multiple shops that are expanding very rapidly as a result of a very clever advertising campaign, and of injecting a nice range of quality products continuously. Examples of this new type of retailer in Italy include Calzedonia, Yamamay, Teddy, and Vestebene' s various divisions (over 1,000 shops) with branches in many countries in Europe and elsewhere.

In this competitive world, how are the department stores going to survive? This is a very important question, and it is interesting to see how some of these big giants have made major changes to keep a good share of the shopper's disposable income.

Now, what is the buyers' approach when they start planning the new season? Again, the interpretation can be very different and it depends on the company, on management directives, and on the way the buyer operates.

I feel that any person in charge of buying should have a good knowledge of the business, the type of customer the goods are intended for, the price range, and the quantity that sells in a certain price range.

Once this is clear, the next important approach when the buyer travels to a foreign market is to analyze the trend, and bear in mind that behind every range, there is a team that has been working for months to put it together in the hope of getting good results. By devoting time to go through the various ranges, the buyer is more likely to spot winners for that particular niche of the market and make a better selection of goods. Very often, it becomes natural for the buyer to make changes to the existing styles, and I often find that changes destroy the item and make it 'average' and uninteresting.

I had a frustrating experience lately with a good customer of mine, a chain of 220 shops. We were working on a range of ladies' suits and the buyer had selected seven lovely styles. All of a sudden, she became a designer and started to make changes to each garment. When I asked why she made all these changes, the answer was that she was adjusting the styles to make them more saleable. Unfortunately, the styles did not sell very well and I had proof that this was due to the changes made by the buyer.

In fact, three months later, another buyer from the same country bought some of the styles without making any changes whatsoever, and they sold very well; so well that the factory received a repeat order."

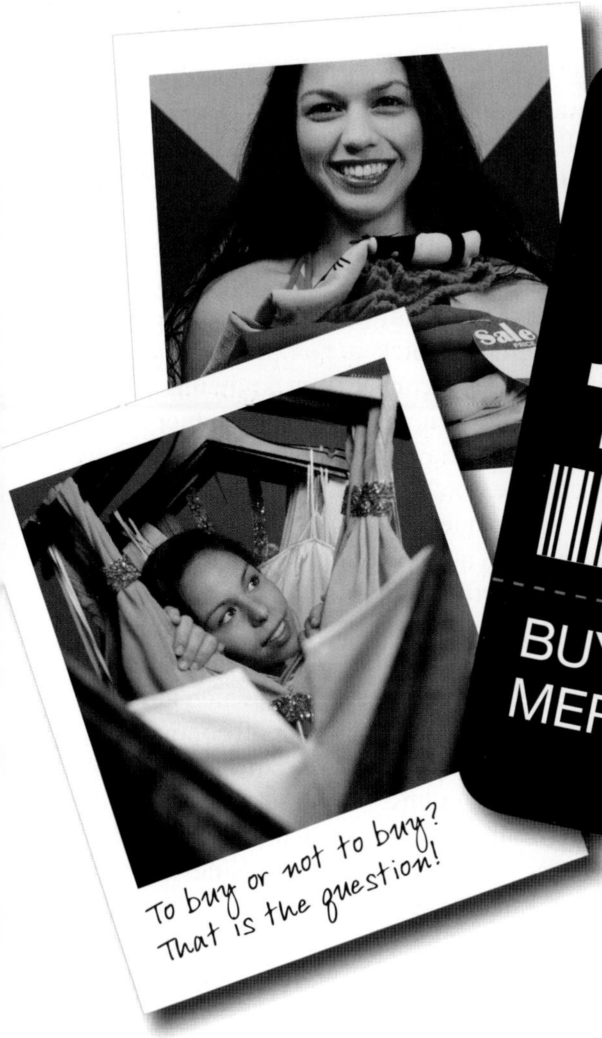

To buy or not to buy?
That is the question!

The Art of Retail Buying

12

BUYING MERCHANDISE

CHOOSING PRODUCTS TO SELL

Choosing products for your retail store may very well be the most difficult decisions you will need to make, especially if you are a newcomer in the retail industry. The choices are limitless and the task may be overpowering at first. Not only should there be a demand for your products, but they must be profitable, and suitable for the market you wish to penetrate. This entails knowing the kind of customers you want, their needs, how much they are willing to pay, and how many of them may want to buy.

If your products appeal only to a limited number of people, it may not be enough to sustain a business. Your product selection doesn't have to appeal to all of the population, but it should be something you can convince a large percentage of shoppers to buy.

When it comes to selecting products, timing is extremely important. New trends and products can be a great boost to your business, but you'll need to be at the beginning of the product cycle in order to be successful. Learning to pick a hot product *before* it becomes hot is a valuable skill that comes from knowing your market. There will always be competition, so finding a product that is unique will reduce the chances of having to compete head-on; finding merchandise that can be exclusive to your store is a successful formula to win over customers.

One way to guarantee having a truly unique product line is to make the item yourself, or to partner with a small business that makes a product that you enjoy selling and attracts a customer base that is just as thrilled as you are with these items. Many department stores have taken the "private label" route, which allows them to brand an item, range or collection. There are small companies around that can help you, without demanding extraordinary high minimums. Finding sources is not as hard as it used to be; it's simply a matter of using search engines such as Google to find exactly what you're looking for.

The key to having a successful business is to know your products and to believe in the merchandise you are selling. If you do not believe in the product yourself, then you probably won't be successful selling it. With persistence, you'll find a product or product line that meets both the needs of your target market and your own ability to locate it, purchase it, and resell it.

HOW TO CHOOSE THE RIGHT MERCHANDISE

Rule number 1: Know your customers. Know the quality levels they expect, the price they are looking for, the types of items you think they will like, the average size ratio they have, and how often they shop with you. The more frequent the shopper, the more often you have to change your merchandise.

In the following pages, we will be looking at several examples of how to evaluate a range, and how and why to select particular items. Each example will take into consideration such things as the type and location of the store; quality positioning and average price points; customer and spending profiles; and the available OTB.

An experienced buyer will know that vendors' collections and ranges are built in different ways. Some collections will be very itemized, where the buyer has to mix and match these items into cohesive ranges. Others pre-plan their ranges in storyboards, making it easier for buyers to select a pre-defined story where the styles, colors and fabrics are well put together. The following examples illustrate a mix of types of buys for different retail formats.

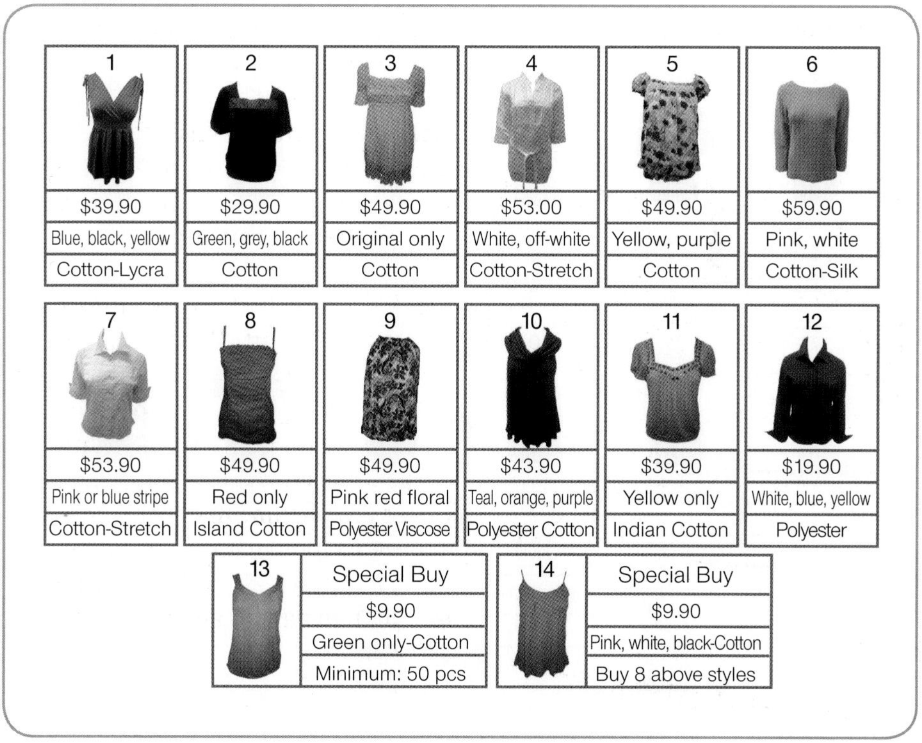
1
$39.90
Blue, black, yellow
Cotton-Lycra
2
$29.90
Green, grey, black
Cotton
3
$49.90
Original only
Cotton
4
$53.00
White, off-white
Cotton-Stretch
5
$49.90
Yellow, purple
Cotton
6
$59.90
Pink, white
Cotton-Silk
7
$53.90
Pink or blue stripe
Cotton-Stretch
8
$49.90
Red only
Island Cotton
9
$49.90
Pink red floral
Polyester Viscose
10
$43.90
Teal, orange, purple
Polyester Cotton
11
$39.90
Yellow only
Indian Cotton
12
$19.90
White, blue, yellow
Polyester
13
Special Buy
$9.90
Green only-Cotton
Minimum: 50 pcs
14
Special Buy
$9.90
Pink, white, black-Cotton
Buy 8 above styles

- **Example 1: Fashion Tops**

The store in question here is a small fashion store in the city, where the average customer is a young(ish) single woman who likes to think of herself as trendy and likes to buy fast, affordable fashion. She is willing to pay between $39 and $49 for a top. While quality is important to her, styling and color take precedence.

The buyer is at the vendor's showroom with a retail budget of $4,000, and plans to buy seven types of tops for immediate delivery. Her size ratio is S-M-L-XL in a 1-2-2-1 split. The vendor has a wide selection from which to choose, so it becomes a process of elimination.

Though #2 is within the retailer's price range, the style doesn't fit the store's customer profile. Style #12 is intended for a customer who would go for a basic shirt style. The price is OK at $49.90 but the look is not what her store is about. Furthermore, 100% polyester is not what she wants to offer her customers.

Next, styles #4 and #7 are eliminated, not because of the $53.00 price point (for a well-made cotton blouse, this is deemed reasonable) but because they are career-wear styles or tops used for office-wear, rather than fashion items.

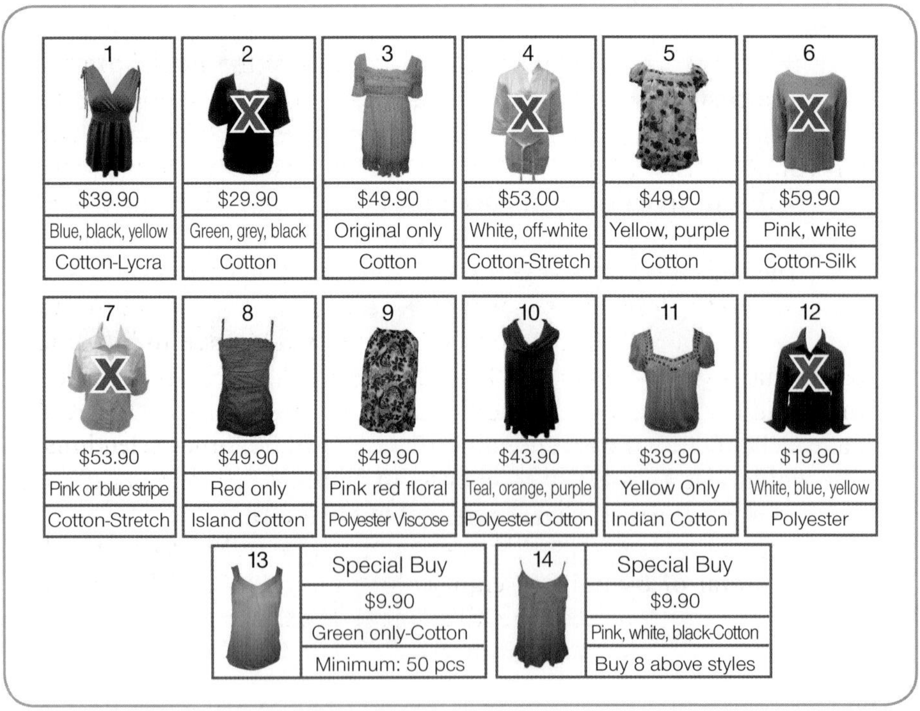
1
$39.90
Blue, black, yellow
Cotton-Lycra
2
X
$29.90
Green, grey, black
Cotton
3
$49.90
Original only
Cotton
4
X
$53.00
White, off-white
Cotton-Stretch
5
$49.90
Yellow, purple
Cotton
6
X
$59.90
Pink, white
Cotton-Silk
7
X
$53.90
Pink or blue stripe
Cotton-Stretch
8
$49.90
Red only
Island Cotton
9
$49.90
Pink red floral
Polyester Viscose
10
$43.90
Teal, orange, purple
Polyester Cotton
11
$39.90
Yellow Only
Indian Cotton
12
X
$19.90
White, blue, yellow
Polyester
13
Special Buy
$9.90
Green only-Cotton
Minimum: 50 pcs
14
Special Buy
$9.90
Pink, white, black-Cotton
Buy 8 above styles

Style #6 is an "evergreen" style but is rejected because it does not fit the particular fashion trend, which in this case is following the baby-doll, soft, feminine look.

This leaves seven regular styles and two promotional items. Before making the final decision, the buyer evaluates the promotional items. Though style #13 is fashionable, it is available in green only. The buyer needs to evaluate if she can comfortably sell 50 of these and if she wants to use up $495 in OTB in the process.

Style #14 is a well-priced fashion tank top in easy-to-sell colors, but the buyer would be obliged to take eight styles, rather than her planned seven, to be able to take advantage of this offer.

Before deciding on the special offer, the buyer makes her preliminary calculations based on the number of styles and quantities she would like to buy.

The initial selection, if she does not go back and adjust, will be an over-buy of $1,256.60. In determining where to cut back, she keeps in mind the best styles and the best colors. She decides to cut away one color from style #1, keeping the black and yellow. She also deletes the purple from styles 5 and 10. Though purple is in fashion, it is not as strong as yellow and orange. Style #8 is an easy-to-sell style but, given her OTB availability, she reduces the quantity from 24 to 12.

After making her adjustments, she returns to the special offers.

The first, #13, of 50 pieces at $ 9.90 in original color and an OTB value of $495, is rejected. She could have bought them if she felt confident in selling all 50 pieces, but this would mean reducing the number of styles or colors from her first pick; she decides to keep to her original number of styles instead.

The second special offer, #14, is tempting. It's an easy-to-sell style in good colors, but she would have to place at least 12 pieces per color to make the buy meaningful, and would have to buy one additional style to be eligible for the offer. If she took up the offer, this would lead to an over-buy (3 x 12 = $356.40), which would have to be met by a corresponding reduction in her other selections. She would also be obliged to choose an additional style from those she had already decided were unsuitable for the store.

Her decision, then, is to stay with seven styles, as planned, giving a total of 84 units in eight colors, a total OTB of $3,855.60 and a balance of $144.40, calculated as follows.

Initial calculation

Style	Item	Color	Size Ratio				Total	Unit Price	Total OTB
Style #1	Top	Blue	1	2	2	1	6	$39.90	$239.40
		Black	2	4	4	2	12	$39.90	$478.80
		Yellow	2	4	4	2	12	$39.90	$478.80
Sub-total		**3 colors**					**30**		**$1,197.00**
Style #3	Top	Original	2	4	4	2	12	$49.90	$598.80
Sub-total		**1 color**					**12**		**$598.80**
Style #5	Top	Yellow	2	4	4	2	12	$49.90	$598.80
		Purple	1	2	2	1	6	$49.90	$299.40
Sub-total		**2 colors**					**18**		**$898.20**
Style #8	Top	Red	4	8	8	4	24	$49.90	$1197.60
Sub-total		**1 color**					**24**		**$1,197.60**
Style #9	Top	Pink	2	4	4	2	12	$49.90	$598.80
Sub-total		**1 color**					**12**		**$598.80**
Style #10	Top	Orange	1	2	2	1	6	$43.90	$263.40
		Purple	1	2	2	1	6	$43.90	$263.40
Sub-total		**2 colors**					**12**		**$526.80**
Style #11	Top	Yellow	1	2	2	1	6	$39.90	$239.40
Sub-total		**1 color**					**6**		**$239.40**
Total		**11 Colors**					**114**		**$5,256.60**
Budget									**$4,000.00**
Over Plan									[$1,256.60]

Amended calculation

Style	Item	Color	Size Ratio					Total	Unit Price
Style #1	Top	Blue [out]	1	2	2	1	6	$39.90	$239.40
		Black	2	4	4	2	12	$39.90	$478.80
		Yellow	2	4	4	2	12	$39.90	$478.80
Sub-total		**2 colors**					**24**		**$957.60**
Style #3	Top	Original	2	4	4	2	12	$49.90	$598.80
Sub-total		**1 color**					**12**		**$598.80**
Style #5	Top	Yellow	2	4	4	2	12	$49.90	$598.80
		Purple [out]	1	2	2	1	6	$49.90	$299.40
Sub-total		**1 color**					**12**		**$598.80**
Style #8	Top	Red [reduce]	4	8	8	4	24	$49.90	$1,197.60
New		Red [new]	2	4	4	2	12	$49.90	$598.80
Sub-total		**1 color**					**12**		**$598.80**
Style #9	Top	Pink	2	4	4	2	12	$49.90	$598.80
Sub-total		**1 color**					**12**		**$598.80**
Style #10	Top	Orange	1	2	2	1	6	$43.90	$263.40
		Purple [out]	1	2	2	1	6	$43.90	$263.40
Sub-total		**1 color**					**6**		**$263.40**
Style #11	Top	Yellow	1	2	2	1	6	$39.90	$239.40
Sub-total		**1 color**					**6**		**$239.40**
Total		**11 Colors**					**114**		**$5,256.60**
Budget									**$4000.00**
									[1,256.60]
Revised		**8 colors**					**84**		**$3,855.60**
7 styles planned and bought.			8 colors				84		$3,855.60
Balance OTB:			$144.40						$144.40

Additional items

Style	Item	Color	Size Ratio					Total	Unit Price
Style #8	Top	Revised							
New		Red [new]	2	4	4	2	12	$49.90	$598.80
Sub-total		**1 color**					**12**		**$598.80**
Additional		Revision		2	1		3	$49.90	$149.70
Sub-total		**Final**	**2**	**6**	**5**	**2**	**15**		**748.50**

She decides to use up her total OTB, and go back to her initial best style, #8, and order three additional units in the most popular sizes, as shown above. This gives a total buy of $4,005.30.

• Example 2: Ladies' Shoes

Buyers can classify their shoe ranges in different ways. It may be by type (flats, pumps, courts, casual sandals, evening shoes, wedges, booties, boots, sneakers, runners, and so on) or by lifestyle classification (career pumps, career courts, contemporary, casual, dressy, occasion, or comfort, for instance).

Our example concerns a ladies' shoe buyer who works for a high-priced shoe chain store. The chain has 10 stores spread over a fairly wide geographic area: three stores with high pedestrian traffic in the downtown area; four in popular shopping malls; two in suburban residential shopping complexes; and one at the international airport. All stores are performing well, though not all have the same customer profile. Most outlets measure approximately 800–1,000 sq. ft.

The downtown stores cater to young office executives who work in the business district. They are savvy shoppers, fashionable and in their mid twenties and thirties, who buy shoes for different occasions. These are the "Innovators" we identified in Chapter 7, who are very "directional" in their buying.

The stores located in the shopping malls have a much wider customer base from different social backgrounds—working professionals, mid to upper management, homemakers, and visiting tourists. They are not too price-sensitive and generally fall into the

"Early Adopters" and "Majority" classifications.

The two stores located in the suburban shopping complexes enjoy a steady and loyal customer base that tends to shop at the stores over the weekend. These shoppers are mixed; where some work and enjoy shopping near their work, for convenience and leisure, some are homemakers living and shopping locally. They often shop for themselves but can frequently be seen shopping and buying with their teenage daughters. The buyer's fashion classification in these two outlets is a mix, as her customer profile is a combination of "Early Adopters," "Majority" and, to some extent, "Innovators."

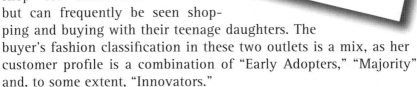

The store located at the international airport has the widest customer range. Many are frequent business travelers, most are aged between 30 and 50, and all have a fairly healthy disposable income. (Note, though, that age is no longer a type classification. A customer may be in her fifties but can also be modern, fashionable, and even directional in her fashion choices. This age group, however, is more likely to have higher criteria for comfort than their younger contemporaries.) Most can be categorized as "Majority," "Late Majority" and "Early Adopters," though 20% of them fall into the "Innovators" category. The fashion classifications here are both "directional" and "upbeat," with some ranges that are conventional or classic.

Prices for shoes offered in the stores range between $239 and $319, with the exception of leisure shoes, which are priced at $99. The assortment quality is good and offers a wide range of full leather shoes. The bulk of the shoe inventory comprises fashionable shoes in leather, leather with PVC appliqué, and some fanciful fabrics.

Under normal circumstances, shoe inventory can be heavy, as a full size ratio spans sizes 34–42, with corresponding half-sizes (18 sizes in total). However, given the restricted size of the outlets in

Man-made footwear materials

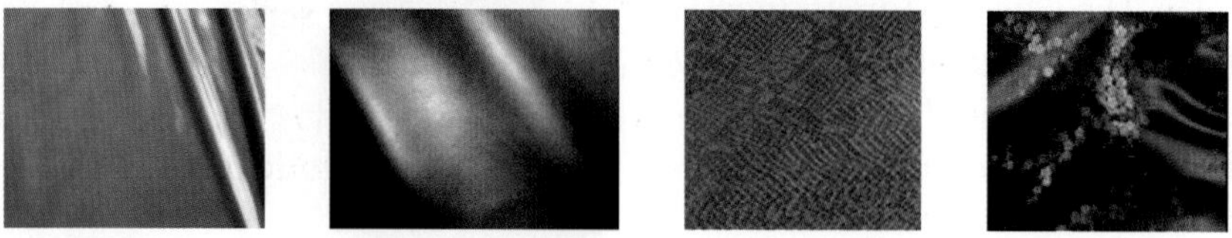

PVC | Synthetic Leather | Synthetic Snake Skin | Fancy Fabric

this example, the buyer does not carry half-sizes and concentrates on the sizes for which there is the greatest demand (in this instance, sizes 36–40). This does cause some customer dissatisfaction and, at times, loss of sales.

The buyer is preparing to place orders for her next quarter (April–June) and has a total OTB for the entire period of $940,000, to be distributed between the 10 stores according to their projected sales, individual stock turns and current stocks on hand. After working out her OTB allocation at cost, the distribution for one of her vendors, Shoe Delight, is as follows:

Store	OTB Allocation at Cost		Allocation Shoe Delight	
City 1	$ 70,000	7.4%	$ 5,180	
City 2	$ 60,000	6.4%	$ 3,840	
City 3	$ 60,000	6.4%	$ 3,840	
Mall 1	$ 90,000	9.6%	$ 8,640	
Mall 2	$ 100,000	10.6%	$ 10,600	
Mall 3	$ 70,000	7.4%	$ 5,180	
Mall 4	$120,000	12.7%	$ 15,240	
Complex 1	$ 50,000	20%	$ 10,000	
Complex 2	$ 60,000	25%	$ 15,000	
Airport	$260,000	27.6%	$ 71,760	
Total	**$940,000**		**$ 149,280**	**15.9%**

Shoe Delight's range consists of 60 assorted styles in two or more colors. The average cost price for the shoes, excluding the leisure shoes, is $133.33 [$150 + $120 + $130 ÷ 3 series = $133.33]. She is looking at placing approximately 500 over pairs of shoes, a bit more if she places some leisure shoes at a cost of $50.00.

To facilitate buys, the buyer sorts out the collection by style types and earmarks them as:

C = Conventional
U = Upbeat
D = Directional
F = Fantasy
L = Leisure

I have purposely chosen to use the above terms rather than shoe type (flats, pumps...) to emphasize the link between merchandise type and customer type. For the sake of simplicity, the styles chosen are general and easy to understand.

Shoe Delight Style Chart 1

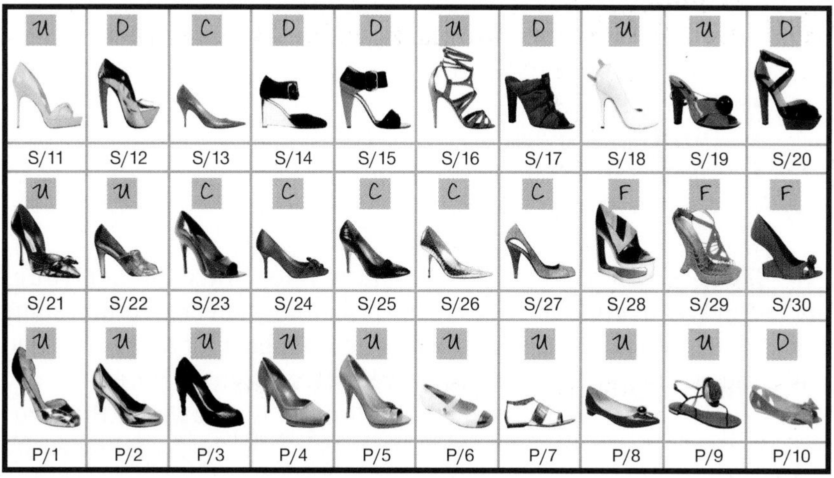

S-Series : Cost $150 Retail $299
P-Series : Cost $120 Retail $239

Shoe Delight Style Chart 2

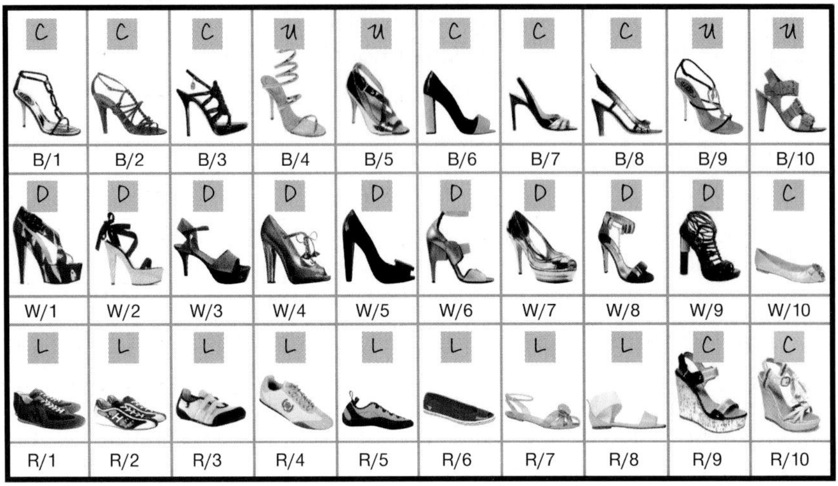

B-Series	:	Cost $120	Retail $239.00
W-Series	:	Cost $130	Retail $239.00
R-Series	:	Cost $50	Retail $99.00

As indicated on the style charts, the collection comprises

- Conventional styles: 15
- Upbeat styles: 19
- Directional styles: 15
- Leisure styles: 8
- Fantasy styles: 3

The assortment and styles required for three of her stores are entirely directional styles. The remaining seven require some directional styles; five will have some upbeat styles; and two will require conventional and leisure styles. None requires fantasy styles, which do not suit her customer profile. As shown on the chart below, directional styles take up the bulk of the buys, followed by upbeat. Conventional and leisure are styles chosen typically for her suburban stores.

Store	Conventional	Upbeat	Directional	Leisure	Approx Pairs
City 1			100%		39 pairs
City 2			100%		28 pairs
City 3			100%		28 pairs
Mall 1		50%	50%		65 pairs
Mall 2		50%	50%		79 pairs
Mall 3		50%	50%		39 pairs
Mall 4		50%	50%		114 pairs
Complex 1	50%		30%	20%	60 and 20 pairs
Complex 2	50%		30%	20%	90 and 30 pairs
Airport		60%	40%		592 pairs

Based on the OTB allocation earmarked for this vendor, she splits the allocation by style types.

Store	Conventional	Upbeat	Directional	Leisure	Total
City 1			$ 5,180		$ 5,180
City 2			$ 3,840		$ 3,840
City 3			$ 3,840		$ 3,840
Mall 1		$ 4,320	$ 4,320		$ 8,640
Mall 2		$ 5,300	$ 5,300		$ 10,600
Mall 3		$ 2,590	$ 2,590		$ 5,180
Mall 4		$ 7,620	$ 7,620		$ 15,240
Complex 1	$5,000		$3,000	$2,000	$ 10,000
Complex 2	$7,500		$4,500	$3,000	$ 15,000
Airport		$43,056	$28,704		$ 71,760

Shoe Delight Color Chart

Napa Leather

Col		SIZE							PAX	TOTAL PAX
		35	36	37	38	39	40	41		
	White									
	Black									
	Red									
	Brown									
	Sand									
	Pink									
	Sky Blue									
	Light Gray									

patent alligator banig croc

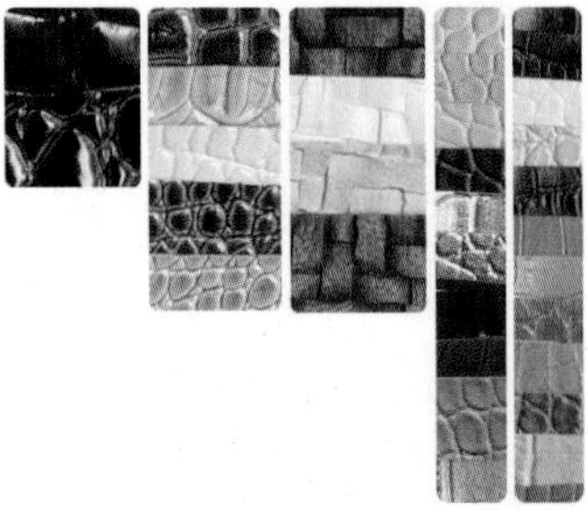

Col		35	36	37	38	39	40	41	PAX	TOTAL PAX
	Black									
	Granite									
	Mocha									
	Rose									
	Teal									
	Gray									
	Bronze									

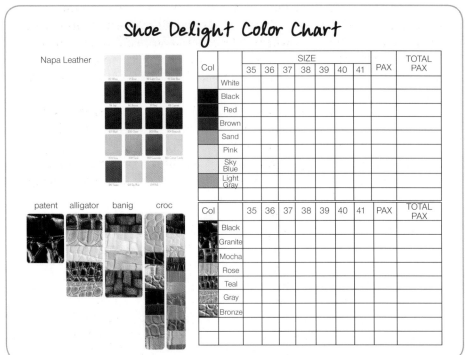

The buyer has now sorted out the vendor's styles by types, with the directional category having the highest proportion. You will notice that there are only 15 directional styles that she can choose out of a total of 60 styles offered by this vendor, and all of her stores require directional styles. Should she go ahead and place her planned OTB with this vendor, given that each style is available in at least nine colors? Much will depend on whether this vendor has a proven sales record that justifies the buys. It is fair to assume that the level of directional styles would be similar to that of previous seasons, and the OTB is a reflection of fewer styles but in higher quantities over several colors.

If this is not the case, and the vendor has changed his merchandise mix drastically, leaving fewer-than-anticipated styles to choose from, then the buyer should re-evaluate her OTB allocation and not compromise. In this case, buying more of the same style may not suit her store or anticipated sellthrough.

- **Example 3: Ladies' Handbags**

Like clothes, shoes and jewelry, handbags occupy a special place in a woman's closet. As the retail market for handbags developed, various designs were introduced, from the very ordinary to the most sophisticated. The biggest change in the handbag business has been color. Gone are the days where 80% of handbags sold were in black. Today, colors, fabrics and adornments are readily accepted and bags are considered very much a part of the fashion statement made by the wearer.

There are several types of handbag shopper. There is the customer who buys only high-end designer brands—Prada, Gucci, Coach, Louis Vuitton, Fendi or Kate Spade—and will readily pay for these status symbols while saving on other consumer products such as clothes. The logic here is that a handbag's brand is easily identifiable; the logo is there for all to see (unlike those of most garments). For such shoppers, an expensive designer bag is like a priceless trophy on display. The latest designs can cost thousands of dollars, making the designer handbag a valuable possession. This makes it a luxury for most but a necessity for some.

The next type of bag shopper is also fashionable and wants to follow the fashion trends. She is still brand conscious but she is expense conscious as well. She is less interested in the brand as a status symbol and her choice of brand is more likely to be linked to the constraints of her wallet. She can typically be seen buying brands such as Guess? DKNY, Esprit, Nine West or Liz Claiborne.

Young or old, the other type of bag shopper is customers that love buying cheap, fun, fashionable handbags. At $29 or $39 each, these handbags are seen as disposable fashion items and customers often buy two or three bags at a time during sales. The most successful bags (in units sold and dollar take) for many department stores in Singapore are brands such as Perllini, Mel, Comoditee, and Guy by Rabeanco.

For the ever-classic lady who prefers quality at affordable prices, the choices—here in Singapore, at least, and possibly other Asian countries—would be brands such as Hilly, Toscano, Renoma or Braun Buffel, which are readily available in many department stores and seldom found at heavily discounted prices.

The newest and hottest handbag trend, however, is Anya Hindmarch's Eco bag. This was more of an accident than an intentional brand, and has an eco-cult following where bags tanned using vegetable dyes to prevent carcinogenic chrome from getting into the water supply are suddenly a cool thing among young consumers. There are other brands following this trend such as Ciel, Doy Bags, Stella McCartney, People Tree, Matt and Nat and Terra Plana, to name just a few. This trend may not persist as obviously as it is now, but I do feel that anything "eco" (vegan handbags made from non-animal products, for example) will be with us for a long while still.

Let's look at the example of a department store buyer preparing her summer sales plans, for which the company has projected an 8% increase over the previous year's event, though the length of the event and the level of A&P support will remain the same.

The buyer's total sales figure for this event is $2,200,000 ($176,000 above the previous year) and she is buying for six stores.

Her sales distribution by store is as follows:

Store	Distribution	Sales	OTB Outright Buys
Store A	20% of total	$440,000	$227,040
Store B	18% of total	$396,000	$204,336
Store C	22% of total	$484,000	$249,744
Store D	15% of total	$330,000	$170,280
Store E	12% of total	$265,000	$136,224
Store F	13% of total	$286,000	$147,576
Total 6 stores	100%	$2,200,000	$1,135,200

Her department merchandise mix consists of 57% consignment and 43% outright. Her total OTB for sales merchandise is $1,135,200. She has seven key vendors that usually support her in sales events, and she allocates the OTB budget in accordance with historical sales data and each vendor's respective sales contribution. Her average price points for special buys are $29–$39, though she does at times buy regular styles at reduced cost, but only if the discount is at least 50%.

Unit Planner

	Distribution	OTB Allocation	Estimated Units	Unit Distribution by Store					
				A	B	C	D	E	F
Vendor 1	10%	$113,520	3,339	668	601	735	500	400	435
Vendor 2	12%	$136,224	4,005	801	722	881	601	480	520
Vendor 3	15%	$170,280	5,008	1002	902	1,102	751	601	650
Vendor 4	14%	$158,928	4,674	935	841	1,028	701	561	608
Vendor 5	18%	$204,336	6,010	1,202	1,082	1,322	902	721	781
Vendor 6	15%	$170,280	5,008	1,002	901	1,102	751	601	651
Vendor 7	16%	$181,632	5,342	1,068	962	1,175	801	641	695
Total	100%	$1,135,200	33,386	6,678	6,011	7,345	5,007	4,005	4,340

In the midst of her preparations, the buyer receives an email from her Italian agent informing her of a special offer of handbags at 50% off. As this brand rarely has such offers, she requests further details regarding the style, color mix and prices, asking also that the agent send her some pictures.

There are 308 pieces in total, 56 of which are in single units. The balance of 252 pieces is assorted over 12 styles, with 21 pieces in each style highlighted in Blue on the chart. Averaging out the cost, the buyer finds that she can sell this lot at a unit price of $399 each. The total value at retail for this offer would be $122,892. She could sell them at a straight 50% off the regular retail price, but decides that a single price would work better, in that it would allow customers interested in this brand and in the market for this price level to concentrate on the choice of styles rather than evaluating the price of each.

When reviewing the pictures and assortment details, she is pleased to see that most of the styles are in full leather, in beautiful shapes and in medium to large sizes. She goes ahead and commits to the offer. She must now decide if all or only some stores will get to sell these handbags.

She could share the units equally between all six stores, meaning that each would get at least 51 pieces, with a retail value of $20,349, or she could allocate them to her three best stores, meaning that each of these would get at least 102 pieces or a retail value of $40,698. She sends the pictures and price details to all six store managers and asks how they feel about the offer. All but one are interested, with two managers feeling they could absorb all 308 pieces. The manager of Store A is not interested, feeling that the retail price ($399) is too high; he is more comfortable with the usual low-priced sales merchandise at $29 to $39.

The buyer checks her sales reports to analyze the average price points for this store and discovers that, outside sales periods, it has a decent business in the bridge (higher-priced) handbags. Further analysis of the brand's monthly sellthrough shows that it ranks number five among the store's higher-priced brands, but is number 17 overall when consignment brands are included. The sales period profile for Store A reveals predominantly low average price points but in very high volume. Having this information gives the buyer a better understanding of the store manager's reaction to this offer, but she is ultimately the one who has to make the final decision on the allocation.

She has several options. She can allocate equal units to all stores; she can allocate the units to the three best stores, which includes Store A; she can split the units between the two stores that feel confident in taking all units; or she can split the units proportionately according to the stores' respective rankings. After checking her sales analysis and brand profile for all stores, the buyer decides to allocate the units in proportion to each store's business profile on higher-priced brands. The allocation follows each store's customer shopping profile on better brands in addition to each store's sales ranking, despite the reluctance of Store A to participate in the offer.

She informs the store managers of her decision, and the rationale behind it. Her choice is based on a sales profile on the bridge handbags, meaning that they have the customers for this brand and price point. She feels that this rare offer is a good one and is willing to chance putting the offer in Store A, but intends to monitor closely the sales for all stores, and action an internal transfer after the first week of the sales event should this be necessary.

Allocation by store and by proportion of total bridge business

Store	Distribution	Sales	Outright Buys	Allocation by store ranking	% Bridge Business	Allocation by % of Bridge Business	Units Allocated
Store A	20% of total	$440,000	$227,040	$24,578	20%	$24,578	62
Store B	18% of total	$396,000	$204,336	$22,121	24%	$29,494	74
Store C	22% of total	$484,000	$249,744	$27,036	18%	$22,121	55
Store D	15% of total	$330,000	$170,280	$18,434	15%	$18,434	46
Store E	12% of total	$265,000	$136,224	$14,747	11%	$13,518	34
Store F	13% of total	$286,000	$147,576	$15,976	12%	$14,747	37
Total	100%	$2,200,000	$1,135,200	$122,892	100%	$122,892	308 pairs

All stores receive an allocation according to their respective strengths in the bridge or higher-priced business. The biggest variances between the general allocation and that for this specific offer are in Store B, which receives 6% more of this offer, and in Store C, which gets 4% less.

The buyer's next step is to revise her initial OTB allocation for the seven vendors accordingly. This entails reducing the initial total allocation of $1,135,200 by $122,892, to $1,012,308. The allocation for each store will be adjusted according to the proportion of the Italian buy. Store B, for example, would have the initial $204,336 lowered by $22,121, or to $182,215. The original total units would be reduced by 651 pieces. (OTB of $22,121 divided by average price points of $34 equals approximately 650 to 651 handbags.) Interestingly, for the same amount of sales dollars, the store need only sell 62 better handbags instead of 651, making this buy much more profitable as there is a great deal less operational cost in storing, handling, moving and pricing tagging.

• Example 4: Missy Coordinated Ranges

"Missy" is a retail term to describe a look that appeals to a customer in her thirties. Bear in mind, though, that age is not simply a number but more a state of mind, an attitude, and a lifestyle.

In coordinating a range or a look, the buyer or brand designer intentionally matches garments that can be worn together. This can be top-to-bottom matches, color matches or complementary contrasts, or by deliberately creating complementary mix-n-match options.

Below is an example of some color theme ranges from Taifun, which is part of the Gerry Weber Group in Germany. The

Charcoal Story—likewise, casual styles yet wearable for work

buyer's selection is made easier as the brand designers create styles complementary to each other.

- **Example 5: Men's Business Shirts**

A menswear buyer from a department store is planning a buying trip to Thailand. His total OTB for the season is $535,000, and he plans to place orders with two of his best Thai vendors. Vendor A is traditionally good at making decent-quality shirts at affordable prices. Vendor B uses prime luxurious fabrics, with 18 stitches per inch, at premium prices. The type of buying he will be conducting is considered product development, which entails selecting a fabric, and either using the retailer's own garment design or adapting/using the vendor's styles on hand.

His overall budget is $375,000 for regular-priced shirts and $160,000 for promotional items. Based on the previous season's sell-through, he estimates that he can allocate $140,000 in total for these two vendors. The OTB balance of $235,000 is reserved for other local vendors. He prepares his plan by brand, class, style, fabric quality, color type, and estimated units he wants to buy within each brand. He has allocated some OTB for some opportunity buys at the desired promotional price points.

He has not plotted the colors at this point, though he expects to be buying lots of whites, blues and novelty stripes. He has forwarded his request on overall units by brand and styles to the vendors. The overall mark-up he wants to make is 48%. For the purposes of this example, we will concentrate on buys from Vendor A.

Initial OTB Plan

Planned OTB Allocation: $ 535,000		**Merchandise Type: Business Shirts**					
Regular: $ 375,000	Delivery:02/08	**Promo: $ 160,000**	Delivery: 10/07				
Plan OTB Thailand	**$ 139,330**	**Planned units: 3,100**	**Balance OTB Reg.**		**$275,302**		
Actual Buy Thailand		Actual units:	Balance OTB Promo				
Brand	**Class-Styles**	**Quality**	**Type**	**Unit Price**	**Promo**	**Pcs**	**Total $**
1. Alex Cross	L/S Button-down	100% Cotton	Solids	$39.90		300	$11,970
2. Alex Cross	L/S Regular	CVC 65%–45%	Assorted		$19.90	800	$15,920
3. Milford	L/S Regular	Cotton Poplin	Solids	$49.90		200	$9,980
4. Milford	L/S Button-down	Cotton Twill	Solids	$59.90		200	$11,980
5. Milford	L/S Button-down	Pinpoint Oxford	Stripes	$79.90		200	$15,980
6. Milford	L/S Button-down	100% Cotton	Assorted		$29.90	1,000	$29,900
Sub-total						**2,700**	**$95,730**
7. Oscar Jacobson	L/S Regular	Herringbone	Solids	$89.00		200	$17,800
9. Oscar Jacobson	L/S Spread	Jacquard white	Solid	$129.00		100	$12,900
10.Oscar Jacobson	L/S Regular	Royal Oxford	Stripes	$129.00		100	$12,900
						400	**$43,600**
Total						3,100	$139,330

FABRIC QUALITIES

A professional buyer is expected to know a great deal about the quality of shirt fabrics. The following should help explain why some shirts are more expensive than others.

Jermyn Street tailors in the U.K. have always measured shirt quality by yarn count. This refers to the length of yarn needed to make 1lb in weight: the higher the yarn count, the finer the fabric. A 200 thread count, for instance, produces a soft, silky feel to the fabric, and is always sold at a premium price.

Two Fold Poplin Dress Shirts

Made from 100% Egyptian cotton, poplins are lustrous, silky fabrics that are cool and comfortable to wear. The shirts get softer, with an even more comfortable wear, each time they are laundered. Smooth, lightweight and durable, poplin always looks smart at work or play.

Cotton Oxford Dress Shirts

"Oxford" is a classic casual fabric; soft, relaxed and durable. Oxford is woven from a heavier yarn than that used in poplin, giving a soft yet strong fabric which is extremely hard wearing.

A Royal Oxford fabric is a two-10 fabric woven to an Oxford construction. Due to the use of a finer 100 yarn, the Royal Oxfords are beautifully silky, and as such, much softer and smoother than classic Oxford.

Cotton Twill Dress Shirts

The fabric is made from two-ply fold, 100% Egyptian cotton. The weft threads pass over one and under two threads to produce a diagonal rib which catches the light, producing a subtle, attractive sheen to the fabric whilst making it soft to the touch. In Herringbone Twills, this fabric features a distinctive "fishbone" pattern where the direction of the twill is alternated to give it a soft, luxurious, classic look.

170's Dress Shirts

Made in two-ply poplin and twill fabrics from the very finest Egyptian cotton and woven to an extremely high yarn count, these shirts have a unique combination of great strength, silky luster and incredible, softness. Shirt connoisseurs know the difference as soon as they touch one!

200's Dress Shirts

200-thread quality fabrics are used by better shirt-makers and are considered the ultimate amongst cotton shirts.

Pinpoint Dress Shirts

Another very popular fabric used in dress shirts is Pinpoint Oxford, which is lighter and smoother than a plain Oxford. There is a wide variety of Pinpoint shirts on the market, starting with a Pinpoint Cotton/Poly blend all the way up to Egyptian cotton, and prices are just as varied.

Broadcloth Dress Shirts

Broadcloth has the same quality and weight as Pinpoint, but has a smoother finish. It is not only very suitable for a custom dress shirt, but is also found in ready-to-wear brands.

Herringbone Broadcloth Dress Shirts

For a dressier luxurious dress shirt, a great option is the tightly woven fine-ribbed fabric called the Herringbone Broadcloth. Shirts made with this fabric are considered fancier than those in the Oxford family of fabric. A Herringbone Broadcloth fabric is heavier than a Pinpoint or an Oxford. The ribbed effect determines the grade and quality of the fabric. The tighter the ribbed effect, the heavier the cloth will be.

Wrinkle-Free Dress Shirts

Back in the 1960's, a wrinkle-free shirt was termed "Drip-n-dry" and was entirely made of polyester fabrics. Generally, consumers consider cotton fibers as their number one choice when they think of comfort. In the past decade, pre-curing, post-curing, drip-spin, and vapor-phase technologies have enabled manufacturers to produce wrinkle-free or wrinkle-resistant fabrics. In each of these processes, the cotton fabric is treated with chemicals which swell and straighten the fabric so that it becomes almost impossibile to crease. The downside of this, though, is that the fabric loses part of its tensile strength and its ability to absorb moisture.

Buy #1: Alex Cross long-sleeve, button-down shirts at \$39.90

Vendor A has a wide selection of 100% wrinkle-free shirts at cost at \$21. At this cost, the mark-up will land at 47.3% [39.90 – 21 = 18.90 ÷ 39.90 = 47.3%], which is 0.7% short against the plan. The selection of solids is good, so the buyer decides to place the order, knowing that he will have to make up the lost mark-up on something else.

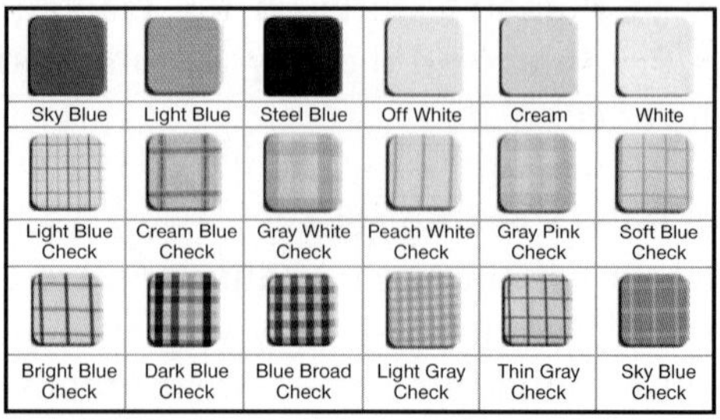

The buyer selects eight colors; four solids and four checks.

- Sky Blue
- Light Blue
- Cream
- White
- Light Blue Check
- Dark Blue Check
- Light Gray Check
- Sky Blue Check

The buyer makes a note that he is short of $90 in mark-up on this buy because the cost of these shirts was 30¢ more than planned. The planned margin is 48%. For him to enjoy that margin, the cost would have to be $20.70 or 30¢ less than he is offered, calculated as follows: 39.90 – 20.70 = 19.20 ÷ 39.90 = 48.1%.

Actual mark-up is $18.90 minus ideal mark-up $19.20 = 30¢.

Total actual mark-up : $18.90 x 300 = $5,670

Total ideal mark-up : $19.20 x 300 = $5,760

$5,760 – $5,670 = –$90.00

This also means that he will be seeking a cost reduction of $540.00 on some other items.

Total actual cost : $21.00 x 300 = $6,300

Total ideal cost : $19.20 x 300 = $5,760

Difference : $540.00

Buy #2: Alex Cross special buy at $19.90

The stock-lot on offer—Assorted Polyester-Cotton [60%-40%] mix shirts in assorted colors at a cost of $10.20—is in good sellable colors. The buyer places the order as assorted colors without specifying each color, with no fewer than 12 per color and no more than 16 per color. This helps condition the buy so that not too many units in odd colors are shipped. For this buyer, the very dark color tones are less attractive.

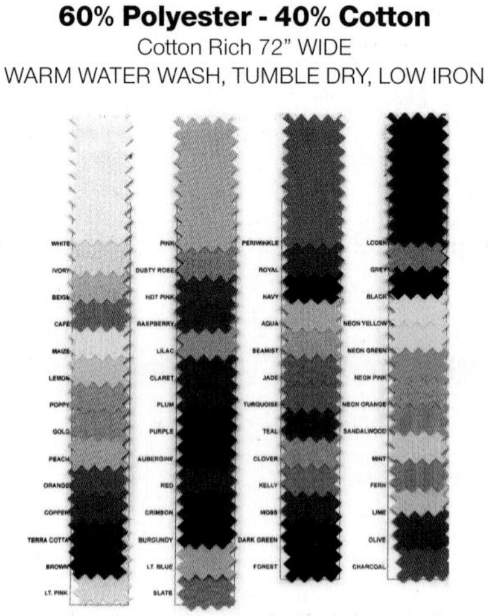

Buy #3: Milford long-sleeve poplin shirts at $49.90

The next range the buyer looks at is Poplin fabrics for his Milford brand. The range shown is available in stripes and solids at $24.00. At a planned retail price of $49.90, his mark-up is 51.9%. He decides to place 300 units instead of the originally planned 200, making the total buy at retail $14,970, rather than the planned $9,980–an over-buy on the original allocated OTB of $4,990.

The split is 65% solids and 45% stripes, or 195 solids and 105 stripes. The range is bought in the four original colors (white, pink, dark blue and blue) and six striped, as shown below.

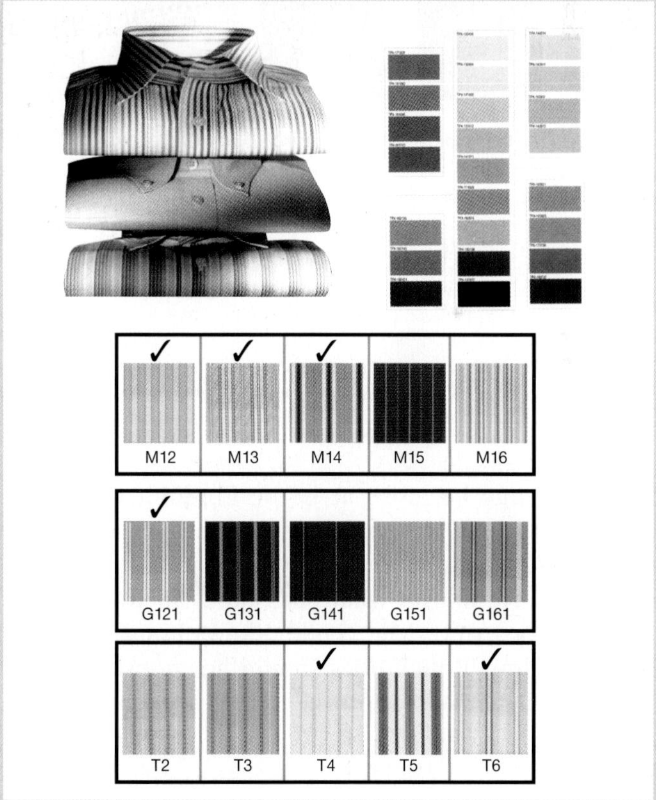

Buy # 4: Milford long-sleeve shirts in cotton twill at $59.90

From the Milford cotton twill range, the buyer selects all colors. The cost of $30.30 each is a mark-up of 49.41% on a retail price of $59.90. The split is as shown below and has an OTB value of $11,980. The buyer re-looks at his quantities and decides to top up on the stone gray, as this color is deemed sellable. He increases the quantity from 20 to 40, bringing the total OTB to $13,178, $1,198 more than planned.

Pure White	Sapphire Blue	Ruby Red	Golden Yellow	Stone Gray
40%	20%	10%	20%	10%
80 pieces	40 pieces	20 pieces	40 pieces	40 pieces

Buy #5: Milford long-sleeve shirts in Pinpoint Oxford at $79.90

The third range he looks at is the Pinpoint Oxford. His plan is to buy 200 pieces of assorted stripes at a selling price of $79.90 each, and he is looking for eight color ways only. He knows what sells but also wants to buy some novelty stripes. The vendor shows him the range of 15 styles below. Which ones should he choose and why? After careful consideration, he settles for the following styles: PT-97, PT-67, PT-68, PT-70, PT-99, PT-58, PT-11 and PT-12.

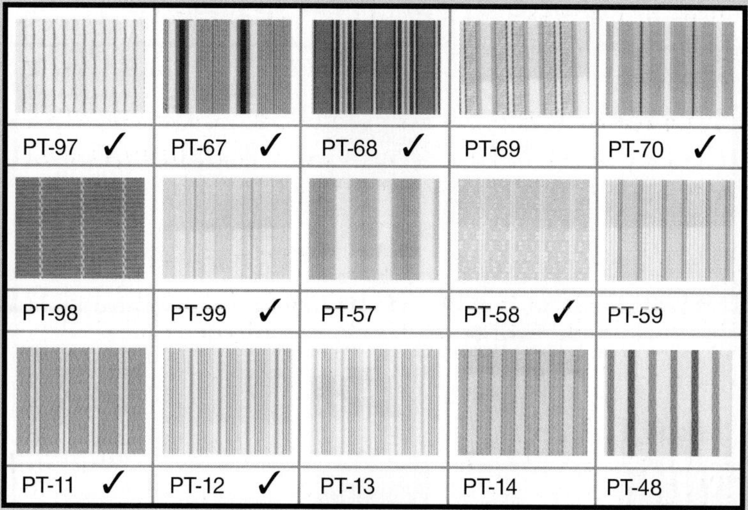

So why were PT-69 + 98 + 57 + 59 + 13 + 14 + 48 rejected? The reasons could be as follows.

- PT-69: too similar to the stripe bought in cotton poplin style # M13
- PT-98: the blue color is too dull
- PT-57: the color is good but the stripe is a bit too broad
- PT-59: good but he has planned to stick to eight ways
- PT-13: preferred the red to the yellow stripe
- PT-14: color combo difficult
- PT-48: too colorful for his customer profile.

Buy #6: Milford assorted shirts at special offer price of $29.90

The last buy with Vendor A is a range of assorted promotional shirts. The grade of the fabrics in 100% cotton is very good. His plan is to buy 1,000 pieces at a retail price of $29.90. The shirts are priced at $15, giving him a mark-up of 49.8%. However, there are very few solid colors in this offer, and he needs at least 450 pieces in solids, or

Fabric offer from Vendor A

	12		36		36		24		12
	24		36		36		24		24
	24		36		36		24		24
	36		36		48		24		24
	36		24		36		24		12
	36		18		24		36		12
	36		12		14		36		26
	36		18		12		12		12
	58		14		12		12		18
	56		12		12		12		16
	36		24		12		12		18
	36		24		24		12		12
	36		24		24		12		12
	24		24		36				
	24		12						
	12		14						
			12						
BR/987	522 pcs	**BR/901**	376 pcs		362 pcs	**BR/681**	264 pcs	**BR/227**	246 pcs

45% in total. Furthermore, he must choose the entire assortment in each lot, a total of 1,770 pieces. So which ones should he choose?

The buyer evaluates each individual strip and sums up the quantities he feels are difficult. The circled swatches (fabrics from which the shirts will be made) are the ones he deems difficult for his market.

1. BR/987 has good color ways but the two dark colors, in quantities of 58 and 56 respectively, are deemed unsuitable.

2. BR/901 is good, with the exception of the checks, which he deems too casual for his customers. Total difficult pieces: 48.

3. BR/115 is the most difficult. As the colors are either very bright or too dark, he discards this lot completely.

4. BR/681 all colors are good.

5. BR/227 all colors are good, with the possible exception of the first, which may be difficult to sell.

Nevertheless, he deems BR/681 and BR/227 to be OK and places orders for the 510 pieces.

The buyer decides to negotiate with the vendor. He knows that some of the colors in BR/901 will be difficult to sell, so he asks for a price reduction of $3 on all. The vendor agrees, but on the condition that he take BR/987 as well, knowing that reducing the cost by $3 is only doable if the buyer buys four out of the five lots.

The buyer recalculates: taking all four complete strips will add up to a total of 1,408 pieces, which is manageable, but he is short of solid colors. He therefore goes back to the vendor with the proposition that he will take all four strips, on condition that the vendor finds him 450 pieces in three or four basic colors in 100% cotton, and at the same offer cost price of $12.

In this case, the vendor agrees, as he wants to get rid of these stocks and can accommodate the request for solid colors.

By buying the agreed lot of 1,408, the buyer is 408 pieces above plan. There are only 174 pieces that are deemed to have a slow selling rate, but with the additional cost cut, there will be plenty of margins to adjust to a lower price later in the promotion. Taking an additional 450 pieces in solid colors means that he will have a grand total

Buyer's selection criteria-rejects circled

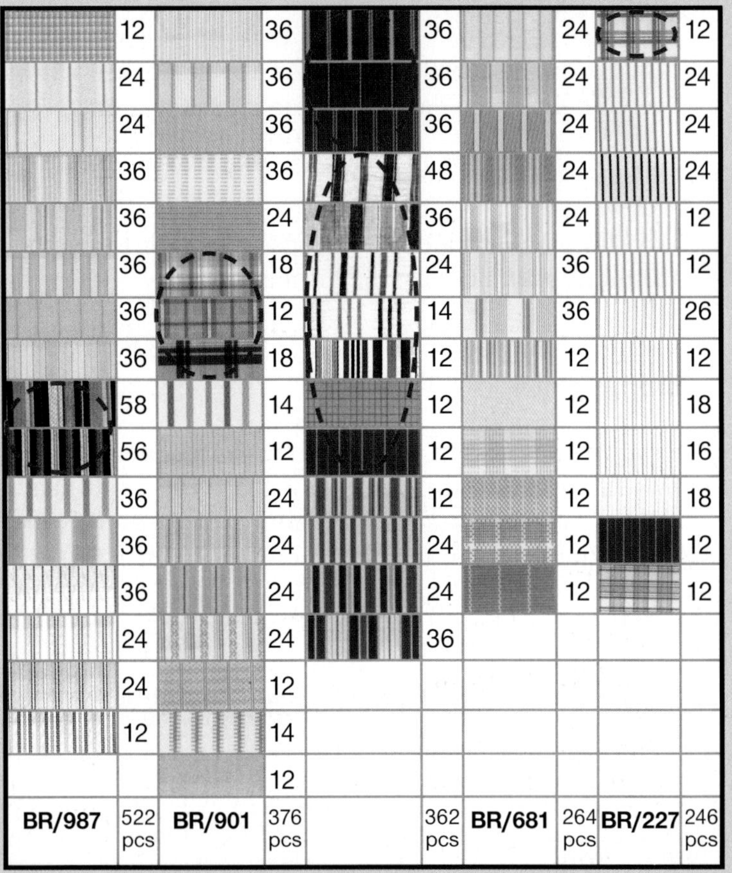

12
24
24
36
36
36
36
36
58
56
36
36
36
24
24
12
BR/987
522 pcs
36
36
36
36
24
18
12
18
14
12
24
24
24
24
12
14
12
BR/901
376 pcs
36
36
36
48
36
24
14
12
12
12
12
24
24
36
362 pcs
24
24
24
24
24
36
36
12
12
12
12
12
12
BR/681
264 pcs
12
24
24
24
12
12
26
12
18
16
18
12
12
BR/227
246 pcs

of 1,858 pieces, with a retail value of $55,554. This is $25,654 more than planned. He agrees to the deal. Why?

Special buys are a bit like a lucky draw. When you find a well-assorted mix of merchandise in good-grade fabrics, in good overall colors, and where you can determine the size ratio in acceptable sellable quantities within your budget, you buy because the opportunity may not arise again.

The buyer's original OTB plan for Thailand was $139,330, but he had a total OTB for special offers of $160,000. While he may have exceeded his buys for Vendor A, he is well within budget for the special-buy allocation. Total special buy is as follows:

Alex Cross $15,920 + Milford $55,554 = $71,474

The new OTB balance for special offer buys is now $88,525.

The other advantage this deal has is a better mark-up. With the new cost reduction, his mark-up is 59.86%, or an average cost price of $17.90 per shirt [total cost $33,258 ÷ 1,858 pieces = $17.90]. As the total units placed are 1,858, he has a total mark-up of $33,258.

The 1,000 units at $29.90 originally offered at $15.00 would have had a mark-up of $14.90 on each shirt, or a total of $14,900. This would have given him a 49.83% margin. Instead, he bought 1,858 pieces at a cost of $12, giving him a mark-up of $17.90 on each shirt, a total mark-up of $33,258 for this buy, and a difference of $18,358 in mark-up between the original plan and the actual buy (original plan 1,000 x $14.90 = $14,900: actual buy 1,858 x $17.90 = $33,258. Actual buy $33,258 – planned buy $14,900 = additional mark-up of $18,358 and a margin of 59.86%) should he sell them all. Even if he should only sell 80% at the intended $29.90, he is still ahead.

The planned budgeted mark-up for his department is 48%. The total mark-up on this buy should not go under $26,755 to meet the budget. (On a buy of 1,858 pieces at a budgeted mark-up of 48%, the mark-up on each piece is $14.40 x 1,858 = $26,755). If he sells 80%, or 1,486 pieces, at full price, this will give him $26,599 (1,486 x $17.90) in mark-up. This being the case, he may decide to sell the remaining 372 pieces at $19.90, a mark-up of 39.69% (retail price $19.90 – cost $12 ÷ $19.90 = 39.69%), or a total of $2,938.80 ($19.90 – $12 = mark-up $7.90. $7.90 x 372 = $2,938.80, rounded up to $2,939).

The total final mark-up for this offer would then be $26,599 + $2,939 = $29,538, or $2,783 above budget of $26,755.

Revised OTB Plan

Planned OTB Allocation: $ 535,000		**Merchandise Type: Business Shirts**					
Regular: $ 375,000	Delivery: 02/08	**Promo: $ 160,000**	Delivery: 10/07				
Plan OTB Thailand	**$ 139,330**	**Planned units: 3,100**	**Balance OTB Reg.**		**$275,302**		
Actual Buy Thailand	$ 171,172	Actual units: 4,078	Balance OTB Promo		$72,526		
Brand	**Class-Styles**	**Quality**	**Type**	**Unit Price**	**Promo**	**Pcs**	**Total $**
1. Alex Cross	L/S Button-down	100% Cotton	Solids	$39.90		300	$11,970
2. Alex Cross	L/S Regular	CVC 65%-45%	Assorted		$19.90	800	$15,920
3. Milford	L/S Regular	Cotton Poplin	Solids	$49.90		**300**	**$14,970**
4. Milford	L/S Button-down	Cotton Twill	Solids	$59.90		**220**	**$13,178**
5. Milford	L/S Button-down	Pinpoint Oxford	Stripes	$79.90		200	$15,980
6. Milford	L/S Button-down	100% Cotton	Assorted		$29.90	**1,858**	**$55,554**
Sub-total						**3,678**	**$127,572**
7. Oscar Jacobson	L/S Regular	Herringbone	Solids	$89.00		200	$17,800
9. Oscar Jacobson	L/S Spread	Jacquard white	Solid	$129.00		100	$12,900
10.Oscar Jacobson	L/S Regular	Royal Oxford	Stripes	$129.00		100	$12,900
Total						**4,078**	**$171,172**

• Example 6: Ladies' Lingerie

Buying ladies' lingerie can be a bit tricky. For many retailers, it is easier and more cost-effective to let brand owners such as Triumph, Wacoal, Blush, Dim, Princess Tam Tam, Wonderbra, Aubade or Maidenform run the business. Inventories can be high, especially in the bra category, where selections of size and cup sizes, styles and fabrications on offer are wide. The sales promoters (selling staff paid by the vendor) play an important role as "brand experts", and this instills customer confidence in choosing the right bras.

Many retailers are attempting to create their own lingerie lines, and these decisions are made in the knowledge that it is extremely difficult to compete head on with strong national brands. The rationale behind such decisions is simple. For retailers to stay competitive, they have to create points of differentiation through private labels or merchandise exclusive to their stores. Secondly, margins offered by most national brands are low and, thirdly, many national brands do not carry bigger sizes.

A good example of a retailer taking the private label route in lingerie is J.C. Penny. Newly launched in 2007, its Ambrielle label covers the entire gamut, from push-up bras, T-shirt bras, no-underwire bras, seamless bras, strapless bras to sports & leisure bras. On average, there are three colors per style and sizes 34A to 42D, where each size carries four different cup sizes.

In my experience of J.C. Penny's business model, it would have conducted in-depth feasibility studies before engaging in this new line, finding the right talent to create it, and applying the 12 rules of successful branding (as illustrated below). These studies would

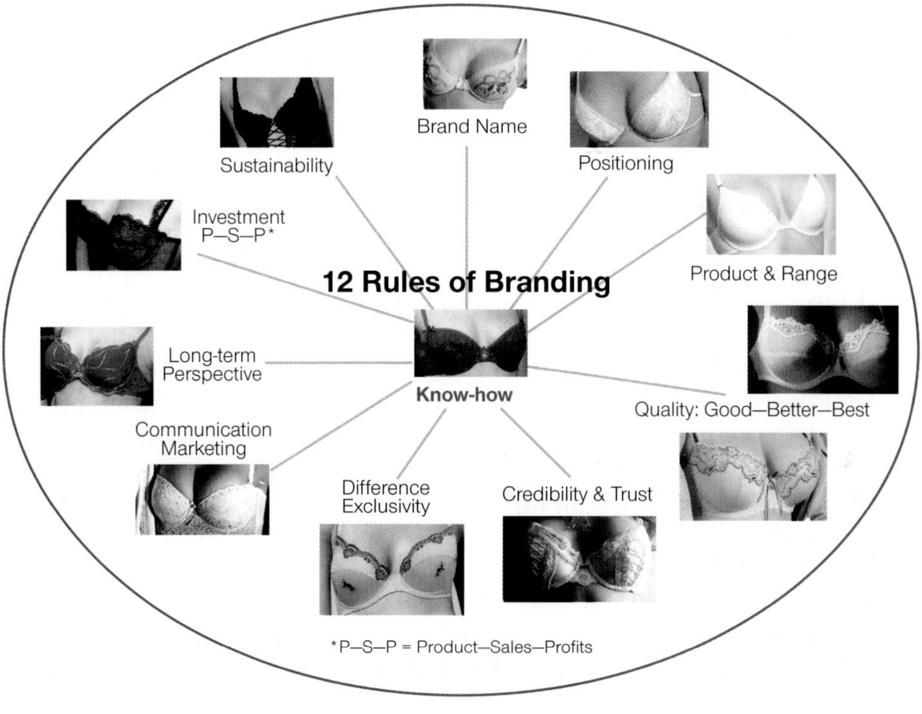

also include consumer demand, and/or how difficult it was for customer to find the right size or fit. So the company found a niche and filled it. Its collections also encompass matching panties in different shapes, shapewear, sleepwear, camisoles, slips and liners, hosiery, and maternity wear.

At the Ambrielle launch, customers were able to find over 4,000 items in free-standing boutiques in every store. The line is actually broken into three sub-brands that appeal to different generations and styles: "Smooth Revolution" (modern and smooth), "Mystique" (sexy and enhancing) and "Essentials" (understated and natural). The lingerie looks modern and sensual.

For retailers that do not have J.C. Penny's size or clout, there are other ways for buyers to find non-national or international branded lingerie at fairly good prices. I found good selections while shopping in the United States market where, with the assistance of local agents, we brought in some lovely ranges of lingerie, in addition to fashion wear, children's wear and shoes. We enjoyed double the margins that we were otherwise getting from national /international brands represented by local agents and selling at half the retail price. The weak point, though, was the selling staff. Traditionally, ours was a department selling entirely consignment goods, and our own staff were used to performing cashier duties; so it took a lot of work getting them from behind the cashier desk and onto the selling floor, selling our own products.

We later introduced special sales commission for these goods to entice the selling staff to push harder. The result was better, but still lower than expected. I concluded that we should have gathered an internal team of specialized sales people to grow this business, as the mindset of existing lingerie staff was too geared towards "Pack & Cash."

Something you have to keep in mind when developing or buying merchandise is the structure of your store. If you currently have very high levels of consignment goods or concessionaire counters staffed by promoters, the smart thing to do would be to hire or find internal talent who enjoy selling and are passionate about customer service; in other words, find people who have "sales in their DNA."

BUYING BED LINEN

When shopping for new ranges of bed linen, a buyer has to first determine the size required and which ones sell best—single, super-single, Queen, Double, King, Super King, California King, European King or a waterbed? This is where the selling staff is required to be equipped with good product knowledge.

A buying plan, as illustrated on the following page, is distributed by brand and by size. The fabric quality within the brand is usually predictable, while the quality of the sales or promotional ranges may vary, as the source for these opportunity buys may change from season to season.

When deciding on the type of material to buy (soft, silky, crisp, cotton, jersey knit, silk, satin...), the buyer should select from a customer's-preference standpoint. Once the materials and the grade of these materials have been determined, the buyer will select the colors (plain solids, tone-on-tone, jacquards or prints).

A print or embroidery, together with styling, is one way the buyer can create themes. The Lulu Guinness brand provides a good example of theme-making, where the designer has taken white-based bed sets and applied black roses and butterfly embroidery, creating a black-and-white theme, as shown below. The store can then add black-and-white props to accentuate the theme. When it comes to selling themes, bigger stores have the advantage in that they are able to create bedroom scenes with matching props, all of which helps customers make their buying decisions.

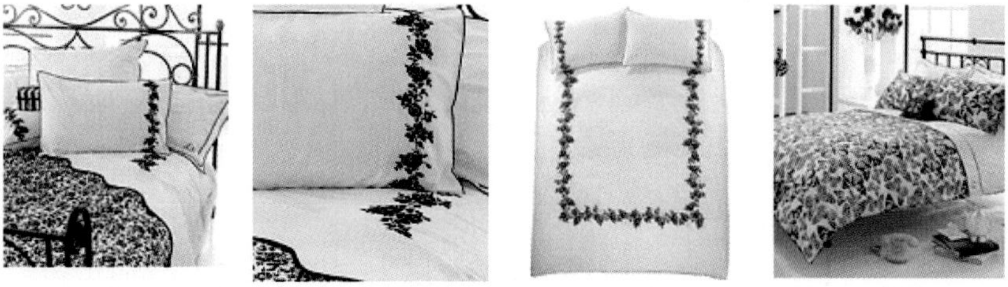

The materials, the grade of the fabric and the thread count are the key factors in determining price. For example, embroidered or jacquard bed sets are more expensive than plain dyed sheets or printed sheets because the embroidery requires more work, and thread counts may be as high as 1,000 (as found in Sheridan's super-deluxe ranges).

• Example 7: Bed Linen

In this example, the store concept is "bed & bath", selling luxury ranges of well-known brands in six stores located in high-traffic shopping malls. In this instance, the buyer's key brands are Aussino, Sheridan, Ditton Hill, Bel Dorm, Christy, and Frette, which together account for 50% of the sales. For the most part, prices are on the high end, except for in-house brands, which are the buyer's entry price points on regular lines and make up the bulk of her turnover during sales or promotions.

The average annual sales turnover per store is $1,334,000, which translates into monthly sales of around $139 per square foot for each of the 800 sq.ft. stores. Her total annual sales for the six stores is $8,004,000.

Family-Tree Planner: Bed Linen Department

TOTAL OTB
$8,000,000

OTB Allocation by Size $8,000,000		
King Size	50%	$4.000
Queen Size	30%	$2.400
Singles	20%	$1.600

OTB Allocation for Private-Label Promotion $2,750,000					
Private Label		King	Queen	Single	Total
Layette Douce	30%	412.5	247.5	165	825
Royal Empress	40%	550	330	220	1.100
Enchantment	30%	412.5	247.5	165	825

OTB Allocation by Brand		**King**	**Queen**	**Singles**	
$4,000,000	Reg.	2.000	1.200	800	4.000
Brand Name	%				
Aussino	20%	400	240	160	800
Sheridan	20%	400	240	160	800
Ditton Hill	15%	300	180	120	600
Bel Donn	15%	300	180	120	600
Christy	15%	300	180	120	600
Frette	15%	300	180	120	600
Total	**100%**	**2.000**	**1.200**	**800**	**4.000**

OTB Allocation Private Label		**King**	**Queen 30%**	**Singles 20%**	
$1,500,000	promo	750	450	300	1.500
Layette Douce	30%	225	135	90	480
Royal Empress	40%	300	180	120	600
Enchantment	30%	225	135	90	450
$2,500,000	SALE	1.250	750	500	2.500
Assorted Brand	50%	625	375	250	1.250
Layette Douce	30%	187.5	112.5	75	375
Royal Empress	40%	250	150	100	510
Enchantment	30%	187.5	112.5	75	375
Total	**100%**	**2.000**	**1.200**	**800**	**4.000**

The buyer has prepared her next year's budgets and has planned a 5% increase against the current year. The projection she is now working on is a budget of $8,404,200 for the year and $4,202,000 for the season. Branded linens represent 50% of sales or $2,101,000.

The full-year OTB budget she has prepared is $8,000,000. The allocation is $4,000,000 for branded bed linen, $2,750,000 for private labels and $1,250,000 for special offers, which can be placed with existing brands or opportunity buys. Each brand will be sorted by type, by quality, and then by price.

The buys for this example are based on sets, comprising one fitted sheet, one duvet cover, two pillow cases, and two bolster covers. The retail prices are by sets.

The OTB is to be split into two six-month periods: January–June (spring season) and July–December (autumn season). The buyer is currently working on the latter, with an OTB of $4,000,000, 50% of which will be distributed between key brands in the following amounts: Aussino, $400,000; Sheridan, $400,000; Ditton Hill, $300,000, and so on.

Within the allocation, the buyer distributes the OTB by size classification. In Aussino's case, this is $200,000 for King-size and $120,000 for Queen-size. However, she does not intend to place orders on the singles, as they have proven to be slow-selling. Instead, she re-distributes the OTB: $240,000 is allocated for King-size and $140,000 for the Queen-size, with the rest being kept in reserve.

When dealing with bigger brands, more often than not, styles can be repeated, making it unnecessary to use up the entire allocated amount at the outset. A basic assortment of the vendor's new collection should be placed and OTB reserved each month for repeats.

The buyer is preparing a selection from one of her best-selling brands, Aussino. She picks five ranges out of a possible nine and concentrates on bed sheet sets which consist of one fitted sheet, one duvet or comforter cover, two pillow cases, and two bolster covers.

First Range: Cotton Prints (average price per set $280-360)

Poppy Field
Top: 100% cotton, 260TC
Color: Pink

Blue Corals
Top: 100% cotton, 250TC
Color: Multi

Color Intrigue
Top: 100% cotton, 260TC
Color: Blue

Fernery
Top: 100% cotton sateen, 280TC
Color: Blue

Second Range: Romantic Embroidery (price range $550-700)

Miss Daisy
Top: 100% cotton with eyelet lace, 260 thread count
Reverse: 260TC
Color: Snow White

Wedding Bliss
Top: 100% polyester georgette with hand-sewn sequins and beaded tassels
Reverse: 260TC
Color: Ivory

Princess Beatrice
Top: 100% polyester faux silk with floral rosettes and hand-sewn beadings
Reverse: 260TC
Color: Ivory

Garden Dream
Top: cotton/faux silk with embroidery. Velvet panel with shell buttons and satin rosettes
Reverse: 260TC
Color: Pink-Blue

Third Range: Royal Symphony (price range $600–780)

Crème de la crème	Summer Nightingale	Imperial Jade	Portrait
Top: polyester/ cotton jacquard	Top: 100% polyester jacquard	Top: polyester/ cotton jacquard	Top: 100% polyester jacquard
Reverse: 100% cotton 260TC	Reverse: 100% cotton 260TC	Reverse: 100% cotton 260TC	Reverse: 100% cotton 260TC
Color: Cream	Color: Ivory	Color: Mint	Color: Deep Red

Fourth Range: Sino (price range $280–360)

Chevron	Desert	Menoya Ivory	Woodlands
Top: 100% cotton sateen with chain embroidery	Top: 100% cotton sateen 370TC	Top: 100% combed cotton sateen waffle 225TC	Top: 100% cotton sateen with embroidery 370TC
Color: Cocoa	Color: Mustard	Color: Ivory	Color: White

Fifth Range: Senze (price range $400-520)

Kinnear Khaki
Top: 100% cotton panel print 260TC with toggle buttons
Color: Khaki & White

La Senza
Top: 100% cotton 260TC with embroidery and pleats detail
Color: Khaki & Gray

Mabella:
Top: Georgette voile with embroidery and faux silk border
Color: Aqua

Mabella: Georgette voile with embroidery and faux silk border
Color: Pink

The buyer will then systematically place her orders according to the prints, colors, size and retail prices, as shown below.

Name of Range	Color	King	Queen	Units	Cost	Retail Price	Total at Retail
Cotton Prints	4	30 sets		120		$360	$43,200
	4		20 sets	80		$280	$22,400
Romantic Embroidery	4	20 sets		80		$700	$56,000
	4		10 sets	40		$550	$22,000
Royal Symphony	4	15 sets		60		$780	$46,800
	4		10 sets	40		600	$24,000
Sino	4	30 sets		120		$360	$43,200
	4		20 sets	80		$280	$22,400
Senze	4	20 sets		80		$520	$41,600
	4		10 sets	40		$400	$16,000
Total	40	460 sets	280 sets	740		Planned Purchase	$337,600
OTB Reserve for Repeats						15.6% buffer	$62,400
Total						Total OTB Available	$400,000

In all stores, Aussino goods occupy an area of 120 sq. ft. or 15% of the total selling area, with a back-wall section. The total number of units that can be placed on the selling floor is 40 sets on two gondolas (fixtures), 40 sets on the back wall, and 10 sets on a display table; a total of 90 sets. The split between King- and Queen-size is 62.1%/37.9%. The average price point for the King-size is $544, and $422 for the Queen-size. Average stocks on the selling floor are approximately 56 units of the King-size (a value of $30,464) and 34 units ($14,348) of the Queen-size. The total value across the six stores is $268,872 ($44,812 x 6) or 79.6% of total planned purchases.

The projected sales for Aussino are $420,210 for the six months. This is derived from the total season's planned sales of $4,202,100 (half of the yearly total of $8,404,200), and the projection for the branded linens, which is $2,101,050, or 50% of the season's sales. As noted earlier, Aussino represents 20% of the buyer's branded linens, giving a value of $420,210, or $70,035 per month.

The projected productivity per square foot for Aussino is $583.63 per month. This is derived by dividing the monthly sales of $70,035 by the selling area of 120 square foot. The buyer's net margin on Aussino is 38%, or $26,613.30, and her profit productivity per square foot is $221.77 ($26,613.30 ÷ 120 = $221.77).

case study

Multi-store Buy

This is another case study related to me by Gianfranco Guidotti.

"One of the stories that I shall never forget took place when I was acting as Selfridges agent. In those days, I had a good account in the U.S., a chain of seven stores in New York State, trading as J.W. Mays. Their flagship store was in Brooklyn and that store alone was taking some $50 million.

Mays' accessories buyer was placing large orders and she was doing particularly well with a leather clutch bag in various colors.

I showed Selfridges' handbag buyer a sample of this clutch and told her that Mays was selling thousands of them in all the colors. Cindy was an impulse buyer; she liked the item and placed a trial order of 500 units. That's a lot of clutches for one store and I was a bit nervous. However, the price was good and Mays was selling the clutch in spite of the cost of transportation, duty, and so on, I convinced myself that I did the right thing in submitting the sample to Selfridges.

When the 500 clutches arrived, she put a large assortment of all the colors on a table ... and in no time, the table was empty. The 500 units disappeared in two days. The buyer was on the phone, and asked me to do the impossible; to send any quantity in assorted colors by air as she wanted to continue to put the goods out for sale.

To cut a long story short, we kept sending large quantities of this clutch by air for months and the item became the talk of the town, so much so that when I started doing business with Debenham's, they also started buying the clutch and they also did very well with it.

Now, what can we learn from this story?

My opinion is that a buyer should also be a merchant and have a feeling for the merchandise. To be guided by figures is correct, but to play safe is not always the answer."

case study

Job-lot Buy

The GM of a low-priced department store was on a European buying trip with his buyers looking for some opportunity buys. His Spanish buying office arranged an appointment with a very popular, young, up-and-coming brand for some clearance merchandise; the GM was thrilled as the brand was known but not yet established in his market.

The job-lot offer had a catch, however. He was not allowed to pick and choose any of the items, but simply required to fill out a form, stating the items of interest—woven tops, knitted tops, pants, jeans, and so on—and the size ratio in each class. Furthermore, to be eligible for the job-lot buy, which was selling at the cost of US$5 per unit, there was a minimum purchase of US$1 million —a total of 200,000 units. Having received approval from his CEO, the GM went ahead with the buy.

Unsurprisingly with 200,000 odd units, when they arrived, the assortments were not all that great: many of the items were several years old, and some had defects. Nevertheless, all the merchandise was priced with a very high margin to allow for any mark-downs required later on slow-selling items.

A street-front selling area was dedicated to the brand, with the branding highly visible. The GM secured a couple of newspaper ads to publicize this "buy of the century" and, with this kind of back up, he was confident of raking in millions. Though the ads generated a huge rush that weekend, the results were very poor. Customers who were familiar with the brand were looking for updated styles and colors, but the assortment offered was deemed old and passé. The sellthrough generated from the first promotion was only 40,000 units, leaving just 160,000 to go.

The offer was publicized a second and a third time with a further discount on the discounted offer, with similarly poor results. As the months dragged on, so did the customers' lack of interest. Recognizing the flop, the GM tried to sell the balance to some jobbers. But the quantities were too huge to absorb, even for them, so he was forced to sell to several at below cost.

The lesson to be learnt from this is never to buy goods unseen in such high quantities. As the saying goes: "For every credibility gap, there is a gullibility fill." (Richard Clopton)

case study

Low-cut Jeans

I've got an ax to grind, but I don't know if it's the designers or the buyers I should go after. Low-cut jeans—some extremely low-cut—can be found in most brands. If you have the body of a goddess, then, yes, these jeans can look sexy, provocative and sensuous. Unfortunately, many chubby girls (sizes 14 to 16) are wearing them too, which make it a sight for sore eyes. The worst part is that the jeans have a tendency to slip down, exposing a great deal of flesh. Where are the fashion police when you need them?

Designers are constantly looking to create newness. Their concepts are usually created with a gorgeous body in mind, and often the garments are suited more to the catwalk than to the sidewalk. Given that such shapes are the exception rather than the rule, it is sensible, therefore, to carry an assortment of jeans that give customers some alternative.

I was shopping a few months ago for a pair of Levi's and there was not one pair that I could buy. They were all low-cut. Not that I am a large person, but I am critical about hiding some minor flaws, but the jeans on offer would have rendered a total exposé!

Recently, at Changi airport, I saw a large girl (about size 16) in her early twenties wearing extremely low-cut jeans and showing more than I cared to see. She seemed flattered that men were looking at her. Well, you can say that it's a lifestyle, I guess; but it's one I find in bad taste.

I feel that some fashion statements are not meant for all. We talked in earlier chapters about size ratios and having the right sizes to fit your customers. That being said, there should also be some size control in some cases. Buyers should run some product-knowledge sessions (PKS) with the selling staff or promoters of these low-cut jeans, and explain the customer profile most befitting these styles. Remember the strength of word-of-mouth advertising. Would you want your store to be associated with such sights?

Many of life's failures are men who did not realize how close they were to success when they gave up.
- Thomas Edison
The Art of Retail Buying
13
BRAND STRATEGY
Idea
Inspiration
Thought

WHAT MAKES A BRAND?

At its most basic, a brand is simply a product or a collection of products. However, successful brands are those which can create a unique set of values whose emotional or functional attributes exert a strong influence over consumers' decisions to purchase. These products/services offer specific benefits by way of performance, quality, price, or status that set them apart from competitors. The values they embody take firm root in consumers' minds and are adopted as their own.

To achieve this status, a brand requires high levels of awareness among the target audience, to whom it can offer differentiated products/services, and fulfill their needs through the perception of superior value, for which they are willing to pay higher prices than those of the competition.

The most effective brands have an almost visionary quality about them. They present to consumers, their employees, and even their competitors an imagined ideal future they often can't enunciate themselves. They guide. They imprint.

Branding is about being remarkable. Branding answers the question of why a company/product exists. Branding is the heart, the soul, and the essence of a company/product. Quite simply, a brand is an image that people trust.

For the retailer, a brand is a promise—a promise that you'll deliver the same important benefits the same way, consistently, time after time; and that you'll deliver high perceived value to your target audience every time they buy or use the brand.

I remember reading several years ago something along the lines that "a brand is something which speaks for itself and which can, in turn, sell itself." A successful brand is one that keeps the promise so that customers will remain loyal. It involves much more than a name, a logo, and slick marketing. It really encompasses every customer contact point. The total brand experience has to work.

TWELVE STEPS TO ORGANIZING AND MANAGING A BRAND

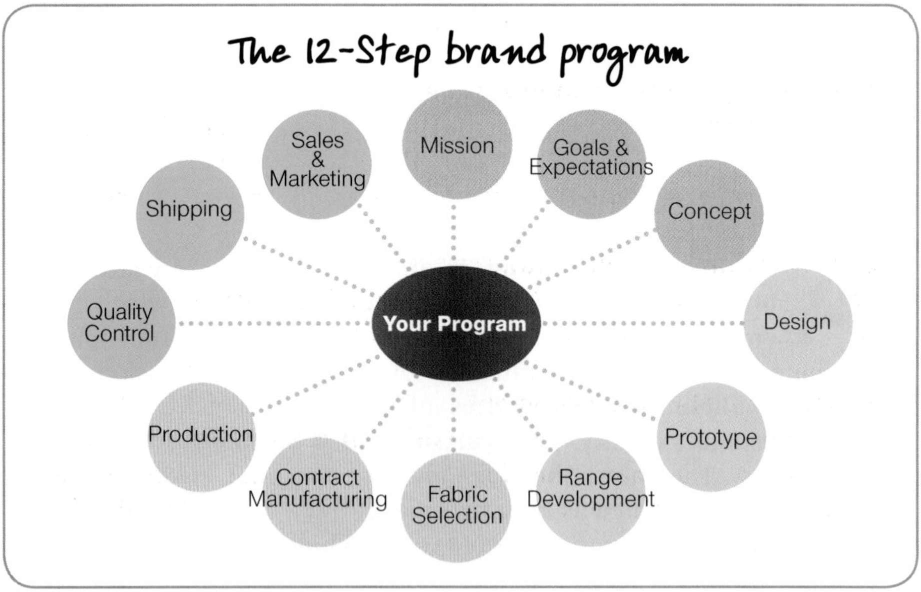

1. Your mission

Have a clear idea of what you want to achieve. Ask yourself whether creating a brand is a matter of positioning/re-positioning your store, gaining more market share, or because owning your own brand will help you to stay competitive. Where will the brand fit in your merchandise mix? Will it add value to your assortment mix? Is it to replace an existing brand or to fill a gap? Is it designed to introduce a new product range, or achieve a price range that is difficult for you to get from existing vendors? Is it a question of achieving better margins?

2. Your goals and expectations

What is the timeline for the launch of the brand, and what are your financial expectations? What kind of investment are you planning to use to support the creation of the brand? Do you have your company's full support in terms of investment and people resources?

3. Your concept

What kind of brand will it be–lifestyle, luxury or basic? Are you trying to add more-moderately priced merchandise to your assortment? Is your aim to create a brand similar to an existing popular brand that is not available to you? What type of products or ranges do you have in mind, and what will they be competing with? What quality level are you aiming at? Who do you anticipate will be shopping your brand?

4. The design/lifestyle of the range

How will the brand suit your customer profile? Is it designed to attract customers shopping elsewhere? Is it intended to attract young and fashionable customers or contemporary sophisticated customers?

5. The development of prototypes

Who will develop the products? How much investment has been reserved to create the prototypes or samples?

6. Range build-up/development

Who will be doing the development? Is it a team, an individual, or in cooperation with a vendor or several vendors? Where will the development take place? Who sets the range component criteria? Who approves them?

7. Selecting fabrics/materials/components

Where and how will you choose the fabrics, materials, or components that fit the entire concept? Quality, color, fabrication, price? Will you be buying the fabrics yourself, then passing them on to the manufacturer, or will you seek the assistance of the manufacturer to source a selection for you?

8. Selecting a manufacturer

Who will manufacture the products? Have you used these manufacturers before? Have you entered an agreement or contract with them, stipulating your company's rules and regulations? (These may incorporate an exclusivity agreement on the product development.)

9. Production and lead time

How much time have you allotted for the development process, from conception to selling? Do you have a fixed schedule?

10. Quality control

Who will undertake quality control before the products leave the factory? Will the quality control take place at your warehouse and, if so, how will you deal with quality failures?

11. Packaging and shipping

Will your products require special packing? If so, who will undertake the creative artwork and manufacturing of the packaging?

12. Sales and marketing

Assuming that all of the above questions have been answered satisfactorily, what will your sales budgets look like? How much money will be reserved for marketing the brand? (Will it be 5% against projected sales turnover?) What media will be used, and what kinds of activities will you use to attract the right attention to your brand?

NAMING YOUR BRAND

When you think about known brands, something is triggered. For example, the word "Rolex" triggers memories of its look, its status, an experience or a perception of what the brand means to you. Strong brands such as this have intrinsic value; they are iconic, engaging and persuasive.

Some brand names are descriptive of the products they sell (Nescafe, Singtel, Microsoft, for example). Others are so strongly advertised (Nokia, Volvo, Google...) that the names becomes synonymous with the products.

Having a great brand name can reduce the costs involved in the launching of new products because it is instantly recognized and carries with it certain expectations regarding quality, function, and advantages. This position of strength communicates its strategy, enables the brand to stand out, and distance itself from its competitors.

These clever brands can have varied intrinsic meanings that can evoke rational, descriptive, imaginative or emotional meanings. For example, for me, Volvo is associated with safety; Cartier with luxury; Ferrari with "oomph"; Google with information.

So when deciding on your own brand name, it should be, in itself, a one-word strategy that communicates the right message. It must be easy to pronounce, easy to remember, and easy to relate to.

Here are a couple of tips:

- Make the name easy to pronounce
- Make sure that it is written the way it is spoken
- If you use a foreign name, make sure that it translates well and that it is appropriate to the concept.

• The naming process

Brand naming is a project, and like any project, it has to have objectives, time frames, budgets and approval. A team should be selected and made responsible for its outcome. Creating a brand name can be fun, creative and stimulating but, most importantly, the outcome (the brand) should have distinctive characteristics that relate to the product(s).

Names can be descriptive (Citibank, General Electric, Singapore Airlines); invented (Aspirin, Lego, Pringles, Zara, Lexus); functional (Land Rover, Aquafresh, Microsoft, Dr. Scholl's); or emotive (Playboy, Pampers, Off!, Blush, Secret) in accordance with the brand's intended purpose.

You may consider several approaches in the naming process: combining words and syllables; using an existing word and abbreviating or twisting it; adopting a credible-sounding person's name to make it appear to be that of the founder or designer; or using a word that will lend itself to rhyming within a specific slogan.

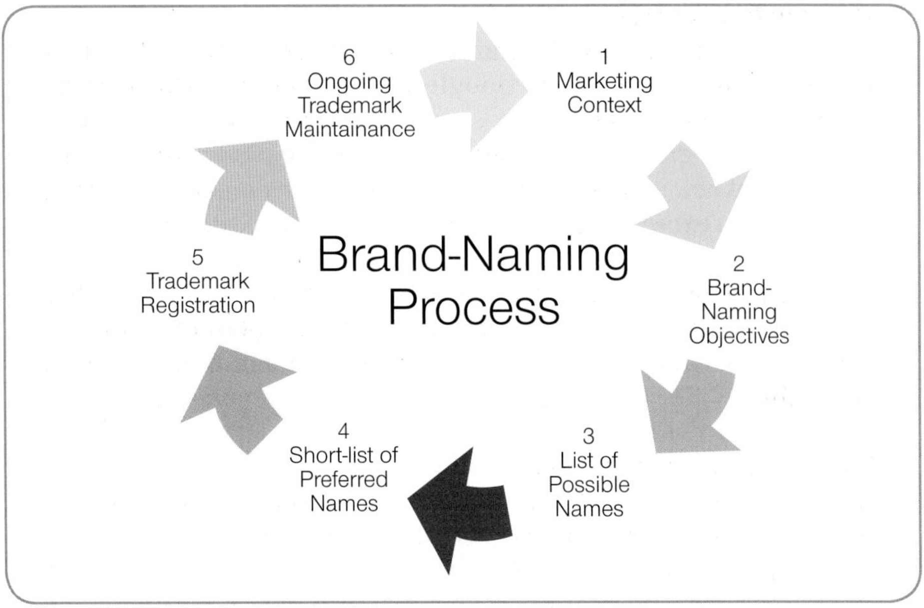

Start off with a well-defined foundation and a clear brand strategy. Brainstorm a list of possible names and create a set of criteria to assess each option. Shortlist the best three or four options and evaluate whether each is credible; that is, whether it is distinctive, motivating, strategic, and enduring. Don't be afraid to ask others for their opinion. Remember that the name should be consumer-friendly. Test whether it touches people's "soft spots."

Make your logo easily recognizable, outstanding, or iconic. Register the name as a trademark in both the country of origin and abroad if you feel that the brand will have a regional or global reach. Having done that, it is important to maintain your trademarks.

- **Registering a trademark**

Trademarks protect words, names, symbols, sounds, or colors that distinguish goods and services. Unlike patents, they can be renewed forever as long as they are being used in business. The shape of a Coca-Cola bottle, the fonts and colors of Google, or Fido Dido as the mascot of Pepsi's 7-UP are familiar trademarks, and are important in marketing specific products or services.

Primary trademarks

The term "trademark" is often used to refer to any type of mark that can be registered with a country's Patent and Trademark Office. There are two primary types of marks that can normally be registered:

Trademarks, which are used by their owners to identify goods–that is, physical commodities–which may be natural, manufactured, or produced, and which are sold or otherwise transported or distributed via interstate commerce.

Service marks, which are used by their owners to identify services–that is, intangible activities–which are performed by one person for the benefit of a person or persons other than himself, either for pay or otherwise.

Using Trademark symbols

If you use the symbols TM or SM, this indicates that you are claiming rights to the marks without having federal registration. However, the use of these symbols may be governed by different local, state, or foreign laws. The federal registration symbol® can only be used after the mark is actually registered in a country's Patent and Trademark Office. This symbol may not be used before the mark is registered, even though an application is pending.

Trademark registration is not easy and may require professional help from legal specialists.

PRIVATE BRANDS AND WHY THEY MATTER

In-house brands or store labels are brands which are specific to a particular retail store. The retailers either manufacture goods under their own label or re-brand private labels into lifestyle brands such as Timberland–rugged, outdoor, and active products that are also worn as casual wear. Store brand merchandise is generally cheaper than national branded goods because the retailer sells directly to the end consumer, eliminating additional handling/profit-sharing. It allows the retailer to optimize production to suit consumer demand and focus advertising costs.

Goods sold under a store brand are subject to the same regulatory oversight as goods sold under a national brand. Store brands are gaining in popularity, and are perceived as major threats to national brand manufacturers in that they have helped shift power to the retailers, enabling them to position their stores as having exclusive merchandise and establish much needed points of differentiation from their competitors.

PRIVATE LABEL RANGE BUILDING

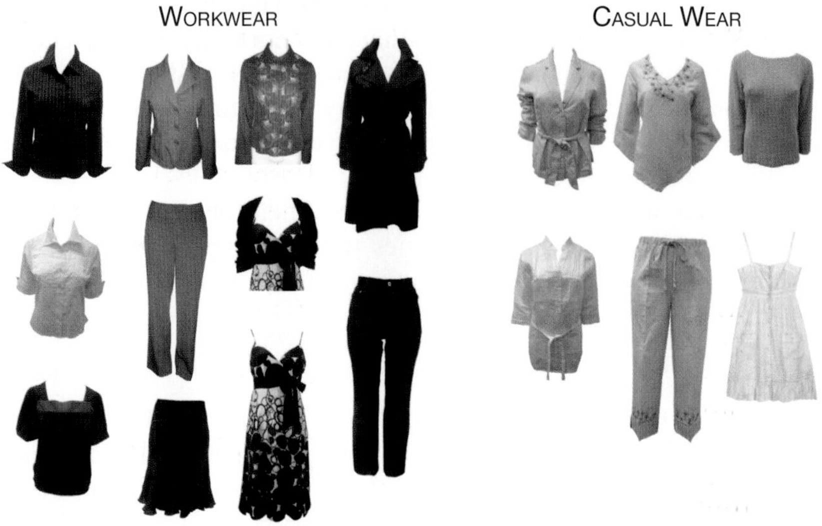

In some retail sectors, store brands can account for as much as 50% of sales. Store branding is a mature industry; consequently, some store brands have been able to position themselves as premium brands.

Range Building ②

World Famous Recognized Brands

1. Abraham & Thakore
2. Adidas
3. Apple
4. Aussion
5. Baccarat
6. Bally
7. BODUM®
8. Bvlgari
9. Calvin Klein
10. Cartier
11. Celine
12. Chanel
13. Christian Dior
14. Canon
15. Dartington Crystal
16. Daum
17. Descamps
18. DKNY
19. Dyson
20. ecoLinen
21. Emporio Armani
22. Ermenegildo Zegna
23. Fendi
24. Fiorelli
25. Gap
26. Georg Jensen
27. Givenchy
28. Gucci
29. Guess
30. Hotpoint
31. Hugo Boss
32. Issey Miyake
33. Jaeger
34. John Rocha
35. Kenwood
36. Kenzo
37. KitchenAid
38. Krups
39. Lalique
40. Laura Ashley
41. Lanvin
42. Levi's
43. Linens on the Hill
44. Louis Vuitton
45. MANGO
46. Marella
47. Marimekko
48. Míele
49. Missoni
50. Montblanc
51. Morphy Richards
52. Nike
53. Orrefors
54. Oshkosh B'Gosh
55. Paul Smith
56. Philips
57. Polo Ralph Lauren
58. Prada
59. Reebok
60. Roberto Cavalli
61. Salvatore Ferragamo
62. Sanderson
63. Samsung
64. Siemens
65. Sheridan
66. Sony
67. Ted Baker
68. Tefal
69. Toshiba
70. Valentino
71. Versace
72. Virgin
73. Yves Saint Laurent
74. Zara
75. Zwilling J.A. Henckels

Sometimes, store-branded goods mimic the shape, packaging, and labeling of national brands and, more often than not, get premium display treatment from retailers.

Retailers realize that it is premium national brands which cause the consumer to select a store. Once the consumer arrives to buy a national brand, the retailer has the opportunity to offer/recommend its own brand.

The retailer typically makes more profit by selling a store brand as he deals directly with the manufacturer and fabric supplier, doing away with any middle-man and designing/developing the items in-house. If the brand's quality and style are what the customers desire and the prices are attractive, there is every chance that the in-house brand is the one that will be purchased.

Developing private labels and store brands enables retailers to differentiate their merchandise with an array of exclusive goods that promise all the virtues of known brands, at competitive prices.

PRODUCT DEVELOPMENT

As seasonal changes in Asia differ greatly from Europe and North America, having seasonally appropriate goods on the shelves is becoming part and parcel of good retail practice. Though consumers will require seasonally correct color palettes, the fabrication and weight of the fabrics also play a pivotal role.

Creating a private brand is hard work because the retail buyer does not generally have the same level of support available to national and international brands. Consumers, however, will expect the same standards of materials, and manufacture as they would from national or international brands. Constructing a range for private brands is usually done through co-operation with vendors who are able to contribute know-how, manufacturing facilities, as well as some design input.

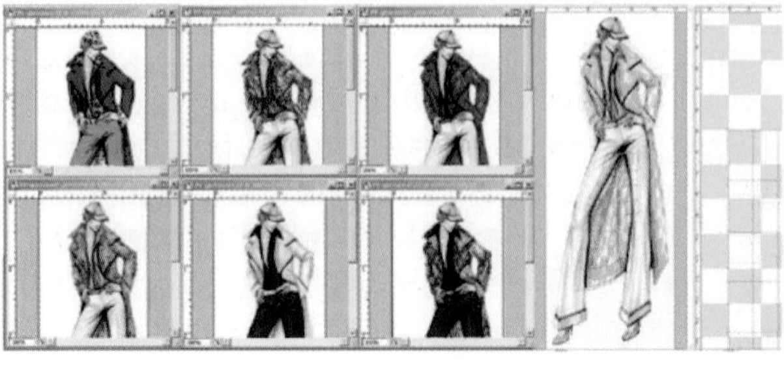

Once a decision is made to go forward with private branding, there are a number of questions to be answered: What is to be the look and function of the brand? Is this a new concept or similar to an existing one? What is the intended target audience and customer profile for the brand? How wide or varied is it to be? In addition, decisions on quality level, on price range, on space allocation and on advertising will also need to be made.

CREATING THE CONCEPT

Let's say that you decide that your brand will be ladies' workwear, a selection from an essentially classic business collection, designed for working women. The emphasis will be placed on the quality of the tailoring, the feminine cut, and attention to detail. Wonderful fabrics have been chosen to co-ordinate, to give the versatility essential for an individual approach to business dress. All the garments can be mixed and matched, and are available in several fabrics and color ways.

The range is considered value for money, as attention to detail and high-quality fabrics are used, and the price is very affordable.

• Conceptualizing

The buyers and merchandisers who are best equipped to develop private brands or private labels are those who have attended design school. Today, technology plays a big part in the speed of creating these designs and styles, and this is reflected in the courses offered by various institutions around the world (see, for example, www.fashionschool.com/computer-fashion-design.htm).

The Istituto di Moda Burgo (IDM) in Milan, Italy, offers courses in, amongst other things, fashion design, pattern-making, and computer-assisted design (see www.imb.it/fashion-stylist.htm). It was created with the intention of transforming its students into real fashion artists. Thus, each student is shown how to reconcile individual imagination with the realities of professional workplace requirements.

To become a fashion stylist requires not only a knowledge of clothes, coloring and manufacturing techniques, but also the ability to give form to a concept in a way that can be fully realized.

The other professional tools that are useful for product development are the fashion technique books found at www.fashiontechniques.com/fashion-book.htm. These provide a step-by-step analysis of the fundamental aspects of fashion drawing and pattern-making.

A buyer hired to do creative work in fashion concepts and design will need to have such a background to develop the skills necessary in producing the high-quality sketches and drawings that are later translated into actual garments. In proposing a concept to management, the buyer or the person in charge of product development has to express the mood, the type of fabrics intended for these collections, the accessories, and so on.

Students at design school are assessed on their written exams; their concepts, drawings and sketches; and the garments they produce. In my experience as a judge of year-end projects for design schools, the main criteria against which a would-be designer's work is measured are creativity, originality, innovation in fabric use, wearability, style, fashion sense and commerciality. The following pictures illustrate the standards produced by some of these students. Also have a look at Temasek Design School at www-des.tp.edu.sg.

Fashion Show: Students' Creations on the Catwalk

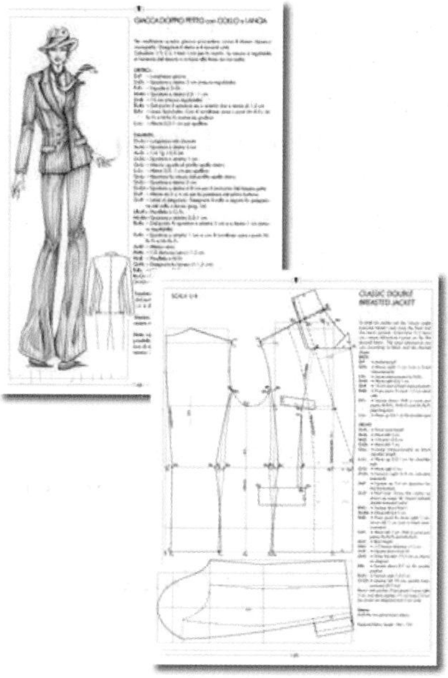

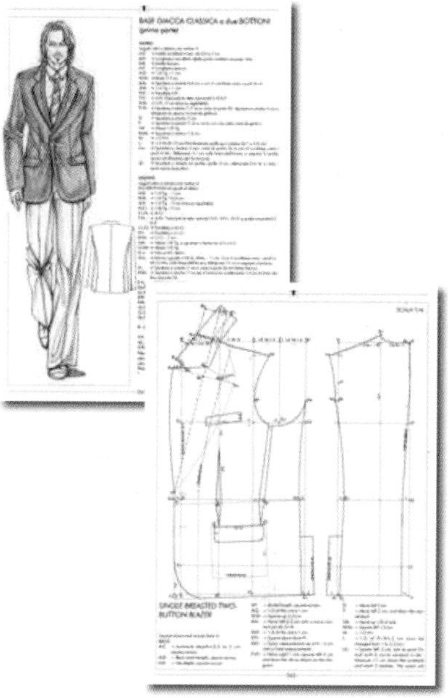

Preview Milan Fashion Week 2007

Emanuele Conza

Ines Anger

Cinzia Monti

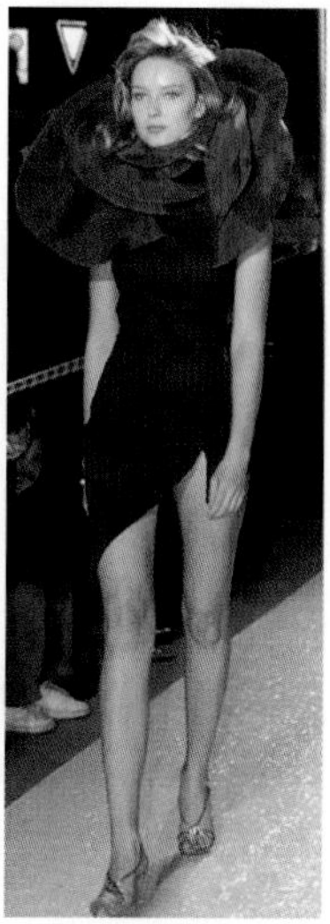

Valentina Di Fronzo

• Determining the concept

When developing private labels, most retailers will start with safe styles that are commercial and basic. This gives experience to the buyers or merchandisers, and allows them to explore the many facets to product development such as choice of vendors, and the selection of fabrics and styles. In most cases, the buyers or merchandisers will develop proven silhouettes (basics) until they are more sure of themselves, and then venture out with more fashionable styles.

• Concept and reality

Whatever the concept, make sure that it suits your customer profile. Only when you have a clear understanding of who they are, what they buy, how much they are willing to spend, their lifestyle, and their brand preferences, are you equipped to put a concept together.

Developing in-house brands requires full commitment from buyers and management. It requires dedication, vision, investment and continuity. If done properly, brand development can reap high financial rewards and give great job satisfaction.

Below is an example of a shirt concept. The buyer would need to have sketches illustrating the body shape, to show the types of collars, fabric swatches in solids and stripes, a size-ratio breakdown of how he will be planning the buys, and some other fashion colors that he intends to add in.

DRESS SHIRTS: EXACT SLEEVE LENGTH

SLEEVE LENGTH	COLLAR 14½	15	15½	16	16½	17	17½	18	18½	19	20
32	•	•	•	•	•						
33	•	•	•	•	•	•		B	B		
34		•	•	•	•	•	•	B	B		
35		•	•	•	•	•	•	B	B	B	B
36			•	•	•	•	•	T	T	T	T
37					T	T	T	T	T	T	
38							T				
SHORT SLEEVE	•	•	•	•	•	•	•				

• = STANDARD B/T = BIG & TALL

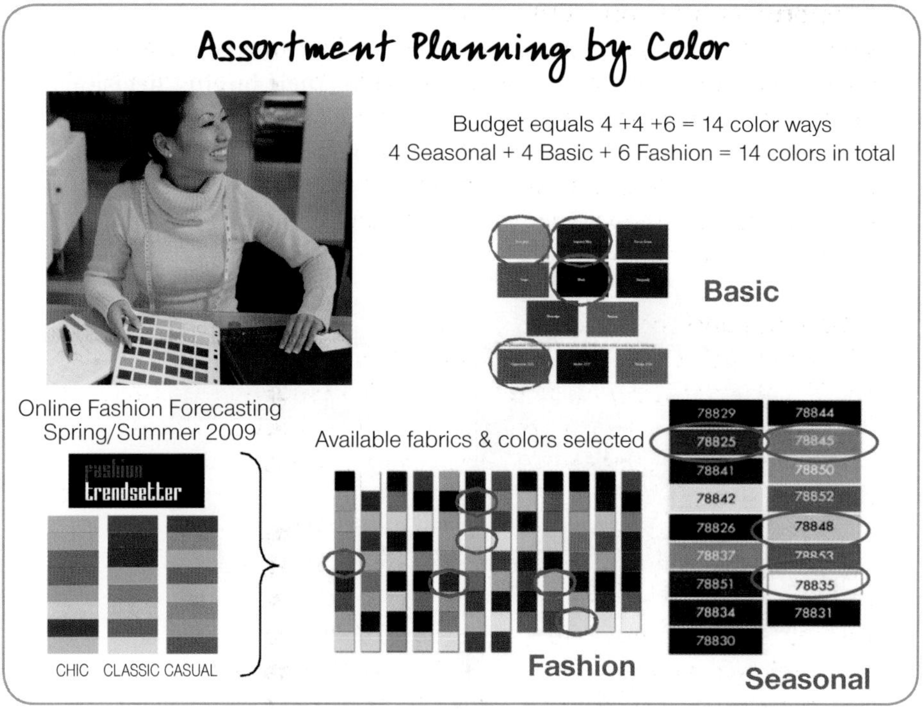

When planning a product development range, besides deciding on the silhouettes or styles, the buyer will need to decide the color ways. If the buyer's typical size ratio for a ladies' range is 1-2-2-2-2-1, this will mean that each time she chooses a color, there will be 10 units.

The other important factor to note is that not all colors will sell equally and, thus, the number of units per color will vary. If the buyer's size range is 10, she might take two or three packs of a commercial color she is familiar with and only one in a new fashion color if she is not sure how the customers will react to it.

The number of colors chosen is also determined by the selling space available. There is no point in buying eight colors if the selling area or the fixtures available can only accommodate six. This is where the question of the number of ways comes in, each way being one style, color and size range. A four-way garment fixture can accommodate four color ways or four different styles in complementary colors of a top, or four color ways/styles of a top with two color ways of a bottom or three tops, one jacket, two bottoms, and so on. The merchandise display on these fixtures is what will attract the customers, so it is important not to clutter them with too many styles and colors. Each item placed on the fixtures should also be complementary. This helps the customers in their buying decisions. The blouses or tops matching nicely with the pants and jackets could help the customer choose both a top and pants.

- **How many?**

Regardless of the type of merchandise involved, it should be evaluated to determine how many of each style to buy. It is advisable not only to work within your budgeted sales and OTB plans, but also to work with a planogram, which is the blueprint or a floor plan of your selling area, with fixture placements shown. Each fixture may represent the location of a brand or a range of products. Each fixture should be planned according to how many units it can take, or how many units would be visually appealing. The assortment planogram shown below is for a regular selling period. During sales, many stores would remove their normal fixtures, and replace them with sales bins or sales tables that can hold a much larger number of items.

The assortment planogram

Shop equipment	Capacity	Number of units on display
Back wall long bar	120 cm	20–30 hanging garments
Back wall straight bar facing	42 cm	10–15 hanging garments
Back wall side facing bar	67 cm	20–25 hanging garments
Back wall shelving	94 cm X 39 cm	4 rows x 15 units = 60 units
Free-standing rail	90–91 cm	30 hanging garments
Free-standing rail	29 cm	10–15 hanging garments
Free-standing rail	45 cm	20–25 hanging garments
Free-standing long rail	114 cm	40 hanging garments
Free-standing long rail	145–147 cm	40–50 hanging garments
Business shirt gondola	8 sections	8 x 20 pcs = 160 units
Promotion tables (two-tier)	120 x 60	2 x 140 pcs= 280 units

Having a clear idea of the available volume on the selling floor enables you to plan your assortments much better. When planning, you need to consider the following questions.

How many colors do I want? How many colors can I have on the selling floor on my existing fixtures? Are all colors equally sellable? If not, which colors are more sellable?

How many units should I buy in each size? Should I buy all sizes or concentrate on best-sold sizes only? How much OTB will this purchase amount to? How much floor space will it need? Each time you place an order, ask yourself: How much? How long? For whom?

UNDERSTANDING THE PRODUCT LIFECYCLE

The illustration below is an example of a sales profile for a fashion product. Assuming that this is based on a six-week period, the initial number of units of the item is 208 pieces. After the first week, the store has sold 28 pieces, and sales peak in the second week, when 92 pieces are sold. In the third week, 44 pieces are sold and the sell-through then declines to 25, 14 and zero pieces respectively in the following three weeks, thus ending the cycle for this item unless the buyer replenishes or initiates a repeat order, in which case a new cycle is created.

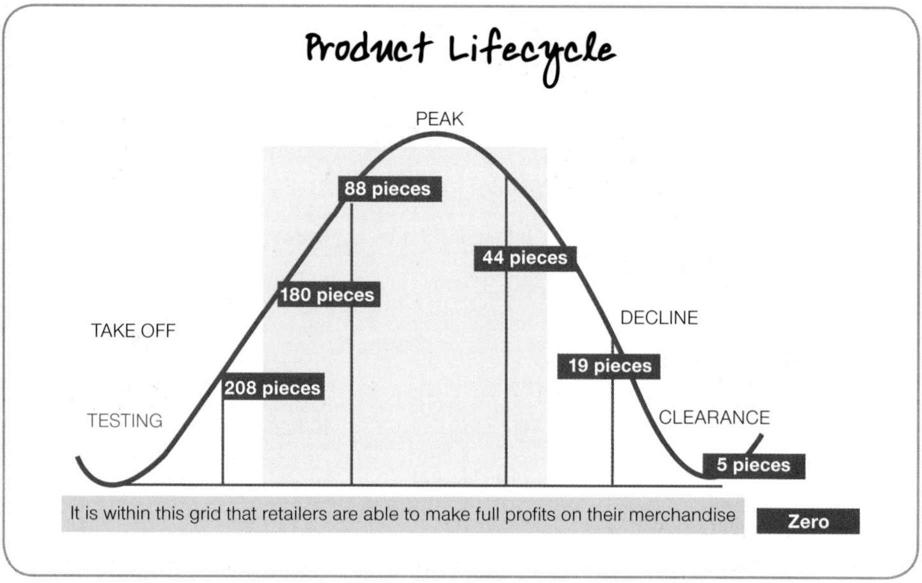

SALES LIFECYCLE

You can estimate sales rates based on historical data, or analyze the sales efficiency of these particular items after the event. The period can be expressed in weeks or in months, but in all cases, a pattern will emerge.

• Example

Let's say that you want to track the profit cycle on the 208 pieces bought at $100 at a total initial sales value of $20,800, and the first part of the cycle shows sales at full retail up to the decline stage. In this case, a total of 189 pieces were sold, giving a sales figure of $18,900. At the decline stage, a price change is applied, the remaining 19 pieces being reduced by 30%, to $70, for a total value of $1,330.

At clearance, there are still five of these pieces left, at a value of $350. There is a final reduction of 50% to clear the balance. All five pieces, at $35 each, sold, for a total of $175. The total sales value is therefore $20,055 (18,900 + 980 + 175).

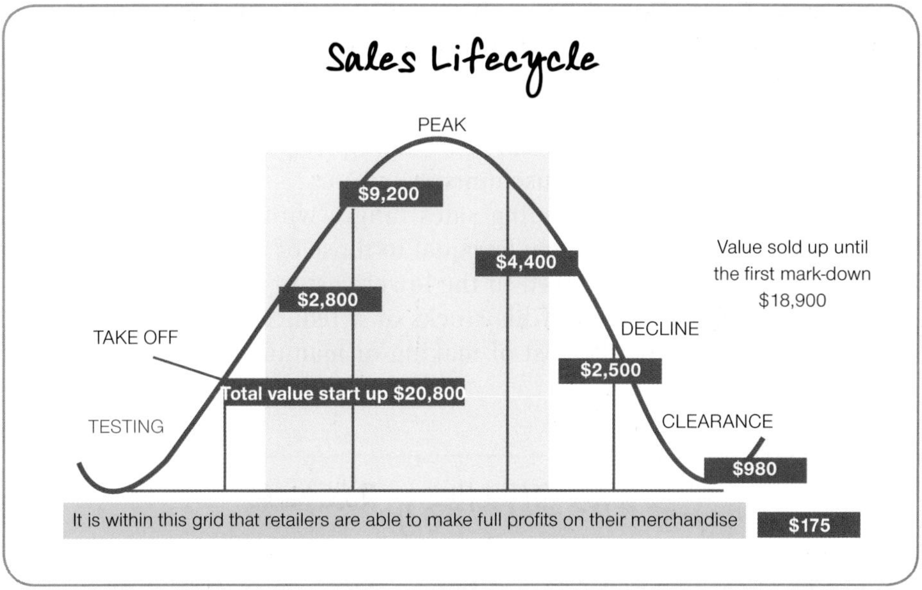

PROFIT CYCLE PROFILE

Having established the selling cycle, it becomes possible to calculate a corresponding margin cycle. Following the above example, let's say that the margin on the items bought was originally 35%. On a total retail value of $20,800, the margin is $7,280, each item potentially generating $35 in gross profit margin. The cost is thus $65 per unit, and the total cost of goods is $13,520.

At the peak and decline stage, a total of 189 pieces were sold at full price, with a profit of $6,615.

The cost of the remaining 19 pieces is $1,235, with a profit value of $665. Applying a 30% reduction shaves the profit to $465.50, each item now having a profit potential of $24.50. A total of 14 pieces are sold, for a profit of $343. The remaining five pieces ($122.50) are further reduced by 50%, and all are sold, with a balance profit value of $61.25. The total profit is thus $7,019.25

($6,615 + $343 + $61.25), which equates to 33.75% ($7,019.25 ÷ $20,800); that is, 1.25% less than the initial full 35% margin.

Not everything that you buy will have equal success, and it is critical therefore that you keep abreast of what is selling and what is not. Appropriate action should be taken to clear slow-moving items as soon as they are identified. Keeping them on your shelves will only block precious OTB that is needed to replenish goods that are selling.

It can take years for a retailer to develop brand equity and just a few to lose it. This can happen, for example, when a store changes its strategy from selling high-quality branded merchandise with controlled season-end sales, to staging frequent sales and price promotions or store-wide discounts.

If the buyer is developing sales ranges with in-house brands, then margins will most likely be equal to those of their regular buys. Lower retail prices are linked to the lower cost of the fabrics, where the fabric supplier sells off his stocks at a reduced price per meter or for an entire roll. The cost of making or manufacturing the items will rarely vary.

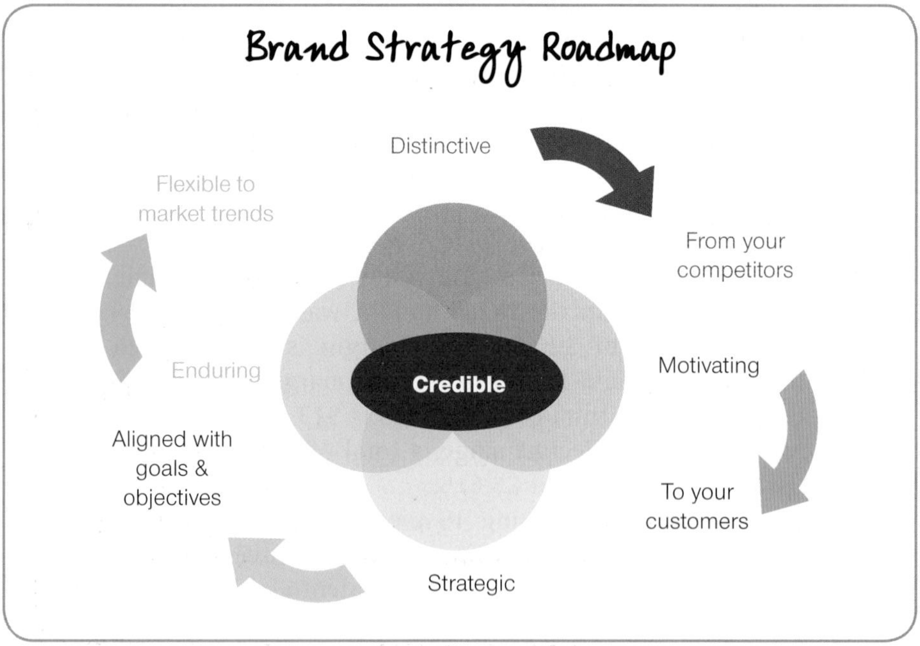

Outright or consignment sales merchandise from local and national brands is placed on items or ranges that these vendors have themselves developed for such events, or on products they wish to discontinue. Margins on these ranges can be lower by between 10% and 30%, but because the sales volume during big sales events can be as much as 10 times greater than in regular selling periods, it is easy to see why some retailers can be tempted to stage more of them.

case study

Hefty discounting and how it can damage your brand

Price reductions are part and parcel of running a retail business. Discounting through sales and promotions can come in many forms and under various names: The Great Sale; Mega Sale; Midnight Extravaganza Sale...

As these events can represent big money, the temptation to have more of them can be very enticing. However, if the retailer is positioned as a better store, having an overload of price events can tarnish the store brand in the long term, and customers will learn to shop only during promotional periods. If a retailer tries to position itself as a better store and yet continues to have promotional activities on a regular basis, then the store will inevitably get a reputation for always having sales.

Another problem associated with having too many promotions is that the retailer creates spikes in sales volumes that have to be repeated the following year. If, say, the anticipated sales are below those of the previous year, the retailer is more often than not tempted to prolong the promotion period to close the gap. So, the spikes in volume during these events are hard to stop, and the sales cycle can look something like this:

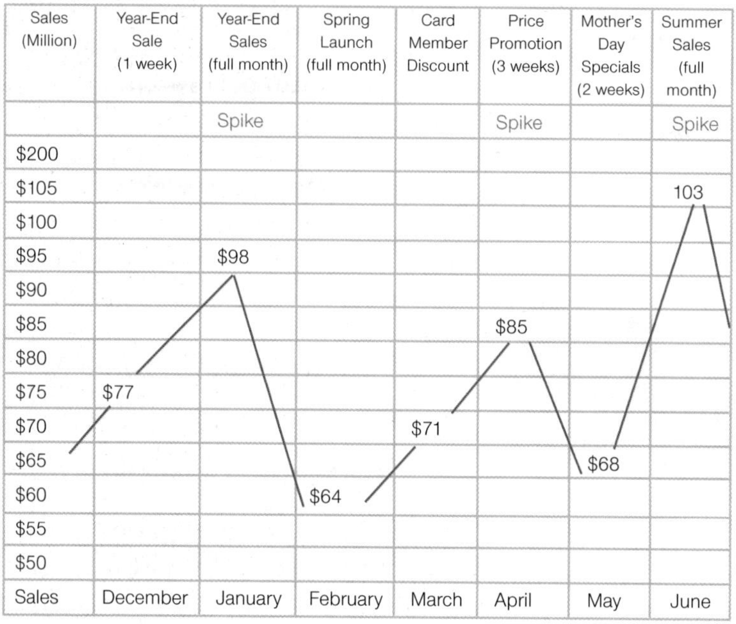

In buying merchandise for such a retail operation, the product lifecycles will also eventually come to look like an erratic heartbeat seen on an ECG monitor, not to mention the stress this puts on the operations people. With so many activities going on, trying to sell regular merchandise at regular prices becomes very difficult. Better brands will eventually resent being associated with such a store as these activities harm their brand positioning. Sales on most regular goods will take a hit as the consumers simply wait for a desired item to go on sale.

The lesson to be learnt from this is that if you have sales and promotions as part of your retail activities, don't have them so often that your store's reputation is jeopardized.

14 MANAGING SUPPLIERS

The performance of its suppliers is critical to any organization. A supplier that performs well can help an organization be more efficient, produce higher-quality products/services, reduce costs and increase profits. One that performs poorly, on the other hand, can disrupt operations, make the organization fail in the eyes of its customers, increase costs and threaten profits.

Managing supplier performance should therefore be a strategic focus of every organization. This chapter looks at how to measure and manage your suppliers' performance.

SELECTION CRITERIA

A buyer's success depends greatly on the selection of resources, which contribute to the company's profitability through steady sales, uninterrupted by late deliveries, poor quality or the supply of merchandise that does not match the buyer's requirements.

The choice of vendors is crucial to success. In the best of worlds, the 80-20 rule (where 80% of the buyer's OTB is allocated to 20% of her suppliers) should be applied, as it has proven to be effective time and again across many types of retail format. With this kind of solid base, the buyer may keep some reserves to conduct trials with new suppliers.

The advantage of working closely with a few proven vendors is that your business becomes important to them, and as a buyer, you can expect a great deal of attention to your orders. You can leverage your position in seeking additional advantages, such as negotiating some level of exclusivity on the ranges or products you are buying, better margins or terms of payment.

The closer your working relationship with key vendors is, the better their understanding of your requirements will be. At the same time, however, you still need to nurture new potential suppliers to replace those who show signs of complacency, or fail to meet your requirements. Nothing should be set in stone. If a key vendor is dropping in performance as a result of problems that are out of your control, it might be time to move some of your business elsewhere.

• Vendor attributes

Quite apart from their merchandise, vendors can contribute to your overall profitability through such things as their distribution policies, shipping and inventory maintenance, promotional merchandise policies, advertising allowances and competitive pricing. In addition, buyers should be looking for flexibility, cooperation and adherence to purchase orders in their vendors. Your business dealings with them should be meaningful at all times so that they can see they are investing in a long-term relationship with you and your company.

• Speed

An important aspect of today's retail buying is speed. Buyers are looking for suppliers who have the ability to react quickly to their needs and deliver the goods within a very short lead time. Herein lies a great deal of additional profits for the retailers, as they are able to improve customer service by meeting customer demand.

Bigger retailers are relying more and more on automated data-linked technology. Electronic Data Interchange (EDI) technology helps retailers communicate purchasing data, sending electronic data in standardized formats between one organization's computers and another's. It eliminates the need for manual paperwork, such as manual purchasing orders, invoicing, shipping details and more, saving precious time for the buyers and merchandisers.

Another area where speed can be enhanced is with delivery of pre-ticketed goods. This service saves time, space and labor in that the goods can move directly to the selling floor, giving the buyer some extra selling time, especially on repeat orders.

- **Purchase-order conformity**

Buyers take time to carefully place purchase orders that have been planned in accordance with their budgets and OTB planners. These orders will reflect buys by class or sub-class which, in turn, translate into actual styles, colors, sizes, inclusive of delivery dates, discount terms, packaging specifications, and other arrangements such as pre-ticketing. These factors are very important in ensuring the right balance of the overall six-month plan and ideal stock model that has been developed for that season.

Conformity to the order specifications is necessary for the buyers to ensure that the right merchandise mix is on the selling floor at the time it is most needed, and it is vital that the chosen suppliers fulfill their part in this diligently. Though simple in theory, this is not always the case. Often, vendors will substitute fabrics, colors, sizes and styles in order to fulfill an order, but without complying with the buyer's specifications. This not only causes delays, with the goods being rejected, but puts a real dent in the buyer–vendor relationship.

The essential elements in managing your suppliers are summarized in the following chart:

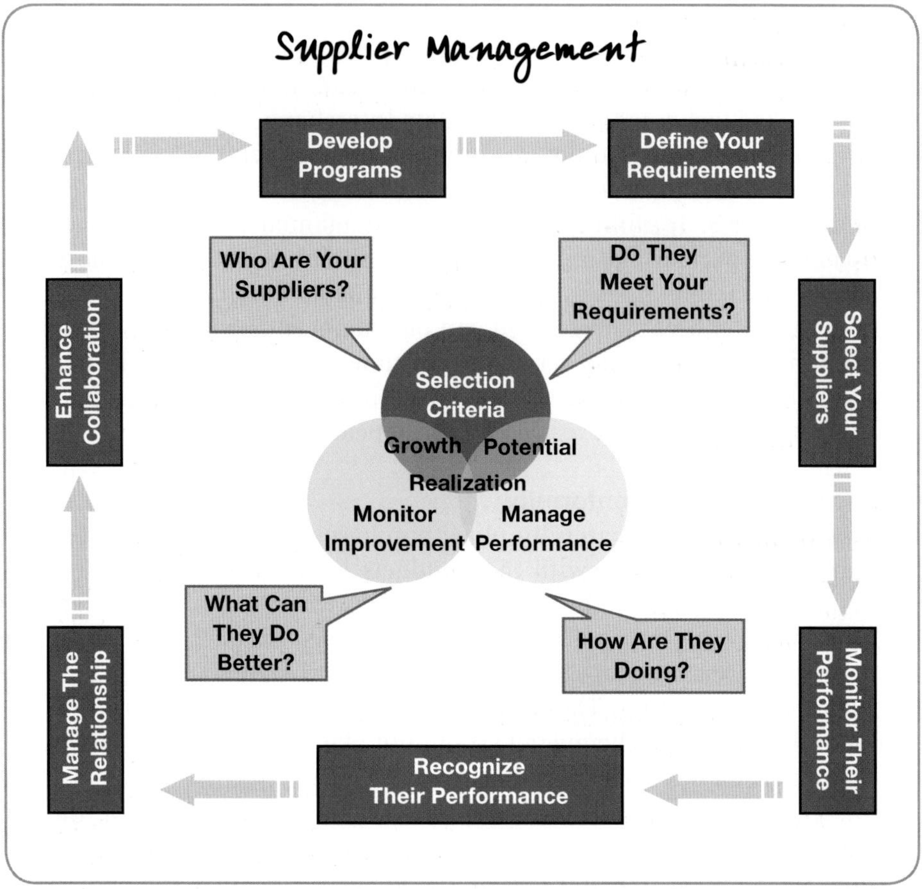

Who are your suppliers?

Your suppliers/vendors on whom you rely for your merchandise are the backbone of your business. The supplier mix varies according to the type of retail operation.

Do they meet your requirements?

Again, requirements will vary greatly from one retailer to another, and from one country to another. However, there are shared criteria that should be met; first and foremost, is that the quality of the goods should match the price being paid for them. If you expect a high quality, expect to pay a premium. Other requirements could include timely delivery, margins, exclusivity, size specs, or promotional support.

How are they doing?

It is advisable to review your suppliers' performance monthly and meet up with them for a performance review at least once a year. This is a good time to discuss growth potential and any other matters arising from your partnership.

What can they do better?

Questions to be asked periodically include whether the suppliers could do better if they expanded their collection or numbers of SKUs with your store. In such cases, this may involve providing more space for them. Could they improve their quality and would you be prepared to pay more for this? Could the margins be improved, or could they improve the level of promotional contributions?

How do you manage performance?

Performance can be managed by set sales targets and/or profit targets. These can be measured as a monthly sales and profit performance in dollars or in percentages, or can be measured against the space they occupy.

How do you stimulate them to do better?

There are unlimited ways to stimulate growth, and by taking time to analyze the strengths and weaknesses of your suppliers, possibilities will always arise. Building towards a strong relationship is key as it facilitates collaboration and willingness to explore new business venues (I call this process "co-creation"). For example, I had a very good men's ready-to-wear supplier that I liked working with very much. He was my top performer, and I knew that he could do more if we explored possibilities together. In the course of our discussions, he agreed to develop a men's underwear concept for me. When he presented his concept the following month, it had everything—quality and color highlights; single briefs; three- and five-piece packs; boxer shorts and undershirts. So good was it that it quickly established itself on the best-sellers list, competing with highly recognized underwear brands.

Rating suppliers

Your key suppliers are those with whom you place a large amount of your OTB budget, and who can thus have the greatest impact on your company if things go wrong (where the merchandise is late or of unacceptable quality, for example). For stores which allocate according to the 80-20 rule, it is all the more important that they choose their suppliers carefully and measure the respective performances of each against certain criteria.

Suppliers can be rated against the quality and novelty of the goods they provide and the resulting sales performance of those goods in the stores. Other major factors to take into consideration in measuring their performance would be such things as cost (including advertising allowances and discounts), payment terms and reliability of delivery.

Supplier scorecards

Some stores use scorecards, such as that illustrated below, to weigh the performance of suppliers. Here, low marks indicate poor performance; high marks good performance. The weight given to each of the factors will vary from retailer to retailer, depending on the degree of importance each attaches to specific factors. If delivery, say, is very important, the buyer may allocate 20% of the total to this.

SUPPLIER:	**Value**	**Score**
Provides competitive prices and meets margin requirements	35%	
Consistently delivers on time	25%	
Consistently provides quality products	20%	
Reacts promptly to stock replenishment demands	10%-15%*	
Contributes to advertising	5%	
Provides efficient and knowledgeable promoter (if applicable)	5%*	
Total Score	100%	

USING PERFORMANCE INFORMATION

There are two sides to using the performance information: rewarding those who perform well, and taking corrective action against those whose performance does not meet expectations.

Rewards can come in various forms: through nomination for your company's Best Supplier Award; suppliers may be invited to a special dinner function, where they are thanked; or you may create a special "elite" that is reserved for the best and highest contributors (see case study below). The advantage of such clubs is that they can reward these suppliers with the best selling space. The suppliers can be featured in window displays or in advertisements. Most importantly, they can be given easier access to additional floor space if they want to launch a new product or brand. When you have a good working relationship with your suppliers, it is not difficult to make them feel valued. Simply introducing them to your management as one of your most supportive suppliers can work wonders.

Correcting poor performers (if you intend to retain their services) takes some tact. As soon as problems become apparent, it is important to meet the supplier in a spirit of collaboration, rather than confrontation, to discuss the root of the problem and the resulting losses. Do not end the meeting without agreeing on an action plan to effect and review improvements within an agreed timeframe.

case study

Working closely with key vendors

During the Asian financial crisis in 1997, I created a concept called the 30% Club. Having experienced a four-year recession while working in Denmark, I knew what should be done to at least maintain our performance.

The basis of this was that each department or division would nominate its best vendors who had a "potential" annual sales growth of at least 30% if we backed them up. They had to be of reasonable size, have control over their own production and have ranges that had potential for expansion. Our backing gave the chosen vendors an edge, and with our support, they felt more confident in investing.

Investing in fashion merchandise was every vendor's fear, but I knew from past experience that if all stores were to carry only basic merchandise, the customers who did want to spend would not have the incentive to do so.

The cooperation gave us the ability to develop existing brands, new product strategies, new product lines that had synergy with the core brand, and marketing strategies to launch these new merchandising concepts. The cost of promotions and launches was either borne by the suppliers or shared between us.

In return, we offered them additional floor space and preferred locations. The cooperation also meant that all merchandise concepts that we created together remained exclusive to our stores, and at better margins.

Our first year results from the 14 members of the 30% Club showed increases in sales ranging from 52% to 137%. The following year, five more vendors were added to the Club, and both sales and profits showed high double-digit growth for all members.

The Club was later re-named "The Million Dollar Club" as all members had reached at least this amount in yearly sales, with the highest growing to six million in just three years.

This is a good example of how building and maintaining close working relationships with your key vendors can have a positive long-term impact on your business.

Negotiations
Sales ability determines your gross revenue, but negotiating ability determines your profits
CONTRACT
The Art of Retail Buying
15
NEGOTIATION

Negotiation's ground rule

Don't let your calculator dictate the retail price. Look at the merchandise and establish its perceived value first. Then negotiate!

Example: If the cost + GP margin = X, and X is greater than the perceived value the item is deemed to have, then do one of two things: either, negotiate down the cost (not your margin) to hit the ideal retail price; or, if the cost cannot be lowered, don't do the deal. Find someone else who can.

Remember: if the merchandise is right but the price is not, be prepared to walk away from the deal ... chances are, your customers will.

WHAT IS GOOD NEGOTIATION?

Most people have the impression that a negotiation is a competition —a contest where one side wins and the other loses. But any negotiation that favors only one party ultimately favors neither. Good retailers know how to build in value so that everyone wins.

The negotiation skills of buyers have a major bearing on the relationships they have with their suppliers, and the profitable successes they bring to the company. Negotiation is particularly necessary when parties depend on one another; when the buyer needs what the supplier is offering, and the supplier needs the buyer to buy the merchandise.

The importance of achieving the best possible negotiation cannot be overstated, especially in the increasingly intensive and competitive retail environment where costs are rising and margins are squeezed. A successful negotiation produces an agreement that will work for everyone concerned. If one party feels that the agreement is unequal, it will often spend a great deal of energy in trying to get out of the terms imposed. In negotiating, perceptions are important. Both parties should leave a negotiation feeling that they have gained something they want or need. In any negotiation, it is vital that you are a careful, clear and concise communicator. The more easily you are understood, the smoother the dialogue will be.

EIGHT GOLDEN RULES OF NEGOTIATION

• Rule 1: Agreements are built on agreeing

It is advisable to start any talks with suppliers by agreeing on certain fundamental points before going on to the heart of the negotiation. For example, you could agree that this supplier has a very good brand that is gaining popularity in the market. You could also agree that his brand would do well in your store because the store has the right retail profile for the brand. You might also agree that the brand's rising popularity warrants a highly visible space on your "precious" selling floor.

Now, for the negotiation part: you are keen on the brand, but not at any cost. You know the margin you want, the sales target you expect from this brand, and who will be paying for the shop-in-shop fixtures that will be required. Be prepared for the fact that the supplier will have the same items in mind, and the negotiation will revolve around who agrees to whose terms for this to happen.

- **Rule 2: Know when to walk**

Suppliers sometimes feel obliged to see how far they can push the buyer. If they can get away with it, they will continue to act this way. Sometimes, the buyer will have to walk away from a bad deal in order to make a good deal. Set the tone. Disallow such behavior, and signal a change in how you want to negotiate. The supplier will follow suit, if he has any hope of making a deal.

Depending on who needs what more, it is wise to know when to talk and when to listen. When negotiating from a position of need, explain your interest in the merchandise, your reason for wanting it and how far you are willing to go (cost price, quantities, exclusivity, and so on). Try not to talk too much; give the other party a chance to express what he is willing to do for you.

- **Rule 3: Lead by questioning**

You control a negotiation by asking questions, not by talking. The person who asks the most questions controls the content and direction of the negotiation.

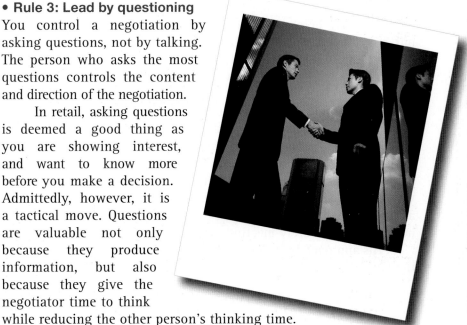

In retail, asking questions is deemed a good thing as you are showing interest, and want to know more before you make a decision. Admittedly, however, it is a tactical move. Questions are valuable not only because they produce information, but also because they give the negotiator time to think while reducing the other person's thinking time.

Sometimes, asking questions to which you know the answer allows you to assess the honesty of the person with whom you are negotiating. If the answers are not honest, you should be cautious. Asking questions may also give the impression that you are not too well informed, and people will often share much more information with someone they feel knows less than they do. It's amazing how much people will tell you about their businesses if they feel they are smarter than you are.

- **Rule 4: Avoid creating conflict**

The person who speaks first sets the tone for the negotiation, and it is much easier to set a positive tone at the start, rather than having to overcome a bad start. The one part of a negotiation that you want to be very at ease with is your opening remarks. How you position the negotiation affects the outcome more than any single factor. Conflict may arise if one or both parties start negotiations by pointing out a weakness, a fault, a past discord or, worse still, an unrelated, unresolved matter. In such circumstances, the chances of achieving an amicable outcome are shaky at best.

This happened to me once with a supplier. The meeting was about an increase in margin, and the vendor started off venting about our slow purchasing order processes, the long wait his driver had to endure before his goods could be delivered and checked at our receiving bay, and the lack of support he'd been given with regard to more selling space. The outcome was simple. I rescheduled the meeting as I wanted to give myself a chance to investigate his problems.

By the time of the next meeting, I had been able to satisfy myself that none of his complaints was justified: the purchasing orders issued in the previous three months were well within our norm (three days); the difficulties he'd experienced in getting goods processed was a special case during the first three days of our sales where all vendors had long queues; and, last but not least, the additional selling space he'd requested was entirely unwarranted because he was barely meeting targets.

His approach in his margin negotiation was to create discord in the hope that we would go easy on him on the margin. Bad idea.

- **Rule 5: Do not negotiate with yourself**

From time to time, a buyer may be given directions from her management to negotiate a deal with a supplier which she knows

may cause the supplier some difficulty. It may be, for example, that the buyer is asked to negotiate a margin increase with a particular supplier who the buyer knows is working on very tight margins himself. While she may have some sympathy with the supplier's position, her mission is to deliver management's instructions, and she has to remember that the supplier is responsible for negotiating his own requirements and concessions. The best outcome for the margin increase is to help the supplier find ways he can make up the difference and, in some cases, this could mean an increase in the selling price.

- **Rule 6: Avoid making counterproposals**

Avoid putting your proposal on the table too soon. Let the other party show some of his proposals and his position. If you want someone to see things your way, you must first see things their way. Ask questions about the proposal: "How would this work? What does this mean, and so on.

When the proposal's shortcomings have been clearly identified, make suggestions to resolve the problems. Skilled negotiators advance their proposals, not in opposition to the other side's proposal, as solutions to problems mutually identified in discussion.

- **Rule 7: Focus on your strengths**

Play to your strengths but do not overplay them. Be clear and succinct in outlining your position. Talking too much can often dilute the strength of that position and undo your case.

- **Rule 8: Negotiate an agreement that is workable**

Good negotiators know it is not in their best interest to slip anything past the other party. In fact, if you feel the other party has agreed to something that is not in their best interests, you should call it to their attention. This builds trust, and puts an obligation on the other party to make the next concession and help you out.

Let me give you an example. A buyer on a buying trip was negotiating the best cost price on a consignment of ladies' shoes for immediate delivery. The supplier was unwilling to reduce the price to the level required by the buyer but, as a concession, offered to pay for the shipping of the goods if his desired cost price was met. The buyer knew, however, that the shipping costs would far exceed those of lowering the cost price, and could easily have agreed to this deal, which would have greatly disadvantaged the supplier. Rather, she took the time to explain to him the financial implications of his proposal, and her straightforwardness was rewarded with a good deal on this consignment, and established a good long-term relationship with the supplier.

NEGOTIATION IN RETAIL

Negotiating favorable terms with suppliers is one of the most crucial of a buyer's many roles. Areas for negotiation include price; quantity and quality of merchandise; discounts and promotional allowances; delivery terms and costs; and the co-sharing of mark-downs on slow-moving goods.

Excellent preparation and a logical approach can help you get the deal you want. To be able to strike the best deals requires that you have researched quite thoroughly the product and the conditions of the market offering it. Clarify your own objectives and make sure you understand what your supplier wants from the deal. By undertaking basic research into potential suppliers, you can work out how valuable your business is to them.

• Plan your strategy

You need to plan your strategy in writing before beginning negotiations. This will help you set clear goals and work out where you will draw the line and walk away from the deal. Decide the overall approach that you will adopt.

Be clear about the type of deal you want and the priority you will give it. Write down your negotiating strengths and how you might use them to get the concessions you require.

Formulate a list of your priorities—price, minimum quantities, colors, delivery terms and discounts, perhaps. To these, add things which you would like to have, but which aren't essential—advertising support or gifts with purchase, perhaps. Decide what you are (and

aren't) prepared to compromise on. Establish your preferred outcome but remain realistic, because if you're not prepared to compromise, some negotiations won't last long.

- **Select the best team**

Once you've decided on your strategy, it is essential that you get your negotiating team right. Make sure it has skills in all the required areas and, where necessary, use a specialist to negotiate in areas outside your expertise (such as in the preparation of contracts).

Ideally, you should select a time and a place for negotiation where you are not under pressure to close the deal. Once you are quite clear on what you want and feel that this is reasonable, make a list of the suppliers—current and new—that you feel would be most able to provide what you want, set up a meeting, and outline the basis for discussions so that the suppliers can come prepared.

- **Outline your requirements**

Open negotiations by outlining your requirements or terms and conditions (knowing that these are merely the starting point of the negotiations, and that some flexibility on such things as margins, sales targets or payment terms has been built in), and try to get your opposite number to reveal their starting point for discussions. You will have considered in advance what offer the other party is likely to make and how you'll respond.

Ask questions and listen closely to answers. Asking questions will help you understand what your opposite number wants to achieve. You may be able to get it to reveal how flexible it is on certain issues.

Don't reveal your exact negotiating position and avoid making unnecessary concessions. If you have to make concessions, look for reciprocation. Concessions should only be made to help you get the things you value. You should also avoid appearing too keen to do a deal.

Once all terms and conditions have been agreed to, the next step is to get a written contract drawn up and signed by both parties. While verbal contracts are legally binding, they are difficult to prove in court. For most retailers, consignment and concessionaire agreements are always based on a one-year contract. Contractual periods when the deal is based on a straightforward leasing agreement, and in such cases the contract would be more than a year.

Both buyer and supplier would view a good deal as one that meets all their requirements, but you should also consider other factors such as whether you want to do business with a particular supplier on a long-term basis. A long-term deal also requires a long-term commitment of space, OTB, and more. Although getting the best possible deal in the short term is important, a good relationship in the future may help you get even cheaper prices or other perks, such as priority delivery or advertising contributions. However, while a long-term commitment is comfortable for both parties, it can dull the senses to a degree, in that buyers may not feel the necessity to shop around for other prospects.

PITFALLS TO AVOID

You need to be attentive to the fact that not all negotiators are clean and upfront. If, for example, the other party keeps referring to urgent deadlines or a person they need to confer with, they might be playing games designed to manipulate you into an unfavorable position. Don't be forced into making rushed decisions or unnecessary concessions, such as false deadlines. Each time a point is agreed, clarify that you've understood it correctly and write it down. Some of the pitfalls to look out for are outlined as follows.

- **Negotiation decoy**

A negotiation decoy occurs when the other party lists as "musts" a whole range of items he insists will need to be tabled, when in reality, there are far fewer items that he is really after. The question is: How can you know whether the other party is being totally honest when disclosing their terms and conditions? Might they be loading the dice in their favor through adding extra, false, interests into their agenda? The danger that comes from a decoy tactic is the potential for an unbalanced exchange that works against you in the long run. You may, for example, be persuaded to trade off some of your real interests against some of his fictitious interests.

However, if you have done the necessary preparation, you will be able to anticipate where the seller's interests lie, and it will quickly become obvious when he is trying to conceal his real intentions, or is trying to manipulate you. Do not allow yourself to be drawn into fulfilling his interests at the expense of your own.

When presented with a list of decoy interests, work together to rank them and get the other party to explain why they are important. If you feel suspicious, trust your hunches and probe further, research more widely or withdraw to regroup. There are always signs to look out for that the other party is being economical with the truth.

Your best method of safeguarding yourself stems from a combination of preparing thoroughly to predict and then understand what they should and will be asking for. Check their expressed interests against your expectations.

- **Extreme offers**

There will be times when the supplier will ask for a lot more than you expected, to perhaps catch you off guard, and thereby gain concessions without having to make any in return. In such circumstances, the risk is that you will be offended and furious, and possibly refuse to have any further dealings with that supplier.

You have to remember, though, that such tactics may be standard practice within particular cultures. A European trading in China, for example, will become accustomed to extreme proposals, and in such circumstances, it is best that you blend in and seek advice on how to play by the local rules.

An Asian buying in Western countries, on the other hand, may have to separate the person from their behavior or tactics. So, if you are surprised, show your surprise and allow yourself to laugh. This can diffuse the situation and facilitate a deal. If a deal is off course,

I don't generally recommend an extreme counterproposal. Let the other side know that their expectations need to be adjusted, and use other deals from other suppliers as precedents to persuade them by how much.

- **The negotiation nibble**

Just when you think you have come to a full agreement and are about to sign the deal, the supplier says: "Packaging and transportation is extra, right?" There may be a strong urge to make this final concession for the sake of signing the deal, but this urge must be resisted. For example, you could say: "Our company has trading principles. We pay for transportation only. Packaging should be included in the price. So, no; if you are willing to pay your own packaging, then we have a deal."

If this omission is simply a mistake on the supplier's part, then perhaps there is an opportunity to meet this need in another creative way that meets both parties' needs.

A great way to prevent nibbling and other unpleasant surprises is through being explicit and thorough in specifying exactly what is included and excluded in the deal.

- **Cherry picking**

Buyers can model their perfect deal through shopping around and getting a range of bids before approaching a particular supplier. They may come up with a proposal that fully satisfies their interests on price and discount structures, quality, service, time scales, and so on, but may have "cherry picked" the most desirable offerings from several sources. They may tell the supplier that "this is what the competition is offering us, so you'll need to at least match it!"

However, I do not encourage such tactics from buyers because this puts their company's reputation at risk. The supplier may talk with other suppliers to check the credibility of the claims. Instead, you may want to say that their goods and prices are very similar to what is being offered by other suppliers, but if they are willing to "add" better terms, you would be willing to work with them.

- **The negotiation flinch**

Physical reactions such as a sharp intake of breath or visible expressions of surprise and shock are common examples of flinching.

What makes the flinch so dangerous is that the flincher cannot retract it, and may have exposed a reaction that was not meant to be registered. Unfortunately, it happens in an instant, and most are not aware of it at a conscious level. Seeing a shocked expression is far more convincing than simply hearing someone saying "I'm shocked."

Flinches can be used, though, as a tactic to influence the negotiation in favor of the supplier. A buyer, therefore, needs to be able to distinguish between genuine surprised flinches and the use of "negotiation flinches." Since a flinch is essentially an expression of disappointment on their side, take the time to ask what seems to be the problem.

- **Take it or leave it**

This tactic is confrontational, and sometimes even hostile: "The minimum per style is 1,000. Take it or leave it!" When confronted by this, it pays to try to get to the reason behind the demand, and then work together to create options that may allow the supplier's interests to be met in another way. Until you know the real reasons, you're not in a position to create alternatives. You may say something along the following lines: "I understand that you sell high minimums per style, but perhaps you could help me to understand why you cannot accommodate 500 units per style?"

It may be that this is how their production is set up, and breaking the lots is both time-consuming and labor-intensive. Having established this, you may then ask how much more per unit they would charge to accept an order of 500 per style.

A good negotiation is creating the circumstances in which both the buyer and the supplier are content with the outcome. If your deal is too one-sided, you run the risk of jeopardizing your future relationship with the supplier. It is important, therefore, that you are fair and reasonable in your approach.

On the other hand, if the supplier has become too confident of your business, and is becoming unreasonable to the point of deadlock, be quite prepared to walk away from the deal. There are many vendors dying to take their place!

case study

Choosing a vendor is like choosing a partner

Good vendors should become good partners. For this to happen, the relationship needs to mature based on mutual understanding and mutual goals. The closer you work with a vendor and communicate what you require, the greater the chances are of getting the right merchandise for your store. The more successful you are in selling those products, the more the vendor's business will grow; all win.

The following provides a good example of such a relationship and involves a menswear supplier known in the market, not so much for the value of his brand as for the quality of his products.

He has great promoters who are enthusiastic about the product and is innovative with the quality of fabrics. He was the first to launch wrinkle-free pure-cotton shirts and the first to launch spot-resistant and bacteria-resistant fabrics. As he worked closely with my buyers, listened to their needs and was never out of stock with sizes or colors, he was considered very dependable.

He took this a step further by planning promotions and product launches with us, supporting sponsored ads, all commercial and all successful. He made an effort to spend time on our selling floor, talking to our customers, motivating his promoters, and getting involved with the business. He knew which styles sold well—even better than my own buyers—and would often call to remind them that they were running low on particular articles.

When it came to events, he planned and executed these with military precision. As I said, he and his products were dependable, so dependable, in fact, that we became dependant on the high sales turnover his goods generated. He was a 20% vendor giving us close to 80% of our business in certain categories. What he lacked in branding, he made up on the integrity of the product. If we had simply judged this vendor on the brand name per se, we would not have engaged and purchased from him, losing out on a great deal of healthy turnover, and very healthy margins. So buyers beware; listen to your customers, for they will be voting with their wallets. If they love the stuff—stock it!

case study

Accepting concessionaire terms

This is a case which illustrates that it is sometimes more profitable to let the vendor run the business.

This case involves a lingerie brand from whom we were buying goods on a returnable/exchangeable basis that depended to a great extent on the buyer's purchasing talent and OTB availability. The brand felt that the business could grow two-fold if we changed our existing terms to concessionaire terms, and was convinced that though the offer meant a lower margin, the sales volume would more than cover this shortfall. It also felt that, being a concessionaire, it would not have to wait for the buyer to produce purchase orders which, more often than not, took forever to get and resulted in lost business in the process.

Much to my buyer's displeasure, I decided to give it a trial period of six months. When the business did grow as predicted, the terms became permanent and the brand requested more selling space. Again, it came with facts and figures, providing us with a business proposal on improved sales return per square foot. We discontinued some less-productive brands and allocated it more space.

Again, the performance matched the promise. The brand knew its business and was aggressive in growing the business with us. I learnt that it is wise at times to let the experts take the lead. As for my buyer, she too saw the benefit as she was eligible for an incentive bonus on improved returns in her division. In this case, all gained.

The Art of Retail Buying

16 RETAIL SHRINK: THE BARE TRUTH

As we noted in Chapter 4, shrink (or shrinkage) is defined as "inventory recorded on a company's books but not on hand, because of theft, loss or accounting error." Whenever I ask buyers if they feel that they have a role to play in helping to control shrink, almost all say: "No; it's an operational issue." Before we look at whether this view is correct, it would be as well to remind ourselves of the extent of the problem, as illustrated in the following graphics.

Losses through crime: A comparison

Auto theft: $8.6 billion
1.3 million vehicles stolen in the U.S. in 2003

Shoplifting: $10.5 billion
Responsible for more than 50% inventory shrinkage

Larceny-Theft: $4.9 billion
7 million cases in the U.S. in 2003

Source: FBI 2003 Uniform Crime Report, 2004 NRSS Study

Global retail evolution through time

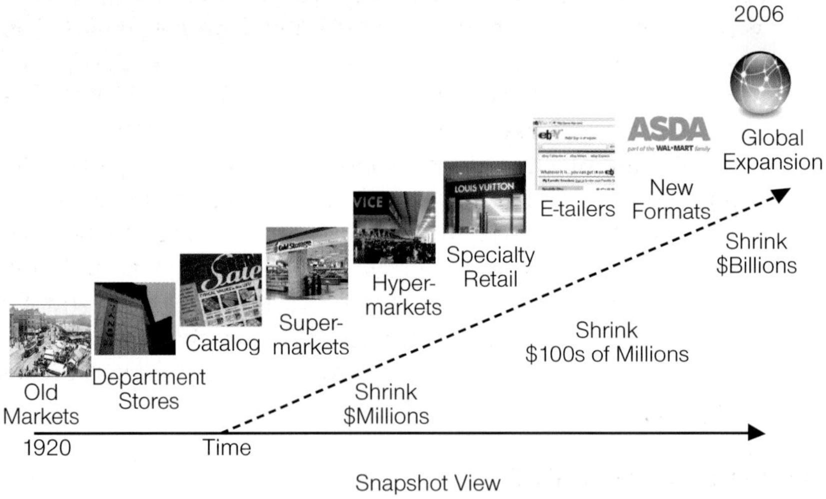

The retail industry is uniquely vulnerable to shrinkage because of the location of stores, the extended opening hours, the volume of goods on display, the high number of transactions and payment methods, the number of suppliers, and the high turnover of staff in this traditionally low-pay environment.

The causes of shrinkage include theft by employees, shoplifting, and paperwork errors, and losses from these add up to billions of dollars which are not listed in crime reports, except for the relatively few cases where arrests are made.

Even though shoplifting is more often publicized than employee theft, security experts are of the opinion that the in-house thief is responsible for at least 50% of shrinkage.

INTERNAL THEFT

The retail industry attracts many unskilled people, who work for minimum wages; whatever their motivation, a fair percentage of workers succumb to temptation and steal. Building strong employee relations through fair compensation, proper surroundings, and employer-sponsored activities can improve morale and concern for the success of a company. Not all will be persuaded by such programs, however, and for some organizations, the only way to dissuade some employees from helping themselves is through having a highly visible security program, and a rigid policy of prosecuting any employee caught stealing.

Prevention of theft requires simple but effective systems for handling merchandise and cash, which not only deter but also leave a trail of documents when any stealing takes place. One important step that the industry can take to prevent or reduce internal theft is to avoid hiring the potential thief or problem employee from the outset. When considering applications from potential employees, the industry must make the effort to determine whether or not the applicant may pose future problems, including dishonesty. Pre-employment investigations are very important and highly recommended.

BACKGROUND CHECKS

It is standard practice to make inquiry from previous employers regarding the job applicant. Since it is rare to get other than positive responses, the reliability of such information is to be weighed against information obtained from other sources.

A background check may be done in-house or through an outside agency. However, since the job applicant is not required to supply very much personal information these days, it may be necessary to seek other sources. There are extensive accumulations of private information about individuals who have credit cards, bank accounts, hospital records, former employment, or paid taxes, but obtaining these is troublesome for the potential employer, and may be considered an invasion of the applicant's privacy. Many firms, therefore, rely on the frankness of personal references supplied by the candidate, which is not a very good way to run any business.

PREVENTING MERCHANDISE THEFT

The degree of employee theft can only be approximated, since inventory shrinkage reflects the losses from all causes. The number of ways in which merchandise can be stolen by employees is limited only by the imagination of those so minded.

The most successful way to combat such theft is to prevent or discourage it. Every company must have thorough systems of control and accountability over merchandise, from the moment it is received, through the various stages of preparing it for sale, displaying it to shoppers, and finally handing it over to the purchaser.

Proper implementation of these controls requires dedication by executives, supervision by middle management, interest and concern by staff employees, and some security presence as a form of insurance.

STOCKROOMS

Employees can find remote corners to idle time away, or to hide stolen merchandise on their persons. Very often, they will discard their own articles of clothing and wear the pilfered items in their place. Once the price tickets have been removed, proof of theft is difficult to establish. Whenever possible, the stockrooms should be kept locked as a security precaution, and as a means of keeping employees on the selling floor to improve customer service. Access should be restricted only to authorized personnel who meet strict identification requirements.

UNAUTHORIZED MARK-DOWNS

A favorite method of theft that many employees regard as practically guiltless is to purchase articles at self-determined discounts. Employees who desire an item at the height of the season, and certainly before discounts are in order, create their own price changes in one way or another.

One way to discourage such activity is to frequently inspect goods that are held or laid away for employees. Alert sales people or cashiers may spot such price changes, but it may not be practical to expect them to deny the mark-downs to co-workers.

When mark-downs are made by the store, various records must be adjusted to reflect the lower value in the inventory records, lest a fictitious shortage be created.

RECEIVING AND SHIPPING

Platform (warehouse) and shipping employees can falsify the various receiving and delivery documents. Sometimes, this is done in conspiracy with truck drivers. Incoming shipments should be physically counted and verified against the accompanying documents.

Receipts given to delivery people should indicate any shortages found. Shipments should be verified again for completeness when they are unpacked and processed for the selling department. Valuable or easily concealable items should be transferred in security bins or racks. Test counts can be done randomly as a security measure.

The documents, which match the merchandise, must be checked for detail, particularly as to retail price. Incorrect ticketing will create shortage, irrespective of whether it is done deliberately or by mistake.

WAREHOUSES

Large companies may have one or more warehouses where incoming merchandise is received for storage and transshipment to retail outlets. Sometimes, the ticketing operations are done in such warehouses.

Theoretically, from a security viewpoint, a warehouse should be easier to control than a store since the environment is closed to the public. Truck drivers should not be permitted within the warehouse. Separate facilities should be maintained for them outside the perimeter, where feasible. Receiving platforms and shipping platforms should be physically separated.

Cargo documents and purchase orders should be matched, so that proper bookkeeping is ensured. Cargo areas for trucks should be locked and sealed when transporting merchandise. Drivers should not have access to the goods. It is a good idea to inspect the trucks from time to time to ensure that they are sound. Within the warehouse, there should be separate storage facilities for merchandise which is most often or easily stolen. Such areas may be specially safeguarded with locks, alarms, and/or CCTV.

If possible, management should reserve the right to search packages and persons. Typical warehouse environments are conducive to such activities as organized gambling or the selling of narcotics, practices that can easily create the conditions that lead to theft.

THEFT OF CASH

The theft of cash by staff whose jobs require them to handle money also presents a major problem to the retailer. Without a program of prevention, there are numerous opportunities for theft by cashiers. These include:

- Helping self to cash from the common drawer register
- Failing to give receipt to the customer and voiding the sale after the customer leaves
- Avoiding ringing the sale; pocketing the cash
- Under-ringing the sale; pocketing the difference
- Failing to close the register drawer after each sale
- Imprinting more than one charge on a credit card transaction; exchanging the surplus charge slip for cash
- Allowing the accomplice to remove cash; reporting the theft later
- Raising the amount of a check taken from a purchaser; pocketing the difference
- Accepting bad checks from the accomplice.

Proper and adequate investigation of such thefts is hampered by the high turnover of staff in retailing. Very often, by the time a particular pattern of shortage is detected, the guilty individual is gone. However, the following procedures may help to prevent such occurrences:

- If shortages exist in common drawer registers, switch cashiers daily and keep "over and short" records to track individual performance

- Frequent voids, no sales, or reports of till tapping should prompt the surveillance of suspects at work. Results may be obtained by interviews and cross-examination

- Conduct spot checks of cashier's funds during working day

- Conduct integrity shopping, as outlined below.

INTEGRITY SHOPPING

The integrity of cashiers can be tested by means of "integrity" or "honesty" shopping. These tests are conducted by specially trained people–in-house or contracted from an outside service–who pose as customers to test the honesty of cashiers about whom there may be doubts. Such doubts can arise about cashiers whose records show that they are consistently over in cash, giving rise to suspicions that they may be creating a surplus for themselves.

The basic test in any integrity operation is the "even money buy." Here, the shopper selects an item and pays for it with the exact amount, and does not have time to wait for the receipt or to have the item wrapped. The idea is to afford the employee who takes the cash an opportunity to pocket it. This transaction is observed by a second test observer.

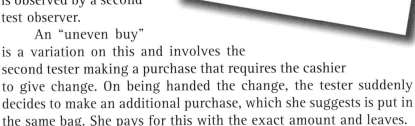

An "uneven buy" is a variation on this and involves the second tester making a purchase that requires the cashier to give change. On being handed the change, the tester suddenly decides to make an additional purchase, which she suggests is put in the same bag. She pays for this with the exact amount and leaves.

Another variation on this is the "exchange buy." Here, the tester hesitates in selecting between two items. Finally, the cheaper one is chosen and paid for, but as the transaction is completed, the shopper opts for the expensive one, pays the difference and leaves. In each of these cases, the testers mark their "buy" money, or record the serial numbers in advance, so that proper identification can be made of the evidence later on.

REFUNDING

Most retail stores have a fairly liberal policy of allowing merchandise to be returned and of refunding the purchase price by either cash or check. In some stores, the refunding is done through the selling department, where the merchandise, the price ticket, and the sales receipt are examined and authenticated.

An authorization for the refund is issued at that point and given to the customer, who presents it at a service desk where the approval is issued and payment made. If price tickets or receipts are not presented with the refund request in such centralized operations, the customer is usually directed to the selling department for verification of correct prices.

There must be at least two employees directly involved in any refund, one for examination of merchandise and approval, and a second to make the payout. Procedures must be established to constantly monitor payouts against related documents and merchandise.

Any deviation from these systems may be indicators of dishonest practice by employees. Price tickets should be found properly attached to merchandise in accordance with company practice. Data on these tickets should match the merchandise being returned. Many people switch to higher price tickets when seeking refunds. Employees, in particular, can do this in comparative safety, since they usually know what sort of information will be accepted as legitimate for certain merchandise. It is advisable to maintain records of refund activity for each employee for possible detection of abuses of the system. Computers can provide such facts to auditors and security departments at periodic intervals.

There is an ongoing problem with safeguarding small items of high value from employee pilferage between point of refund and return to selling departments. Control records must be maintained for such items and special locked storage facilities provided. Supervisors must make daily inspections of records and facilities, and see to the secure in-store transfer of the items. Since the refund operations are particularly vulnerable to employee dishonesty, particular care should be taken in personnel selection.

Temporary vacancies due to illness or vacation should not be filled haphazardly. Proper and adequate training of all employees involved in the refund procedure should be rigid company policy.

CASHIERS

Cash shortages, failure to ring up sales, and failure to give receipts are not proof of theft. Prosecution is not recommended unless there is a direct observation of stealing and recovery of some tangible evidence in merchandise or money.

Identifiable cash recovered from the person of the suspect is the best kind of evidence. This is often referred to as a "pocket case." Proper questioning based on observation of highly suspicious actions can often result in admissions of theft.

Without further evidence, the best course of action is to explore the feasibility of obtaining restitution. Often, the employee admits to frequent thefts going back over a period of weeks or months. The amount of money involved can be significant. Very often, restitution can be ordered and arranged through the courts. It is unwise to seek restitution without legal advice.

UNDERCOVER INVESTIGATION

Undercover investigation has long been used for providing intelligence information and is no less applicable to retailing. With sophisticated retail security, improved training and techniques, and the utilization of modern technology's latest advances in equipment and devices, the value and effectiveness of undercover investigation cannot be overstated. As a loss-prevention tool, it can provide information to security and other management that is not easily obtainable by any other means.

In practice, investigators posing as employees are placed within a firm. This should be done through normal placement procedures, with as few people in the know as possible during the term of the investigation. These investigators then blend and mingle, developing relationships with their associates for the purpose of locating and identifying employee dishonesty. Where such practices are uncovered, this information is conveyed to those executives who can put it to work.

While some information comes from occasional observation of isolated spontaneous thefts, the major portion of criminal information is developed over a longer period through confidential conversation, initially with the use of comments and remarks specifically designed to elicit a response. This, of course, must always remain within legal boundaries regarding entrapment.

The loss-prevention aspects of undercover investigation apply not only to criminal loss, but also to loss by other means—failure to adhere to policy and procedures, supervisory inadequacies, systemic deviations, and so on. Such loss is generally insidious, but can have devastating financial effects.

Ordinarily, the information from undercover operations is used to develop cases in an independent manner, so as to avoid exposing the original source. The identity of the undercover operatives should be protected at all times, and only when it is impossible to proceed with a case without breaking their cover should this be done.

KEEPING A LID ON LOSS

The most effective way to deal with a crime is to prevent it from happening in the first place. Although it is unrealistic to expect to eliminate all crime, the proper use of people—security guards, plain-clothes detectives and fitting-room attendants—and equipment—EAS (Electronic Article Surveillance) security tags and labels, and CCTV surveillance systems—can help reduce the total incidence of theft and destructive acts.

- **Security involvement by staff**

A successful security program is one which helps prevent theft. Since the commission of crime cannot be wiped out, recovery of merchandise can assist in minimizing losses. There are many retail stores that do not have a security staff per se. In such companies, the security effort depends on the vigilance of sales help, cashiers, stock persons, and other retail staff.

Even where a security staff exist, the total security effort will be more effective if the other employees are involved too. They must be trained to spot shoplifters and to take action to prevent the loss of merchandise. Ordinarily, these clerks and sales people are not expected to apprehend wrongdoers. However, if specially trained and instructed, anyone may be expected to take necessary action, including detaining shoplifters.

The actual apprehension of a person attempting to steal merchandise from a store requires knowledge of penal statutes and codes, which must be strictly obeyed. The safest policy to follow with all employees, except those specifically employed in a security role, is to design programs aimed at preventing theft.

Many employees perform better if there is an incentive program that encourages interest and participation. When a bonus is given to a salesclerk who points out a shoplifter, other employees sit up and take notice. While it is reasonable to expect wide participation in combating shoplifting, the average worker will hesitate before turning in a fellow employee. Although cash awards for such information are usually larger than shoplifter awards, such incentives are not very successful. Some firms pay bonus money to security people also, since this usually keeps productivity at a high level. However, this practice has been criticized as a bounty system leading to overzealousness and false arrests.

- **Loss-prevention procedures**

Although some shoplifting is inevitable, there are things that can be done to keep it to a minimum, and all employees must be committed to enforcing these procedures. Some obvious things to keep in mind might include:

- Keeping articles of high value under glass or locked away. If taken out to show customers, they should be returned immediately.
- Wherever possible, EAS anti-theft tags should be used.
- Displays should be set up in such a way that they do not block easy viewing by employees.
- Price tags should not be loose or easily removed. Look out for price switch. Read the text on the screen at the point of sale to ensure that it matches the description of the item being scanned.
- Customers should always be given prompt service, and sales people should not turn their backs to the customers.
- ID should be requested of any strangers in non-sales areas.
- All discarded sales receipts should be picked up.
- Sales people should be alert to the fact that luggage, legitimately purchased, may be filled with stolen merchandise.
- Frequent inventories of expensive or desirable merchandise should be taken.
- Employees should be alert to suspicious behavior and the possibility of mass shoplifting.

Many people who steal for the first time do so on impulse, and if they are caught, there is a good possibility that they will quit. On the other hand, those who get away with theft will most likely steal again, since it becomes easier to pilfer each succeeding time. Shoplifting is similar to many other crimes in that the lawbreaker will tend to return to the same place he or she was previously successful.

Shoplifters come from all walks of life, of any age or sex. They can be categorized as professionals, amateurs, juveniles, addicts, kleptomaniacs, or opportunists. Those who get away with theft will most likely steal again. Shoplifters are like satisfied customers. If they get what they came for ... they will be back!

The methods used by shoplifters are many and varied. These include concealing merchandise in boxes, bags, purses, or clothing (oversized garments may be worn to afford easy concealment); wearing stolen garments in plain sight, and to boldly walk out of the store; concealing small articles in the hand; or simply snatching articles and running out of the store.

Store personnel should be alert to the following signs that should give rise to suspicion of shoplifting.

- People wearing overcoats out of season, or raincoats on a clear day.

- People carrying boxes, bags, or umbrellas which could be used to conceal merchandise.

- Nervous-looking people who are constantly touching the backs of their heads, tugging at sleeves, or adjusting socks.

• Exceptionally fussy people, who cannot seem to make up their minds about a purchase, or do not appear interested in purchasing an article that they have been examining.

• People who walk around and keep one hand in pocket.

• People who come back to the same area of a store several times.

• People who are busy looking about, rather than at merchandise.

• People who walk into stockrooms, or behind counters, and have no business in such places.

MISCELLANEOUS GUIDELINES FOR CASHIERS

Employees who handle sales transactions must be constantly alert to render efficient service, pay attention to prices, and safeguard the contents of registers. Staff training and instructions covering some or all of the following areas is essential.

Cashiers should be familiar with the merchandise and the pricing because the switching of price tags is common, particularly in department stores. Paying attention to the description of the merchandise when scanning the bar code is good practice. The bar code will, more often than not, state the brand or the merchandise type and department code. Descriptions that do not tally should raise immediate suspicion and prompt further enquiry of the sales staff.

It should go without saying that the cashier should never turn away from an open register drawer. The drawer should be kept closed between transactions, and neither should it be left unlocked and unattended. Cashiers should refrain from counting the contents of the cash register on the selling floor, and should be alert to any attempt to distract their attention away from the register. Where a customer claims to have been shortchanged, the cashier should request assistance from a colleague.

REFUND OPERATORS

Some shoplifters find it more lucrative to seek a refund on stolen goods than to sell them. Professional thieves are quite adept at obtaining cash by obtaining refunds on goods purchased with bad checks or on credit cards, and some find it less risky to seek a refund for stolen merchandise without ever leaving the store.

Useful policies to counteract these practices include:

- Insisting on the customer to produce price tickets and sales receipts, and verifying the sale in the appropriate selling department before a refund is made.

- Examining all documents for alterations or erasures.

- Making refunds payable by check in the mail.

Shrinkage is an illness which cannot cure itself. Proper systems will contribute toward prevention of losses, but there must be constant follow-up and re-evaluation to ensure that what was adequate yesterday is still applicable today. Crime is on the march, and new schemes are constantly being devised. Expertise in loss prevention is as essential in today's retail world as fashion and salesmanship. Retailers have recognized and accepted the fact the money spent to protect company assets contributes to overall profits. In my opinion the provider that is most likely to give the best return on investment is ADT/Sensormatic.

THE ROLE OF THE BUYER IN PREVENTING LOSS

Most retailers today have some sort of loss-prevention system in place, be it CCTV, access control, EAS (Electronic Article Surveillance), or a simple burglar alarm. EAS systems require hard tags and labels, increasing the cost of protecting the merchandise. Hard tags are used mainly for garments, and soft tags or EAS labels are used by retailers of hardgoods, by hypermarkets and supermarket.

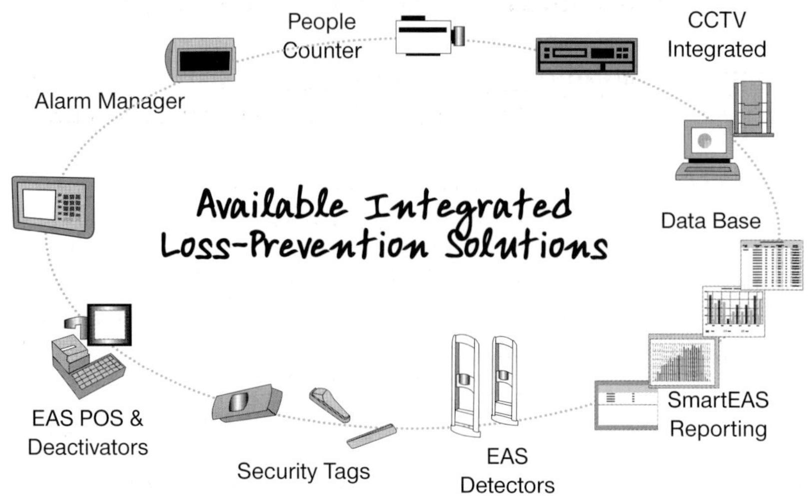

Source: www.sensormatic.com & www.adt.com

Buyers can make a substantial contribution to reducing loss through shrinkage by championing the cause of source tagging. Each time a buyer negotiates for the vendor to pay for EAS tags or labels to be attached to the merchandise, the buyer is directly contributing to the retailer's bottom line in that the company saves on the cost of labels/tags and the labor involved in attaching them; the goods are shelf-ready, and the shrink on tagged goods is drastically reduced.

In looking to improve profit levels, retailers want their suppliers to take over the task of delivering goods that comply with source tag requirements. As with any negotiations, this takes time and determination but, as shown in the graphics opposite, benefits are there to be enjoyed by all concerned.

When a retail company embarks on a loss-prevention program, besides investing in the anti-theft systems, it should draw up a task list of the people and divisions responsible in working with the system.

The first in line are the buyers. This is because without the buyers' negotiations with their suppliers, the full cost of the EAS tags will be borne by the retailer. It is becoming increasingly common for suppliers who are on consignment or concessionaire terms to share this cost because they have full responsibility for their inventory and, of course, the loss of inventory through theft.

Source Tagging: Retailer Benefits

Buyers	Benefits to the Company
The best team to Initiate, negotiate, implement and follow are the buyers	Controls and minimizes shrinkage
	Saves labor cost of in-store tagging
	Moves tag cost from company to supplier
	Allows open merchandising
	Improves sales and profit margins
	Maintains consistent tagging compliance
	Provides hidden labels
	Floor-ready merchandise
	Ensures product availability
	Gives more accurate best-sold item (SKU) statistics
	Enables decision-making on merchandise catalog
	Allows best-sold merchandise more prominent space

Source Tagging: Supplier Benefits

Brand Managers	Benefits to the Suppliers
Suppliers need to be orientated on the change of corporate standards. Suppliers will be willing to pay for the tags because they want to set the consumer price, have favored status with your stores, retain their market share, have higher sales volume, and never be out of stock	Increase sales performance
	More accurate replenishments, less aging
	Increase market share
	Increase sales and profit margins through open merchandising
	No need for empty box displays
	Competitive advantage value-add
	Floor-ready merchandise
	Ensures product availability
	Reduces out-of-stock caused by theft
	Promotes selling new high-ticket products
	Improves product appearance
	Allows more prominent space in store
	Allows the supplier to set the retail price

Second in line, and most in contact with the systems, are the operations people. They are the ones who ensure that the merchandise is properly tagged; who remove and deactivate tags at point of sale; who analyze the people-to-sales ratio (integrated people counter/ CCTV systems); establish improved staff cover; as well as dealing with shoplifters.

Action & Implementation of Solutions

Champions	Source Tags	Deactivator	People Counter	Alarm Mgt	CCTV
Buyers	Convert from some to all				
Operations	Tag Compliance	Deactivation Standards	People to Sales Ratio	Non-negotiable standards	Case Review
LP	Alarm Mgt	System Compliance		Acknowledged Alarms	Case Review & Reporting
HR		Training		Training	Case Procedure
Audit/Finance	Cost Savings		Report Review	Report Review Theft & Fraud	Case Audit
IT	Integrated System			Connectivity	
Marketing	Application		Promotion Effectiveness		
Logistics	Tag Compliance				
Solutions Provider	Train the Buyers	Train the Trainer	Hosted Reports	Hosted Reports	Hosted Viewing

The loss-prevention, human resources, IT departments, and others all have a part to play, with specific tasks and responsibilities. For many retailers, the time, people and systems investment is small in comparison to their yearly losses. As a rule of thumb, a loss-prevention system pays for itself after 18–24 months, and thereafter starts bringing in profits in the form of reducing losses through theft.

SUCCESSFUL RETAILING FORMULA

Let's face it; retail is not the most glamorous industry around. The hours are long, the job is physically demanding, and excellent customer service is demanded at all times. Perhaps not surprisingly, in the past, for a $30 wage increase, retail staff would change jobs. While the poaching of retail staff still goes on, the tide has turned and, today, having a great employer is more valuable in the industry than a few more dollars in the employee's pockets.

Employers who provide security and stability, a competitive salary and benefits, the possibility of career progression through training and development opportunities; who support the work/life balance; and who foster a sense of belonging, are those who are more likely to engender loyalty in their employees. All of these factors are central in creating a culture that supports good relationships. The more a company shows trust, respect and recognition for individuals, the less likely it is to experience loss through the dishonesty of its staff.

As John D Rockefeller Jr once said in another context: "The success of each is dependant upon the success of the other."

17 LEADING BY EXAMPLE

As we have seen, because buyers are largely instrumental in creating and buying the concepts around which a store is built, they are in the best position to guide the selling staff on how those concepts are to be presented on the selling floor.

You, as a buyer, should know the feel of the store and the image you want to project to the general public, your customers, your competitors, and your internal staff. You should recognize that everything you do must be done with a view to romancing your customers. Your products must stand for something and this must be reflected in the display. Successful stores are not about selling low prices, nor should they be about promotions and sales. Successful retail is about creating a market and pampering the customers with an ambience that shows that they have made the right choice in shopping with you.

The image that you portray builds business. Just as it is important for the buyer to find and select the right merchandise, so it is important for these goods to be presented at their best. By getting involved and sharing your views with how the merchandise should be displayed, you help create the right mood or surroundings for the goods; further supporting the growth of the business.

You may argue that this function belongs to the operations team or the visual-merchandising team, but you have good reason to be involved. With each new season, you have six months' worth of merchandise coming in, with new themes, color ranges and styles, and you should work out a plan for each key arrival.

When ranges are selling down (where colors and sizes are no longer in full assortments), it is amazing how you can freshen up the displays by re-coordinating the merchandise through blending the old with the new. This is an effective way of merging basic stocks and trendy merchandise to give the displays a fuller look.

Re-organizing the merchandise on the selling floor also helps showcase the merchandise in a different way. A blouse can now be displayed with another jacket and pants, giving these three pieces a new look altogether. Negotiate with your vendors on getting some trans (a picture or a frame from a series of pictures), or postures that can be placed in the department to support the look or lifestyle that you are trying to sell.

PROMOTING YOUR MERCHANDISE

In collaboration with your MM/DMM, prepare advertising plans, budget allocations and schedules for promotional activities for a new theme, brand or product line. You must ensure that all sales managers and staff are given detailed information of the promotion and expected sales targets well in advance. Ensure, too, that your deliveries are secured and timely. It also helps to take account of the experience of similar promotions from the past and to keep details for future use.

• Conducting product-knowledge sessions (PKS)

Knowledge is power. For retailers product knowledge can mean more sales. It is difficult to sell to a consumer effectively if you cannot show how a particular product will address the shopper's needs. I am a great advocate, therefore, for buyers taking the time to conduct well-prepared product-knowledge meetings with their selling staff.

A PKS, in fact, constitutes the buyer's first attempt to sell the merchandise. If the sales staff are thrilled and excited about the merchandise, chances are that they will sell it with similar enthusiasm. As you generate excitement for the product, you remove any uncertainty that the customer may have about it.

Having a thorough understanding of the products on the shelves can allow a retailer to use different techniques and methods to present the product to customers. Stronger communication skills will allow a salesperson to recognize and adapt a sales presentation for the various types of customers. Explaining the features and benefits of these many products not only adds value to the products that are being offered, but also provides a good opportunity for excellent customer service.

If a customer is indecisive about a purchase, it is helpful to have sales staff who are able to remove the doubts. Successful selling lies in knowing the products well and selling them with confidence. Becoming educated in the products and their uses will help cement that confidence.

Planning a good PKS takes time and preparation. You have a captive audience, and a very short time in which to deliver important information. The more information that sales staff have about a product, the better. The buyer should be well-equipped to convey that knowledge, not only about the company's own products, but also about those of competitors. However, your suppliers, the vendors themselves, may well be in an even better position to conduct some sessions, to the benefit of all concerned. It is important to understand how the product is made, how it can and should be used, and what products work well together. These meeting can be animated through role-play, demonstrations and comparisons.

A great deal of practical information must be shared as well. This can be distributed and shared during the PKS, and reinforced with handouts covering such things as the history and manufacture of the product and how to use it; servicing, warranty and repair information; the styles, colors or models available; pricing structure; delivery times, and planned promotions or launches. It's even more beneficial if you can show samples of the new items or pictures of the merchandise that is on its way.

You travel and are exposed to the latest concepts and trends. Share that knowledge. Take pictures of how other retailers are displaying their merchandise. Remember, a picture is worth a thousand words!

Well-prepared product-knowledge sessions would include showing the staff the new trends applicable to their specific portfolio. These can be shown as collages to set the mood. Just as importantly, it is always a good idea to show pictures of the actual merchandise that is forthcoming, which gives you the opportunity to talk about features and benefits of these products, price positioning, and competition positioning.

Think of such sessions as part of your strategic plan to achieve your sales goals. Each season is like preparing for a new battle where you equip your army (sales team) with the right ammunition (knowledge) to win the battle (sales goals) that wins the war (customer satisfaction and customer retention)—all good reasons to plan them well and conduct them well.

These meetings also provide a great opportunity to ask the sales people how they feel sales could be improved. If they feel their views are respected and, wherever practicable, used, they will be more than happy to give you information. Nothing is more discouraging than providing feedback, and then having it ignored. Many of the ideas that sales staff provide are very workable because they are usually an accurate reflection of customers' reactions.

OTHER DUTIES

• PO matching

A tedious task and one less favored by buyers, purchase order (PO) matching entails checking that the goods received from vendors match the goods ordered from them, or that the cost price on the invoice matches that shown on the PO. While an accounts department can easily take care of this task, many companies are of the view that the buyer is responsible for contacting their vendors for rectification of any errors.

The task becomes trickier when problems arise with imported goods, since losses can occur in transit. Though many retailers have insurance coverage with their shipping agents, it can be a messy and time-consuming business. Companies that have buying agents are in a better position, as these agents would be the ones chasing the vendors and resolving such problems.

- **Warehouse visits**

Occasional warehouse visits by buyers are recommended, even though they may receive regular reports from the warehouse on all units stored there. However, these reports do not reveal the condition of the merchandise. In fact, some buyers tend to overlook the dollar value of the goods sitting there, and look at it as a percentage of total goods on hand. It may be that a buyer has 5% of her goods stored at the warehouse, which sounds reasonable enough, but not if that same 5% is attached to a very high inventory, representing a fairly high dollar value or high units.

The other advantage of visiting the warehouse and seeing the merchandise yourself is that evaluating ageing stocks helps determine the mark-down you will need to use to clear these goods. The buyer may discover current sellable stocks that could and should have been used by operational staff to replenish floor stock and prevent out-of-stock situations occurring.

Such visits also enable the buyer to assess whether there are high volumes of low-priced merchandise that ought to be sold off.

- **Range reviews**

Many companies require buyers to prepare merchandise presentations and range reviews. These presentations can arise where the buyer needs a final approval before placing orders, or for the introduction of a new brand, range or vendor, or when management needs to select merchandise to be used in advertising for sale purposes.

Merchandise presentation is a good motivation tool that can be used for the selling teams. Remember that the basis for good sales is knowledgeable sales people, so the effort of doing such presentations works in your favor.

- **Stock checks**

My views on the importance of buyers spending time on the selling floor should be clear enough by now, and one good habit to acquire while on the selling floor is to check for sizes, and then to gauge the reactions of the sales staff to questions about the availability/non-availability of stock. Often, you'll be told that it's out of stock. The kind of answers you should be looking for and should expect would include: "Let me check the storeroom/other outlets" or "Let me call the warehouse/buyer/vendor to see if it's available."

Similar checks can be conducted for styles, colors or ranges, irrespective of the merchandise being sold.

Whatever the scenario, inventory reports can give you answers (if you can digest them all,) but the fastest and easiest way of finding out is to check the situation yourself. Always look at it from a customer's point of view, and ask yourself whether you have the stocks available to satisfy the customer's needs.

- **Managing broken ranges**

Managing ranges that are sold down or broken is important as it will save mark-downs later. Some vendors would have prepared their ranges and range deliveries with colors that can easily blend in with previously shipped merchandise. However, in most cases, buyers will have to undertake this task with the help of the selling staff. With a bit of imagination, products can be re-merchandised during a regular period, and still be sold at full price, or with a smaller discount than would be required during a sale or a promotion. The following examples illustrate what can be done.

A table with knits in four colors has been selling well, but the number of units left no longer justifies the display. In this case, the buyer can sort out the colors and hang them with existing woven garments on the selling floor, improving the chances of selling even if all of the colors can't be accommodated.

Ranges of garments from different vendors can also be merged in colors or in style types. Though some stores would have designated areas for certain brands, when it comes to the tail end of a season, buyers can make room for these oddments with a discount.

In the homeware department, a theme consisting of tableware, cups, glasses, vases, and table mats in solid black-and-white can no longer be repeated, and the ranges are now incomplete. Besides offering a discount, the buyer could re-merchandise these products

by category, placing the vases together, or displaying the table mats with others from different ranges. Another option might be to top up the theme with other types of merchandise found in the store, matching the table mats with other black-and-white items such as candy bowls, candle holders, and so on.

As mentioned in a previous chapter, the first mark-down is the cheapest mark-down: that is, in the circumstances outlined above, the buyer may be able to get away with a 10% or 20% discount. However, if they have to be put on sale, these oddments will be competing with bought-in sales merchandise, and will require much higher discounts of up to 50% before they are sold.

ALIGNING YOUR GOALS WITH THE COMPANY'S

When conducting product-knowledge sessions or group meetings with your staff, buyers should take the leading role in refreshing company goals which have an influence on the merchandise buys. When discussing customers and their needs, it is important to update how these are defined, how they are measured, and how they will be gratified. This will provide a clear indication of your current position and whether this is in sync with emerging customer trends.

The next set of quantifiable measures focus on sellthrough, merchandise differentiation and service, which indicates whether and by how much each is adding value to the total offering.

Customers

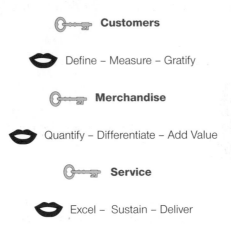

Define – Measure – Gratify

Merchandise

Quantify – Differentiate – Add Value

Service

Excel – Sustain – Deliver

The last set of measures to consider is the service standards. Though these are primarily the responsibility of the operational manager, it is sensible that you take the time to discuss these issues with the selling staff directly, sharing your ideas for promoting the merchandise you have bought. Many retailers today operate with high levels of consignment goods that are sold by individual promoters, which makes it all the more important that the merchandise you have bought receives the best possible attention from your own sales staff. Raising the level of selling skills is a real team effort.

You may be very familiar with the kind of merchandise display illustrated in this picture. At best, it's very average, lacking mood, direction and distinction. The placement of merchandise looks almost haphazard. But it needn't have been so. It would have been just as easy to arrange by stories (thematic collections) or by color matching or by type, which would have been much more eye-catching.

As the buyer, you can have a great influence on how your merchandise is displayed by working closely with the operations people.

case study

PKS Feedback

A new shipment of imported twin-sets had just arrived. They came in four styles, in four color ways (in retail terms, one color purchased = one color way. This, in turn, translates to the selling space a color or several colors will occupy) and were very well priced. The goods were stacked on a table in front of the department with a "New Arrival" sign. During the weekly product-knowledge session, the buyer shared the sellthrough with the selling team and voiced her concern that the merchandise wasn't selling. Why? What was wrong?

The sales people readily gave the buyer their feedback. The merchandise itself was of high quality and in sellable colors, but the way it was presented cheapened the entire offer. In addition, having all 16 SKUs out at once made the selection difficult for the customers, many saying that they would think about it and come back later.

The buyer agreed that this was possibly the problem, and arranged for the changes to be made in time for the weekend trade. The table presentation now incorporated two styles in all four colors, and only two pieces per size. New signage was put up:

Season's Hot Classics

Exclusive only at...

Though a lot of replenishing of stock was required, this wasn't too much of a hassle because the goods were stocked next to the department. The strategy worked, and the first two styles were sold out by Saturday evening. The sales manager had already requested the remaining two styles, which were rushed in late Saturday afternoon ready for Sunday's trade. The change in customers' attitudes towards these knits was quite remarkable. They were buying several pieces, over the same styles in different colors, or one in each style and color.

This was definitely a case where less means more. Though the goods were the same, the customers' perception of them had changed. This was captured in one customer's reaction to the offer: "Exclusive knits in trendy colors in a beautiful quality and at such a good price; it was a steal!" It was all about perception.

There are many such examples where teamwork and good communication can make things happen. Here, each had a role to play, but each had the same goal of achieving high customer satisfaction by creating a higher perceived value for these knits.

The Art of Retail Buying

18 BUSINESS COMMUNICATION

Management requires feedback on current sales trends, monthly sales results, stock holdings, mark-downs and profit margins in regular written reports. Though writing reports is part and parcel of a buyer's job, not many buyers are good at it. Presenting facts and figures in an accessible way is an essential skill and one that can be learned.

This chapter is about writing concise and precise reports. But before you can do so, you need to know what's going on, which means having a firm grip of what is happening on the selling floor. Regular weekly meetings with sales staff will keep you up to date on such issues as missing sizes, colors or items, as well as on customer response to the merchandise you have bought in. If sales are slow, you'll find out why and will be able to work out a plan of action to rectify the matter.

BUYERS' COMMUNICATION TOOLS

Buyers are called upon to communicate with a whole range of people, using a wide range of tools and formats. There are face-to-face presentations, meetings, reviews, conferences and interviews. There are also phone calls, emails and SMS messages on a daily basis. They will also be called on to prepare written reports, proposals, contracts, minutes of meetings, brochures, press releases, newsletters and advertisements.

It is essential, therefore, that buyers have good spoken and written communication skills.

TEN STEPS TO WRITING REPORTS

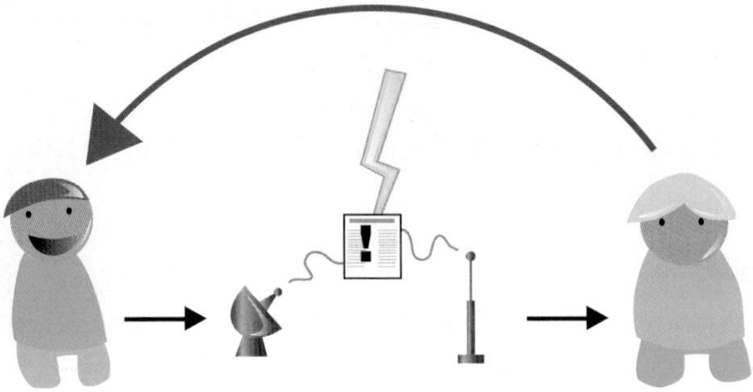

1. **Define the subject**
2. **Gather the necessary information**
3. **Identify the problem/situation**
4. **Analyze the information**
5. **Organize the information**
6. **Propose the recommendations**
7. **State the requirements**
8. **Propose the timeframe**

9. **Write the report**

10. **Determine the recipients**

(If this is a routine report, then ensure the usual recipients are on the mailing list. If in doubt, think about the people receiving this information and ask yourself whether this is a case of need-to-know or nice-to-know.)

WRITING STYLE

Good reports are short, precise and informative. In the following examples, note how, through condensing ideas and combining sentences, the second version in each case becomes much more effective.

Example 1:

Triumph's main objective is to increase sales. Specifically, the objective is to double sales in the next five years and become a more successful lingerie business.

Triumph's objective is to double sales in the next five years.

Example 2:

Sales last month were disappointing because we had planned a promotion which was supposed to give us a 10% increase in sales but we just managed to hit overall budget.

Sales were on plan without the additional 10% expected from the promotion.

Example 3:

We would have achieved our budgeted gross profits this month if it weren't for the fact that we took $5,300 worth of mark-downs on some slow-moving merchandise.

(Here, the obvious point is that buyers will use mark-downs to clear slow-moving merchandise. What needs to be reported is how much and what the percentage effect of the price reduction to the overall budgeted margin was.)

CONTENT AND STRUCTURE

A formal report will normally consist of cover and title pages, a table of contents, and an executive summary. These will be followed by the body of the report, which usually includes case studies or illustrations. Reports can be structured as follows:

Introduction: *Purpose–Scope–Limitations–Assumptions–Methods*

History: *Background–Conditions–Circumstances–Status*

Body: *Data–Position–Analysis–Interpretations*

Recommendations: *Advises–Suggests–Proposes*

Conclusion: *Summary of facts and potential outcome*

References: *Material–Work Scope–Information*

Appendix: *Interviews–Transcripts–Questionnaires–Printouts–Previous Reports*

SALES PROGRESS REPORTS

Monthly progress reports are part and parcel of any buyer's job. Management will require the buyers to report on the previous month's performance in detail. Here, we look at an example of a progress report based on the information in the chart opposite.

• Sales

State the **reason** for an improved sales performance against last year's. The budgeted sales indicates that you may have planned a promotion or launch for that month. If so, state the **nature of the promotion**, brand and products. If advertised, state the **media** used and whether **additional floor space** was given. State the **number of items sold** vis-à-vis the **number of customers** (did the customers buy the advertised items only or did they buy add-ons?). Mention any areas (speed of replenishment or staff levels, perhaps) that **need to be improved** next time.

When reporting on sales, present both the highlights and the low points; by department, by brand/vendor, by class and, if necessary, by SKU. It may be that your overall figures are up, but

Monthly Progress Report

Example **Reporting for the month of September**

Department	Sales Actual	Sales Last Year	Plan	Actual vs Last Year +/-	Actual vs Plan +/-	GP$ Actual	GP$ Last Year	GP$ Plan	Actual vs Last Year	Actual vs Plan
108 Accessories	$266.8	$135.4	$264.2	+$131.4	+$2.6	$114.4	$60.1	$108.3	+$54.0	+$5.8
Actual GP %	**GP % Last Year**	**GP% Plan**	**Actual. vs Last Year**	**Actual vs Plan**	**Plan Stock**	**Actual Stock**	**Variance**	**Stock Turn**	**ROI**	**MKD Mth**
42.7%	44.3%	41.0%	-1.6%	1.7%	$177.2	$107.4	-$69.8	12.0	10.25	$5.2

Note: Unit = $000s

Monthly Sales Report	
Sales	
GP$	
GP$	
Stocks	
Next Mth Activities	
Vendor	
Activity	

that a particular brand is lagging behind; or a class is performing particularly well, but another is performing poorly.

In addition to explaining the dynamics of what's going on, you should set out a proposed plan of action. For example, you may decide to back up your winners by giving them more OTB and/or space, which will require management approval. You may identify why a particular class is underperforming and explain how you are going to rectify the problem. Or, it may be that though a class is underperforming, it has merchandise that your customers expect you to carry. Be explicit.

- **Gross profit dollars**

Comment on the profit performance (GP$) vis-à-vis gross profit percentage (GP%). Here, the GP$ is above plan; however, the GP% is below last year (–1.6%). **Explain why.** One explanation could be that this year you planned a gift with purchases above $100 on the promoted brand. Or, it could be that during the course of the month, you brought in some product at a lower margin that proved to be a fast-seller. Whatever the reason, be **precise** and **accurate.**

- **Stock levels**

Stocks are below plan by $69,800. **Explain why.** This could be due to some late shipments, or poor replenishment. In any case, you need to explain how you will rectify the situation, or state your delivery schedules going forward.

An overstock situation can arise for any number of reasons: for example, a lack of sales over a period of time, or goods brought in for a promotion on a sale-or-return basis where the balance was not returned to the vendor before month end. However, critical to management is if the overstock position arises from stocks being overbought. Obviously, the reason(s) for this will need to be explained, together with **plans of action** that will be taken to get back on track.

- **Stock turn and mark-downs**

Here, both are on plan, so no elaboration is needed. Where stock turn is lower than plan, state why. This is usually linked to having too much stock. So, after reporting on the stock levels, talk about the impact these have had on your stock turn, elaborating further on the remedies.

- **Next month's store activities**

If you have activities planned for the coming month, **explain** what they are and your **anticipated outcome.**

- **Market news**

If there are any major market shifts that may affect future sales, **explain** what they are, the **possible consequences,** and what **plan of**

action you propose to take to buffer their impact. Mention only the critical factors.

- **Vendor management**

State if you have adopted any **new vendors** and the **reasons for doing so** (better margins or price points, or to fill a category gap, perhaps). Likewise, if you have **terminated a vendor**, explain why. If a vendor or manufacturer is closing down, explain how you intend to replace that source.

MULTIPLE-STORE REPORTING

If you are buying for a chain of stores, your progress report will be different. The reporting should be as detailed, as shown in the previous example, but may require additional information. There are numerous data that can be analyzed, evaluated and compared. Most retailers will give their buyers guidelines on what to report, as the previous example showed.

In the example illustrated on the next page, performance is evaluated according to the overall performance of all stores, and then by comparison of individual stores. In this example, we look at two of the six stores because they generate the same sales turnover.

City Central and Grand Plaza Mall each represent 20% of the total stores combined. If the total sales turnover were to be $1,000,000, then each store has $200,000 in sales. This does not mean, however, that both stores are performing equally well. The size of the store is one attribute to be examined; the composition of the merchandise is another.

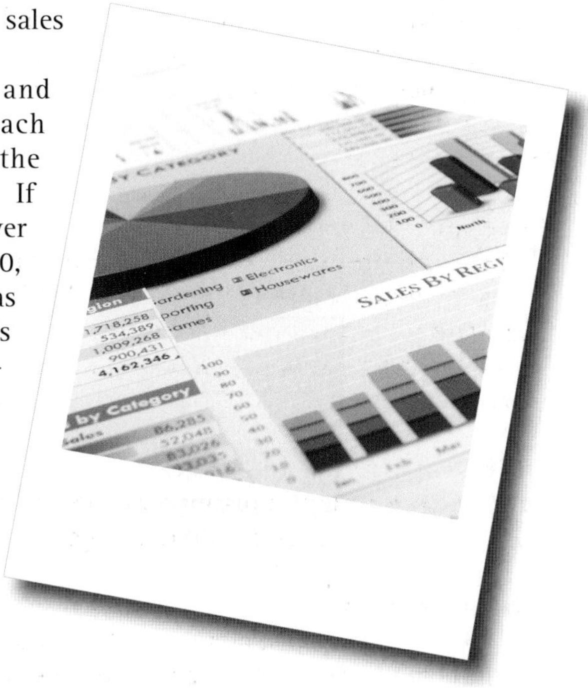

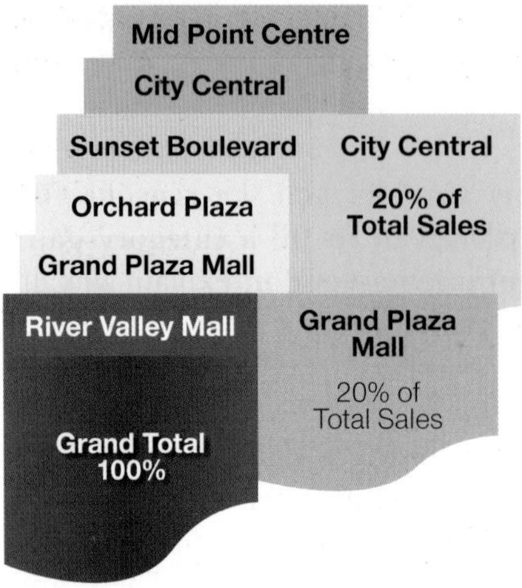

If Grand Plaza Mall's selling space is 800mt² and City Central's is 700mt², then City Central is performing better on a sales-per-square-meter basis (Grand Plaza Mall: 200,000 ÷ 800 = $250 per square meter. City Central: 200,000 ÷ 700 = $285). If the total selling space of all stores is 4,000 mt², then the total sales per square meter is $250 ($1,000,000 ÷ 4,000). In this case, City Central store is performing 14% better than average ($285 – $250 = 35 ÷ $250 = 0.14 or 14%).

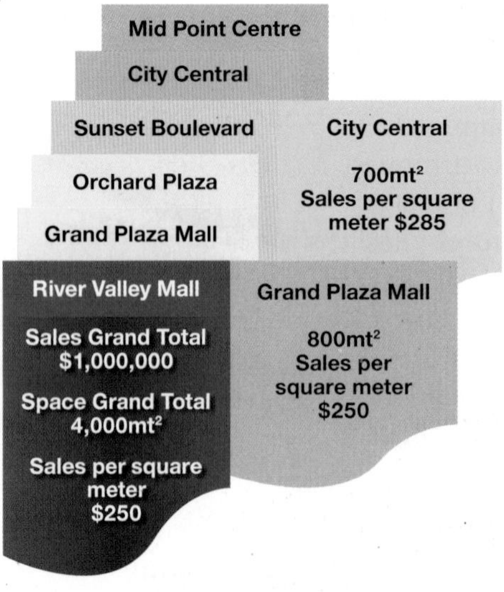

The merchandise mix will also make a difference to the store's performance. Let's assume that City Central is operating with 60%

consignment goods at 30% margin, and 40% outright goods at 45%. Grand Plaza Mall is operating with 80% outright goods at 45%, and 20% consignment goods at 30%.

City Central's sales turnover is $200,000. The merchandise composition is 60% ($120,000) on consignment and 40% ($80,000) on outright. Total profit margin generated is, therefore, $72,000 ($120,000 x 30% margin = $36,000 + $80,000 x 45% margin = $36,000).

The profit per square meter is, therefore, $72,000 ÷ 700 mt^2 = $102.85.

Grand Plaza Mall's sales turnover is $200,000. The merchandise composition is 80% ($160,000) on outright and 20% ($40,000) on consignment. Total profit margin generated is, therefore, $84,000 ($160,000 x 45% margin = $72,000 + $40,000 x 30% margin = $12,000).

The profit per square meter is, therefore, $84,000 ÷ 800 mt^2 = $105, making it more productive than City Central.

The six stores combined have sales of $1,000,000, and their total average gross margin composition is 70% outright (GP margin 45%) and 30% consignment (GP margin 30%). They thus generate an average of $405,000 in profits ($700,000 x 45% = $315,000 + $300,000 x 30% = $90,000). The total store space of 4,000 mt^2 thus generates profits of $101.25 per square meter. Both City Central ($102.85) and Grand Plaza Mall ($105) are, therefore, producing above-average profits per square meter.

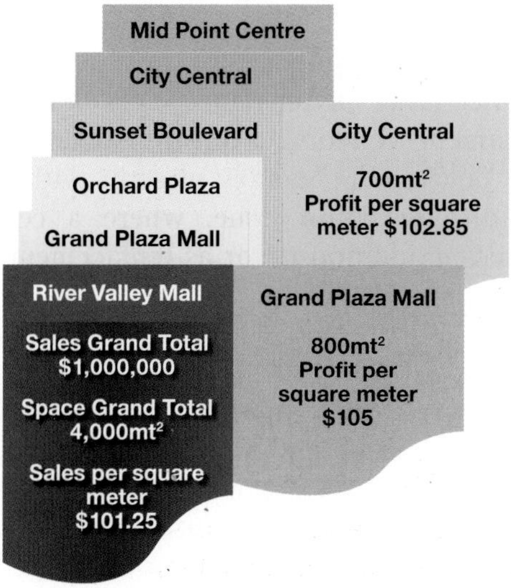

BUSINESS EXPANSION PROPOSALS

• Budgets

As we saw in Chapter 6, budgets can be created either from the top down or from the bottom up. If prepared from the bottom up (that is, by the buyer,) these figures are submitted to management. If the total budget is below expectation, then a written explanation will be required; likewise, if the total budget is greatly above expectation.

If your budgets are part of a business plan, then a written proposal will be required.

• Strategy and tactics

If your proposal is linked to a specific strategy, state as much. Your higher-than-expected target may be linked to a repositioning of a merchandise category, or involve expanding an area of business or developing a new one. It could be that you want to reduce the number of consignment vendors and expand the current level of outright purchases, giving your store more exclusive lines and an edge over your competitors. It could also be a case where you wish to expand a merchandise category that is showing some growth potential.

If space allocation is part of the strategy, state the sales and profits currently generated from that space and those that you propose generating with your new strategy. Explain if the vendor occupying the space will be re-located, shrunk or removed totally. This enables management to evaluate the feasibility of your proposal.

The tactic that you propose for this new strategy may, for example, be a price issue (better retail prices than currently offered by your consignment vendors), a profit issue, higher margins as you propose to develop the ranges directly with a manufacturer, or a point of differentiation issue, where a certain quality or styling is required in addition to, or as replacement for, the current merchandise mix.

• Objectives

State your objectives clearly. In the case of a business proposal, your objective may be to obtain management approval for a higher level of OTB in a certain category, department or division, for additional sources or vendors for your existing list. Also, approval may be sought for additional selling space or selling staff or for some additional buying trips. Management will evaluate your target vis-à-vis the additional cost they will incur if they go ahead and support your budget and the strategy that goes with it.

- **Schedule**

State the timing for these proposed changes—from the time of conception to the time of delivery, to the time the merchandise is positioned on the selling floor.

- **Results**

State what will be needed for you to achieve these results. This could be some advertising support, visual merchandising support, and/or additional selling staff. State the possible effect if one or more of these items were not approved.

- **Closing**

When closing your proposal, summarize the benefits vis-à-vis the effort, the investment and additional cost. If your proposal shows a healthy increase in overall profits, you stand a good chance of it being accepted.

MEETINGS

As a buyer, you will be required to hold meetings with various people within the company and with external suppliers. To be effective, your meetings should have a clear purpose and you should know exactly what you want to achieve. Having determined this, invite only people relevant to your purpose and supply them with a proposed agenda in advance, inviting them to suggest any other items they may wish to have included.

Establish a clear time for the meeting and make sure that it starts promptly. Don't waste time waiting for people to arrive. Make sure that somebody is appointed to take minutes for the meeting. Actions should be clear and concise, and an owner and target completion date set for each. Try to complete and distribute the minutes within 24 hours of the conclusion of the meeting to give people adequate time to complete their actions.

Before the next scheduled meeting, obtain updates on actions taken to date and incorporate them into the agenda for the meeting. This will help to significantly reduce the length of the meeting.

• **Keeping/writing minutes**

These days, many of us find ourselves in the position of taking minutes without a clue of how to go about it. Try not to be intimidated by the prospect. Concise and coherent minutes are not that hard to do if you have the topics already written down.

This allows you to note down the key points raised, and to jump right on to a new topic without pausing as the meeting progresses. In essence, good minute-taking is all in the preparation, and here are some tips on how to go about it.

First, ensure that all of the essential elements are noted: date, time, venue, names of participants and chairperson/facilitator, topics discussed, and time of adjournment. For formal and corporate meetings, include approval of previous minutes, and all resolutions. Have a list of expected attendees ready, and check off the names as people enter the room. Or, pass around an attendance sheet for everyone to sign as the meeting starts.

Don't record every single comment. Concentrate on getting the gist of the discussion and take enough notes to summarize it later. Think in terms of issues discussed, major points raised, and decisions taken. Leave plenty of white space next to the topic headlines for additional comments or notes to self.

Also don't wait too long to type up the minutes; do it while your memory is fresh. Be sure to have the minutes approved by the chairperson or facilitator before distributing them to the attendees.

• **Taking notes**

You may find it useful to use abbreviations in your notes, but you need to be consistent with them. There's nothing worse than re-visiting your notes the next day and trying to figure out what you meant. You can make up your own codes or use some commonly used ones, as shown opposite.

Abbreviation	Meaning
DK	Don't know
DPI	Disposable personal income
ENP	Expected net profits
F & B	Features and benefits
FAQ	Frequently asked questions
FIS	Free in store
FMCG	Fast-moving consumer goods
FOC	Free of charge
4 P	Product, price, promotion, place
HTML	Hypertext mark-up language
Imp	Important
IDI	In-depth interview
IM	Instant messaging
ISP	Internet service provider
JIT	Just in time
KISS	Keep it simple and straightforward
KIV	Keep it in view
KPI	Key performance indicators
KIP	Key influential people
LAN	Local area network
MBO	Management by objectives
EG	Email group
MEG	Moderate email group
MR	Market research
NA	Not available
NAP	Not applicable
NPD	New product development
NSPF	Not specifically provided for
OTC	Opportunities to check
PDM	Product differentiated marketing
Prep	Preparation or Prepare
PIN	Personal identification number
PLC	Product Life cycle

Abbreviation	Meaning
PoS	Point of Sale
PoP	Point of Purchase
PR	Public Relations
R&D	Research & Development
ROI	Return on Investment
RTS	Ready to serve
SBU	Strategic business unit
SKU	Stock-keeping Unit
SWOT	Strengths, Weaknesses, Opportunities, Threats
TA	Target Audience
U&A	Usage and attitude
UPC	Universal product code
VO	Voiceover
NW	Networking
WWW	World Wide Web
!	Caution
~	Approximately equal to; proportional to
=	Equal to
!=	Not equal to
= =	Equivalent
!= =	Not equivalent to
>	Greater than
>>	Much greater than
<	Less than
<<	Much less than
+/-	Plus or minus
| |	Parallel
@	At
* or x	Multiplication
%	Percentage of
&	And

Using short-hand abbreviations saves time and helps you concentrate on what is being said. Using the above short-form examples, your minutes could go from looking like this:

Statement by Chairperson, Mark Grey:

"The minutes of last month are approved, let's move on to the second item of the meeting. Sales last month exceeded budget by 7% and profits were well ahead by 12%. Month-to-date sales, however, are behind plan by 19%. I would like our sales and marketing teams to discuss amongst themselves and come up with a promotion activity to boost sales."
[63 words]

to something like this:

MG: prev mths min OK. sales in prev mth > bud by 7% and Prof by >12%. Sales mtd bud. < <by 19%. Ops & A & P to OTC 4Promo.
[31 words]

or from this:

Statement by Head of Operations, Kevin Hoe:

"The renovations of the men's department at Raffles City are progressing slower than anticipated. Though the cost is well controlled and within budget, we may have to postpone the re-opening by eight days. The delay is caused by the removal of the old floor and the laying of the new marble flooring."
[52 words]

to this:

KH: reno late by 8 days – new flr. Cost OK.
[10 words]

Example 1: Simple Minutes

Once all topics have been tabled, the minute-taker can proceed in condensing the topics, comments and decisions.

Topic	Comments	By	Decision
Last month's Minutes	OK	MG	Approved
MA - Agent's Visit	Went well	MD	None
Last Month's Sales	On budget	MG	None
Marketing Plan	Looks good	MG	Approved
Sales m-t-d	Behind plan	MJ	Action a promotion
New Hires	Good	AJ	Training in progress
Renovations	Late but on budget	KH	Follow-up to speed

Organizing minute-taking can simplify the task. If the minute-taker is prepared with, for example, a pre-organized form, then the flow of information that needs to be recorded is straight-forward.

Example 2: Detailed Minutes

The meeting is a normal monthly management meeting, where the subjects tabled are predictable. A pre-organized form could look like this:

Company Logo

Minutes Management Meeting

Attendees	Enter the names of the people who attended
Apologies	Enter the names of the people who advised on their absence
Absent	Enter the names of the people missing
Cc	

Date				**Time**		**Venue**	

Ref	Issue	Action	Owner	Status	Timing
1	Sales Progression				
1/1					
2/1					
3/1					
2	Profit & Loss Statement				
1/2					
2/2					
3/2					
3	Promotional Activities				
1/3					
2/3					
3/3					
4	Human Resources Activities				
1/4					
2/4					
3/4					
5	Renovations				
1/5					
2/5					
3/5					

Comments:

The subject matter raised may not necessarily be in the same sequence as your form; however, if the subjects are formatted sequentially, it makes it easier for all to read, prepare and action. Here is an example of what the minutes might look like:

Company Logo

Minutes Management Meeting

Attendees				KC - JO - KT - SW - JC - PT - LJ - SS - WP - AY - SF			
Apologies				EC			
Absent							
Cc				PP - JL - TT			
Date	8	10	07	**Start Time**	10.00 am	**Venue**	Management Office
				End Time	11.50 am	**Minutes**	SF

Ref	Issue	Action	Owner	Status	Timing
1	Sales Progression				
1/1	Last month's sales were up 8% against last year and 2% above target				
2/1	Month-to-date, cummulative sales are below target by 16%. KC proposes a promotional activity or price event	Propose mechanics of promotion	GMM-MM Mkt	New	12-10-07
3/1	Merchants to create a promotional activity to boost sales. Less 10% store wide or less 20% on selected categories	Promotional activity based on discounts to be proposed	KT SW SS	Approval Launch	12-10-07 15-10-07
2	Profit & Loss Statement				
1/2	Last month's net profits were above budget by 5% and cumulatively year-to-date by 3%				
2/2	In view of the proposed price event, Accounting to submit new sales & margin forecast		WP	New	13-10-07
3/2	Forecast top-line sales increase. Overall effect on the margin	Prepare profit diagnosis with merchants, input	WP		13-10-07
	Merchants to seek vendor co-op on the discounts. Propose promotion duration	Vendor List: All bearing or 50/50 bearing?	KT SW		11-10-07
3	Promotional Activities				
1/3	A & P to prepare 1-page advertisement on the storewide discounts. Insertion date: 15/10/07	Propose ad layout	JC		12-10-07
2/3					
3/3	Advertising Department	Create theme - Submit cost	JC	New	12-10-07
	Human Resources				
1/4	Operations to increase staffing during the promotional period. Submit total requirement to HR	Additional staff needed to support the event	SF		10-10-07
2/4					
3/4	HR	Submit additional staff cost	AY		12-10-07
5	Renovations				
1/5	NIL				
2/5					
3/5	Operations to submit additional store fixture requirements	Wagon or tables	SF		10-10-07

Comments:

- All department heads to submit their individual requirement by 10-10-07
- Additional costs to be submitted to management by no later than 12-10-07
- Merchandising to submit promotional mechanics and list of co-operating vendors by 11-10-07
- A & P to propose ad layout - Theme based on approved promotional mechanics
  Submit advertising cost by 12-10-07
- Accounts to submit P & L forecast 13-10-07

Minutes are important, especially when buyers are having discussions with their suppliers. They are a formal record of what has been agreed to, who is to action what and when, and can prove invaluable should disputes arise.

MIND-MAPPING

Another way of keeping track and noting down what is being said during meetings is mind-mapping. A mind map is a diagram used to represent words, ideas, tasks, or items linked to a subject or idea. It is used to generate, visualize, structure and classify ideas as an aid to organizing, problem-solving and writing.

Using mind-mapping techniques for minute-taking can be fun, especially for creative people. Though in the following example, the notes may, at first glance, look like a bunch of scribbles, the minute-taker is actually keeping track of what is being said.

Statement by Chairperson, Mark Grey (MG):

"The minutes of last month are approved. Let's move on to the second item of the meeting. Sales last month exceeded budget by 7% and profits were well ahead by 12%. Month-to-date sales, however, are behind plan by 19%. I would like our merchandising and marketing teams to discuss amongst themselves and come up with a promotion activity to boost sales. Submit your proposals by the 14th".

Statement by Head of Operations, Kevin Hoe (KH):

"The renovations of the men's department at Raffles City are progressing slower than anticipated. Though the cost is well controlled and within budget, we may have to postpone the re-opening by eight days. The delay is caused by the removal of the old floor and the laying of the new marble flooring."

Statement by MG:

"I will not accept any delays in the opening date for this department. Get your contractor to beef-up the manpower to complete the job on time!"

Question from MG:

"Our European agents were visiting last week. How did your meetings go?"

Statement by Merchandise Manager, Mac Doran (MD):

"Everything went on well. They were pleased to hear that the merchandise bought last season sold well."

Statement by Buyer, Penny Lee (PL):

"They would like to know our travel dates for this coming buying season. I told them that we will let them know as soon as our budgets have been approved."

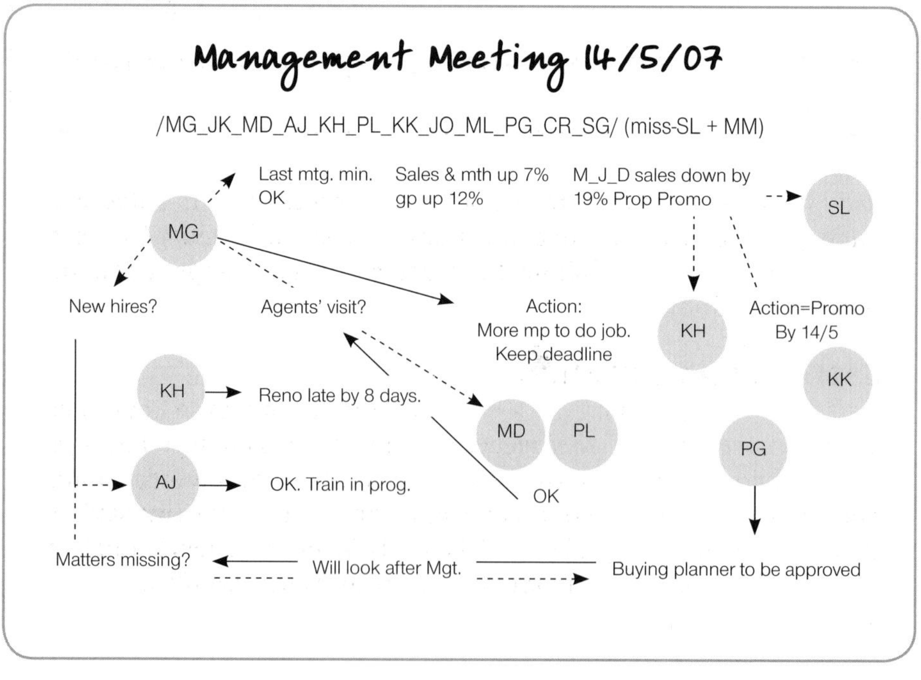

After the meeting and before you start writing, you may find it helpful to read through your notes to refresh your memory of what has been said. Highlight any comments or issues that you feel should be included in the minutes, especially those with action plans or deadlines. This will help you sort out any unnecessary notes you have and give you an idea of what you need to write.

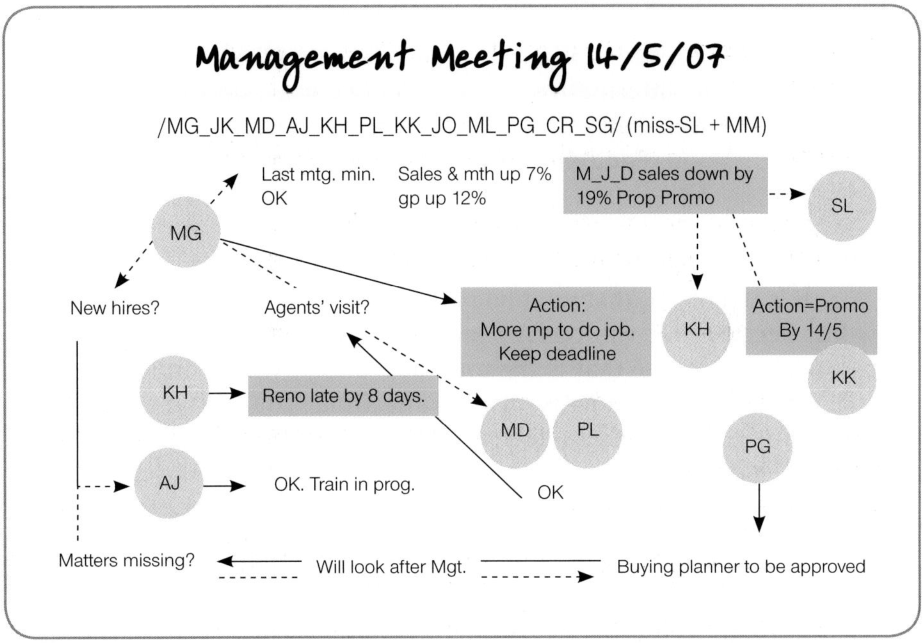

It is important to remember at all times that minutes are an important form of communication and, as such, must be clear and concise so as to allow little room for misinterpretation or misunderstanding.

SPOKEN COMMUNICATION

In face-to-face communication, it is easy to convey a message: words, expression, tone of voice, gestures, body language and eye contact all combine to make meaning clear. It helps, too, if you are concise and precise in your statements, and it goes without saying that an enthusiastic speaker will hold his listener's attention better than one who speaks in a monotone or who is long-winded.

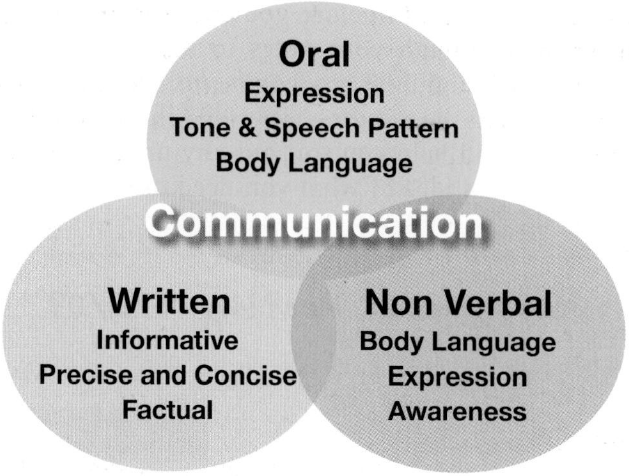

It is important that your body language is not at odds with your words because this can convey mixed messages at best; at worst, it can relay a message that is the total opposite of what you intend.

To elicit the response you want from your listeners, it is important to make them feel as if they are participating in the task at hand. Explain your objective and engage the listener, perhaps by asking how they would go about the task, and thus pre-empt possible objections.

If speaking clearly, concisely and precisely is important in face-to-face communication, it is even more so when communicating by telephone, where you have fewer tools at your disposal to get your message across. Just as important, though, is the ability to listen carefully to others, to read the signs from the words, tone and silences of the person to whom you are speaking. This ability to read the verbal signs will steer you away from potential problems, and make it more likely that you will achieve the outcome you have in mind.

CONCLUSION

As we come towards the end of *The Art of Retail Buying*, I trust that you have found it useful, even though the case studies or examples may have been drawn from a retail format that is not familiar to you. Whichever format you currently work in or aspire to work within, the principles involved remain the same and applicable across the retail industry.

Whichever branch of the industry you work in, you may find it useful to use some of the tips given throughout this book. For example, conducting a SWOT analysis (see Chapter 9) on yourself, using the questions set out below, could help clarify your specific strengths and weaknesses and help you attain your future career goals.

- Did I identify my fast-selling items in time to re-order?
- Did I identify slow-selling items and take timely action to dispose of them?
- Did I ensure that I maintained well-balanced stocks and assortments?
- Did I ensure that my basic stocks were in full size and color ranges throughout the season?
- Did I ensure that my planned deliveries were met, and did I take appropriate action when they were not?
- Did I take enough time to visit the selling floor to check assortments, prices and merchandise presentations, and to consult sales staff on problems and solutions?
- Did I take the time to check my goods at the warehouse, and take necessary action on price changes or price reductions to get rid of oddments?
- Did I take the time to conduct regular market surveys on competitors to evaluate their prices and merchandise assortments, thus giving me a better understanding of my own strengths and weaknesses?

This exercise may help you to set clear goals for yourself. Write the down following:

Improve work habits...
Upgrade skills...
Seek new opportunities...

Ask yourself what you need to do to get there. Remember that whatever you do to improve your skills that later translate to better performance, you are investing in your own future. You will be known in the market for the excellent job you are doing and become a desirable asset. This puts you in a good negotiation position with your own company when your salary and bonus are being discussed, as well as when other retail companies are scouting for talent.

Your performance is an achievement that no one can take away from you. Couple that with a great attitude and you have a winning formula that will give you greater freedom to shape your own future.

APPENDIX 1

INTERNATIONAL TRADE FAIR

The following is a list of some of the most useful and influential international fairs and trade shows that will be of interest to buyers from a wide range of retail categories.

- **Ambiente (Frankfurt)**
  The largest European housewares fair. Featuring many categories including housewares, kitchen trends, and high-end tabletops, it draws an impressive audience of buyers from around the world.

- **Bread & Butter (Barcelona)**
  An international tradeshow for selected brands representing a strong global marketing and communication platform for

progressive contemporary fashion culture: jeans & urban wear, sports & street wear, and high-level street couture.

- **BIG+BIH (Bangkok)**
  The Bangkok International Gift Fair & Bangkok International Houseware Fair is a dedicated event showcasing the finest in giftware and homeware products. Promotes high-quality gifts and home-related products to international buyers.

- **Canton Fair (Guangzhou)**
  Operating on a twice-yearly trade basis since 1957, the Fair (full name, the China Import and Export Fair) is organized by the China Foreign Trade Centre and is the largest in China. Boasts the largest assortment of products, the highest attendance, and the largest number of business deals of any Chinese fair.

- **CIFF (Copenhagen)**
  Copenhagen International Fashion Fair has become Europe's leading fashion fair on all counts: visitors, space and collections.

- **CPD (Düsseldorf)**
  With more than 1,000 exhibitors representing more than 1,430 brands from 38 countries, CPD embodies the best from the world of women's ready-to-wear.

- **GDS-Shoe Fair (Düsseldorf)**
  One of the most important shoe fairs, it has more than 1,350 exhibitors from 58 countries and rates a 90% satisfaction score from visitors, whose main interest is to source young fashion and known brands, wellness & comfort, and lifestyle & sports brands. High-end labels such as Hugo Boss, Goffredo Fantini and Robert Clergerie were represented for the first time in March 2007, along with brands such as Bikkembergs, CeFouShoo, DKNY, Ed Hardy Shoes, Etro, GUESS, Graffiti, Marc by Marc Jacobs, Strenesse, Stuart Weitzmann and Vialis.

- **Hong Kong Houseware Fair**
  Showcases top-of-the-range brand names and designer products in an exclusive and grand setting. Products range from artificial flowers, gardening & outdoor accessories and

green products to bathroom accessories; from hardware & DIY products to health & personal care items; from home decorations, kitchenware and gadgets to lighting, small electrical appliances and bar accessories.

- **Magic (Las Vegas)**
  Held twice a year as part of the MAGIC Marketplace, it provides a complete sourcing and supply-chain venue for the international apparel industry. Offering more than 700 companies from 30 countries, it is the largest apparel sourcing & fabric show in North America, connecting branded apparel and fabric wholesalers, designers and product development teams to the largest selection of global contract manufacturers, original design manufacturers, fabric and trim suppliers, and service companies. Also offers comprehensive educational seminars and workshops, and a match-making service, connecting buyers and sellers.

- **Macef Fair (Milan)**
  Macef, the international exhibition dedicated to the world of the home, has been a point of reference for over 40 years for a range of retail sectors: tableware, furnishing accessories, fancy goods, interior decoration, silverware, decorative ceramics, textiles, candles, gifts, bonbonière, Murano glass, outdoor furnishings, kitchen and household goods, artificial plants and flowers.

- **Maison & Objet (Paris)**
  Operating for just over a decade, the fair displays the latest in home interior design. While French design dominates proceedings, there is an increasingly strong presence of Japanese, American, British and German companies.

- **Micam (Milan)**
  Micam SHOE EVENT is the prime showcase for medium-high and high-end footwear, with the most exciting new footwear fashions for men, women and children. The increasing presence of internationally known footwear stylists attests to its growing importance.

- **Mipel (Milan)**
  The most important international showcase for leather goods. Held twice a year, it presents the best creations in leather, fabric and alternative materials from around the world for all seasons.

- **Modamont (Paris)**
  Primarily focused on all fashion sectors of ready-to-wear, sportswear, lingerie, footwear, leather goods, millinery and jewelry, it is also connected to other sectors such as design, packaging, and automotive.

- **Moda Prima (Milan)**
  Exhibitors—producers of fashion and accessories collections for men and women—are drawn mainly from Italy, though other European textile countries are represented. Italian exhibitors represent the best of high fashion from Capri and the Apulia region, and the exhibition attracts representatives from Italian and international department stores, chains, large-scale retail, wholesalers, buying hubs, importers, mail-order and trading companies.

- **Prêt à porter (Paris)**
  This internationally renowned fashion fair showcases a wide selection of fashion and accessories from the most contemporary and cutting-edge designer brands and new arrivals from around the world. Presenting fashion for today and tomorrow, PRÊT À PORTER PARIS® is a trend hub that is ahead of the pack, deciphering markets and anticipating the new fashion impulses.

- **PURE (London)**
  One of Europe's most exciting fashion events and the U.K.'s largest, PURE is entering its twenty-second season. A total one-stop-shop buying experience, with more than 800 women's wear, unisex and lifestyle brands, it gives visitors a chance to see brands that won't be found at any other U.K. fashion show.

- **Spring Fair (Birmingham)**
  The biggest gift and home trade event in Britain, it brings together some of the world's biggest brands and more than 80,000 of the best buyers in the business. Products and services on display include art, antiques & handicrafts, bags & travel

gear, building materials, electronics & electrical appliances, fashion wear & accessories, fast-moving consumer goods, fresh, frozen & canned foods, furniture, gifts & novelties, leather products & footwear, lights, lamps & fixtures, office equipment, promotional giveaways & plaques, perfumes & beauty products ...

For more information on international tradeshows, see www.biztradeshows.com/trade-events/

The Art of Retail Buying

APPENDIX 2

COMMON TERMS FROM THE WORLD OF FASHION

Below is a list of some of the more common terminology used to describe the type and cut of clothing in the world of fashion design.

- **A-kline skirt/fit-and-flare skirt**
  A skirt that is fitted at the waist and flares out in an A-line or tulip shape at the hem.

- **A-line gown**
  A form-fitting bodices that flares out from the waistline to a full skirt. The gown has a seamless waist.

- **Back drape (i)**
  A skirt that is fitted at the waist and flares out in an A-line or tulip shape at the hem.

- **Back drape (ii)**
  A length of material attached either at the shoulder or the waist that flows over the back to floor length. In some cases, it is removable.

- **Back yoke**
  A fitted or shaped piece at the top of a skirt or at the shoulder of various garments.

- **Ball gown**
  Characterized by a very full skirt that begins at the waist and continues to a formal length. The skirt waist is seamed and can be of various styles.

- **Ballerina neckline**
  This is a low neckline that usually occurs with strapless or spaghetti-strapped dresses.

- **Bandeau/tube top**
  A band-shaped covering for the breasts.

- **Bateau neck/boat neck**
  A high, wide, straight neckline that runs straight across the front and back, meeting at the shoulders; the same depth in the front and back.

- **Besom pocket**
  A pocket sewn inside the garment with access through a welted slit-type opening.

- **Bias cut**
  Cut diagonally across the grain of a fabric to create garments that follow the body curves closely.

- **Bike tard**
  A close-fitting, one-piece garment from the top of the torso to the hem of the shorts.

- **Blazer**
  A long-sleeved sports jacket with lapels.

- **Bolero jacket**
  A loose, waist-length jacket open at the front.

- **Boot-cut**
  Cut below the belly button and slightly flares from the knee to the ankle.

- **Box-pleated**
  Two folds of fabric brought together to form a pleat.

- **Boy-leg**
  Shorts, undergarments, or swimwear that has a close-fitting leg that reaches halfway down the thigh.

- **Broomstick**
  A skirt or dress that is characterized by numerous pleats and crinkled material.

- **Camisole**
  A short, sleeveless garment for women.

- **Camp pockets**
  Pockets that are sewn to the outside of the garment, usually squared off and characterized by seaming.

- **Cap sleeve**
  A small, short sleeve which sits on the shoulder, either forming a stiff cap or falling on to the arm to provide minimal coverage.

- **Capri pants**
  Fairly straight-cut pants, tapered to the mid-calf.

- **Cardigan jacket**
  A usually collarless sweater or jacket that opens the full length of the center front.

- **Cargo**
  Characterized by sporting a large pocket, usually with a flap and a pleat.

- **Carpenter pants/shorts**
  Five-pocket pants characterized by a "hammer holder."

- **Cathedral/monarch train**
  A cascading train extending six to eight feet behind the gown, for the most formal weddings.

- **Chapel train**
  The most popular of all train lengths, it flows from three to four feet behind the gown.

- **Chemise/skimmer**
  Simply a straight, unbelted dress with varying sleeves and length.

- **Column/straight skirt**
  Also referred to as a pencil skirt, this skirt is a straight line with no flare or fullness at the hem or waistline.

- **Concealed snap/velcro/button placket**
  A slit in a garment where closures are hidden.

- **Convertible collar**
  Rolled collars that can be worn open or closed. Sewn directly to the neckline.

- **Corset top/boned bodice**
  A form-fitting, usually strapless, bodice with boning and either laces or snap closures; styled in the fashion of the ladies' undergarment of the same name.

- **Cowl neck**
  A neckline featuring a piece of material attached to a garment at the neck, which may be used as a hood or draped loosely in a swag from shoulder to shoulder at the front neckline or back.

- **Crew neck**
  A round neck with ribbed banding that fits close to the base of the neck.

- **Crinoline**
  Petticoats stiffened with horse-hair to enable the bell-like skirts of the early nineteenth century; was eventually replaced with the bustle.

- **Cropped top/jacket**
  Hem is cut just above the waist.

- **Diamond neck**
  A diamond-shaped cutout that fastens at the front or back neckline.

- **Dolman/batwing sleeve**
  Cut as an extension of the bodice, the dolman sleeve is designed without a socket for the shoulder, creating a deep, wide armhole that reaches from the waist to a narrowed wrist.

- **Double-breasted**
  Having one-half of the front lapped over the other; usually has a double row of buttons and a single row of buttonholes.

- **Double-tee top**
  A layered look with one T-shirt over another.

- **Draped bodice**
  An extra piece of material is draped over the bust line.

- **Dropped /low waist**
  A waistline that is sewn below the body's natural waistline.

- **Dropped shoulders**
  Characterized by the shoulder/sleeve seam falling off the shoulder.

- **Empire bodice**
  A bodice that ends just below the bust; sometimes low-cut and gathered.

- **Empire seams**
  A seam that is sewn directly below the bust line.

- **Empire waist**
  This waistline begins just below the bust.

- **Fishtail train**
  Fitted around the hips and flares out from the knee to the hemline.

- **Fitted point sleeve**
  A long, narrow sleeve that tapers to a point which rests against the back of the hand.

- **Flat-front pants**
  Straight pants, often seamless and pocketless.

- **Form-fitting/slim-fit**
  Straight from waist to ankle, except for a slight curve around the hip.

- **Frog closure**
  Chinese closing of decorative cording or braid. A soft ball of cording or a button is used to complete the closure.

- **Gauntlets**
  Dress gloves extending above the wrist.

- **Gaucho**
  Wide-legged pants or divided skirt reaching mid-calf, and worn with boots.

- **Halter top**
  A sleeveless bodice with a high choke or wrap neck that may be backless.

- **Handkerchief style**
  The hem of a blouse or skirt that is gently jagged to form flowing points.

- **Hip pockets**
  Pockets which are sewn on the front of the garment at hip height.

- **Hollywood waistband**
  Characterized by a full elasticized back and a side zipper/button closure.

- **Hook & eye closure**
  A two-part fastening device (as on a garment or a door) consisting of a metal hook that catches over a bar or into a loop.

- **Leg-of-mutton/gigot sleeve**
  A loose, full sleeve, rounded from the shoulder to just below the elbow, and then shaped to the arm, often ending in a point at the wrist.

- **Maillot**
  A women's one-piece bathing suit.

- **Mandarin collar**
  A short, stand-up collar, adopted from the close-fitting Asian collar.

- **Mermaid**
  A skirt that hugs the body until it reaches the knees or just below and then ends in a dramatic flare.

- **Natural waist**
  A seam or waistband that secures or falls at the natural curve of the body, which is the indentation between the hips and the ribcage.

- **Notched collar**
  A two-piece collar that can be only worn open.

- **Off-the-shoulder neck**
  A neckline that lies gently hovering across the top of the bust line, with the shoulders uncovered or able to be seen through the sheer yoke of net or organza attached to a high collar.

- **Overskirt**
  A skirt worn over another skirt.

- **Peasant top**
  Romantic style often characterized with a low neckline, ruffles, or free-flowing material.

- **Peek-a-boo**
  Any part of the garment which has been cut out to reveal skin.

- **Petticoat**
  An underskirt, usually a little shorter than outer clothing, and often made with a ruffled, pleated, or lace edge.

- **Pieced**
  A look created by sewing several pieces of material together to form the garment, much like a quilt.

- **Pinafore**
  Originally used to protect dresses from dirt, it was adopted as a fashion piece and worn as a sleeveless dress or over a blouse.

- **Placket**
  The piece of cloth that reinforces a split or opening in a garment; usually also serves as the closure.

- **Point collar**
  A collar with ties used to attach women's sleeves to their gowns.

- **Princess seams**
  Seams that can be found in the front or the back of a garment to create a form-fitting shape.

- **Puff/pouf sleeve**
  A full sleeve of varying length, created by generous gathering around the armhole.

- **Puckered bodice**
  Usually associated with tube tops, it provides a scrunchy look.

- **Push-up jeans**
  Spandex in the jeans helps to lift and shape the wearer's rear.
- **Romper**
  A one-piece garment with the lower part shaped like bloomers.
- **Sarong skirt**
  A length of cloth which is wrapped around the entire body.
- **Scoop/round neck**
  A low, U-shaped or round neckline.
- **Shawl collar**
  A one-piece collar turned down to form a continuous line around the back of the neck to the front.
- **Sheaths**
  Usually a straight or close-fitting skirt, accompanied by a form-fitting bodice. The skirt is often ankle length, and sometimes has a slit in the front, side, or back to make walking easier.
- **Shelf bra**
  A bra that is built right into the garment.
- **Shirred waist**
  A decorative gathering (as of cloth) made by drawing up the material along two or more parallel lines of stitching.
- **Shrug**
  A woman's small, waist-length (or shorter) jacket.
- **Skant**
  Pants that have a sweater-like attachment around the waist.
- **Skort**
  Shorts that have a front covering to resemble a skirt.
- **Spaghetti strap**
  A thin tubular strap that attaches to the bodice; named for its likeness to a strand of spaghetti.

- **Split neck**
  A round neckline that looks like it has been cut in the center to form a small "V."

- **Square neck**
  An open-yoke neckline shaped in the form of a half square.

- **Straight legs**
  Pant legs cut an equal width from waist to ankle.

- **Sweep train**
  The shortest train, barely sweeping the floor.

- **Sweetheart neck**
  A graceful, open yoke, shaped like the top half of a heart.

- **Tank top**
  A short, sleeveless top with wide armholes.

- **Tankini**
  A two-piece bathing suit with the upper portion resembling a tank top.

- **Tapered legs**
  Pant legs become progressively narrower toward the ankle.

- **Tea length**
  A gown hemmed to end at the shin.

- **Tear-away shorts**
  Feature versatile side snaps that allow quick removal of a top layer.

- **Tie-cinched waist**
  The waist is pulled tight around the body with a tie.

- **Trapeze top**
  Tank-top style with flared bottom.

- **Tulle skirt/bouffant gown**
  A sheer, puffed-out skirt often made of stiffened silk, rayon or nylon net.

- **Tunic style**
  A simple slip-on garment made with or without sleeves, and usually knee-length or longer, belted at the waist, and worn as an under or outer garment.

- **Turtle neck**
  A high, close-fitting, turnover collar used principally for sweaters.

- **Unitards**
  A close-fitting, one-piece garment for the torso, legs and feet, and often for the arms.

- **V-neck/V-back**
  An open yoke coming to a "V" shape midway down the bodice.

- **Variegated**
  Having streaks, marks, or patches of different colors; distinguished or characterized by a variety of different colors.

- **Wedding-band collar**
  A collar featuring a yoke that is either open or of sheer net, with an ornate band fitting snugly on the neck, creating a choker effect.

- **Wide legs**
  Pants or jeans that are cut extra-full through the legs.

- **Wing collar**
  A collar with projections which cover shoulder seams of bodices and doublets.

- **Wrap/surplice top**
  A bodice created by the cross-wrapping of fabric; may be in front or back, and associated with a high or low neckline.

A good source of information on fashion terms is www.youlookfab.com/fashion-glossary

STYLE DEFINITION & FASHION TERMS

- **Active wear**
  Attire worn for sport or for casual wear.

- **Beach wear**
  Clothing worn in connection with the beach and the swimming pool; consists of swimwear, T-shirts, shorts, and large shoulder bags usually made of cotton twills or straw.

- **Body wear**
  Close-fitting clothing, as in leotards or bodysuits, made of lightweight, usually stretch, fabrics and worn for exercising, dancing, or leisure activity.

- **Business attire/career wear (men)**
  Wearing a suit to work daily is often an indication of managerial or professional status. Some men do not wear a suit and tie to work. Manual workers, for example, may wear uniforms or other inexpensive, sturdy clothing that can be easily laundered. However, many men, who would not otherwise wear suits, will dutifully wear one to a job interview or when attending business meetings, as a mark of respect and formality.

- **Business attire/career wear (women)**
  The standard for women is also in flux. In the 1970s, women aspiring to managerial or professional status were advised to "dress for success" by wearing clothing that imitated the male business suit: jacket and matching skirt, worn with a plain blouse and discreet accessories. The plain blouse is designated as a long-sleeve button-down shirt, tucked properly into the skirt at the waist. Some women wore pantsuits, substituting pants for the skirt, but in doing so, they risked the displeasure of many who felt that women should not wear pants. Now, even conservative Western workplaces are more accepting of pants on female employees. However, they may still expect female employees to exhibit the formality of men's suits. Women in "creative" professions, such as advertising or fashion, can usually dress with more color and flair. In fact, their eye for the current fashion could be a subtle proclamation of their competence as leaders who set the fashion for others.

- **Business casuals/smart casuals**

  A popular dress code that emerged in white-collar workplaces in Western countries in the1990s, and which has partially supplanted formal business wear (suits and neckties) as the standard apparel for managers and professionals. In general, it means dressing professionally, looking relaxed, yet neat and pulled together. In a sense, it is the middle ground between formal wear and street wear. Examples of combinations for women considered appropriate by some organizations include capris, long shorts if they are "tailored" and of a dress-pant material (usually not denim or heavy cotton), or a tennis shirt and trousers. For men, a combination of collared shirt (perhaps a polo shirt instead of a business shirt) and cotton trousers (such as khakis), and shoes such as loafers and dress sandals, with socks, are generally acceptable. Neckties are generally not part of business casual dress unless worn in a very non-conservative way. The acceptability of jeans is variable: many organizations frown upon them as too casual, but will accept men who wear jeans with a sports jacket.

- **Casual wear**

  In the European tradition, casual is the dress code which emphasizes comfort and personal expression over presentation and uniformity. It includes a very wide variety of costume, so is perhaps better defined by what it isn't than what it is.

  The following are not considered casual wear: Jeans and a T-shirt have been described as the "casual uniform," but in most workplaces, clubs and, even, restaurants they are not acceptable. If you're working in the garden or cleaning the house, you can wear whatever works for you, but many companies consider them too casual for the workplace.

  With the popularity of spectator sports in the late twentieth century, a good deal of athletic gear has influenced casual wear. Here again lies a fine line. For example, a polo shirt worn with a pair of chinos may be acceptable for the workplace, while a collarless, sleeveless T-shirt worn with baggy sweatpants is not.

While utilitarian costume comes to mind first for casual dress, there is also a wide range of flamboyance and theatricality. Punk costume is a striking example. Madonna introduced a great deal of lace, jewelry and cosmetics into casual wear during the1980s, which today is accepted as casual wear.

More recently, hip-hop fashion has played up elaborate jewelry and luxurious materials worn in conjunction with athletic gear and the clothing of manual labor, and this would be another example of crossing that fine line, where these would be considered too extreme for work, or other formal, or conservative establishments.

Casual wear is typically the dress code in which new forms of gender expression are attempted before being accepted into semi-casual or semi-formal situations. An obvious example is masculine jewelry, which was once considered shocking or titillating even in casual circles, and is now hardly noteworthy in semi-formal situations.

- **City chic**
  Associated with sophisticated business wear for women–generally high-quality branded garments.

- **Club wear**
  A general term for the type of provocative, revealing, or fetish clothing that is worn to sex clubs, or other nightclubs featuring a sensual atmosphere with a very relaxed dress code.

- **Cocktail dresses**
  Usually short, sexy dresses used at parties or informal functions.

- **Contemporary wear**
  Up-to-date, current, "right now" fashion collections that are sophisticated and stylish. Mostly seen as trendy coordinates rather than dresses. Distinctively modern in style.

- **Couture**
  As in "haute couture"; garments made by a highly recognized designer. Also known as "Designer Wear".

- **Cruise wear**
  Light casual clothing appropriate for pleasure cruises or hot weather while on vacation.

- **Day wear**
  Daytime attire or clothes for wearing during the day; usually not used in relation to work.

- **Errorwear**
  According to Wikipedia, this comprises "T-shirts that fuse geek culture with high fashion" (see http://en.wikipedia.org/wiki/Errorwear). It deals exclusively in error messages printed on shirts (see also www.errorwear.com/index.php).

- **Fantasy wear**
  A style of clothing, including lingerie, worn in the bedroom.

- **Folklore**
  Describes an old-fashioned European look. It can also be used to describe a tribal look.

- **Formal wear/dress**
  A general fashion term to describe clothing suitable for formal events such as state occasions, weddings, funerals, debutante cotillions, and so on. Western formal wear has had a pervasive influence on styles in many countries, and is almost always the standard used in countries where there is no formal version of the national costume. Traditional "rules" govern men's formal dress; these are strictly observed at socially conservative events such as royal weddings, and serve as starting points for the creative formal wear seen at high school proms, formal dances, and the entertainment industry awards shows. Men's styles include court dress–for wear at the Royal court–white tie (tailcoat) and black tie ("dinner jacket" in British English, or "tuxedo" in American English). For women, formal evening wear would include full-length ball gowns.

- **Golf wear**
  Garments in which to play golf–polo shirts, loose-fitting cotton trousers with large pockets or knee-high Bermuda shorts; usually conforms to a specific dress-code of golf clubs.

- **Informal wear**
  A dress code in the European tradition, it is more presentational than semi-casual, but offers more room for personal expression than full semi-formal. Usually indicates a suit for men and a dress or suit with either trousers or skirt for women.

- **Innerwear**
  Clothing worn next to the skin—undershirt, briefs, boxer shorts.

- **Jeanery**
  All garments made of denim—jeans, jackets, shirts, skirts or shorts. In many shades of blues or black, it is often associated with a Western or cowboy look.

- **Leisure wear**
  Informal clothing designed to be worn when relaxing.

- **Lounge wear**
  Clothing worn when relaxing, usually at home.

- **Lux sports**
  A term for expensive branded sportswear; Ralph Lauren, for example.

- **Modish**
  Fashionable or conforming to the latest fashions or styles, especially those considered fads.

- **Nautical**
  A distinctive look normally found in red–white–navy. It can be a "sailor" look, or a type of garment people would wear on a cruise. For many years, European stores launched their spring season with a nautical theme as a break from the winter colors, but without launching true spring colors.

- **Retro**
  Use of past styles; the practice of modeling clothes or music on styles from the past; also refers to the '60s era.

- **Punk**
  The classic punk look among male musicians harks back to the T-shirt, motorcycle jacket and jeans ensemble favored by 1950s greasers associated with the rockabilly scene. During the 1980s, tattoos and piercing became increasingly common among punk musicians and their fans.

- **Safari**
  Applicable for both men's and ladies' lines, this term is used for a specific look, colors and fabric selections, which are almost always pure cotton. Shirts usually have two breast pockets and lapels on the shoulders; cargo pants have multiple pockets; colors are beige, camel, sand, or with some variations of green shades.

- **Sportswear**
  Clothing, including footwear, worn for sport or exercise. Typical garments include shorts, tracksuits, T-shirts, polo shirts and trainers. Specialized garments include wetsuits and salopettes. Sportswear is also often worn as casual fashion clothing. Generally, easy to launder and not too bulky.

- **Street wear**
  The style is very close to urban, hip-hop culture and skateboarders, with a strong sporting influence. Born in the ghetto and making its way into mainstream youth culture through MTV, the look has to be comfortable, yet define a status. Denim will always be a part of it because it's easy (strong material that won't stain easily), as will baseball caps. Has spawned many sub-cultures, such as Hipsters.

- **Swimwear**
  Garments used for swimming—one-piece, two-piece (bikini) or tankini, a tank-top with swim shorts or bikini bottom.

- **Urban wear**
  A dictionary may define this as "a variety of subgenres of popular dance music, chiefly associated with black musicians, including R&B, hip-hop ... and frequently reflecting inner-city

social themes and attitudes." To those stylishly in the know, "urban" has come to have a much more inclusive meaning: anything young, hip, forward-thinking and multicultural. Urban customers are those who know what the next trend is going to be, and adopt it before anyone else they know, according to clothing designers, trend forecasters and magazine editors. See http://jscms.jrn.columbia.edu/cns/2006-5-02friedman-urbanmeaning

- **Vintage**
  A fashion style from the 1920s and '30s, it consists of delicate fabrics, laces and embroideries in powdery pastel colors.

APPENDIX 3

CATALOG OF COLORS

Below is a list of some of the many colors that you will come across in the course of your career as a buyer in the retail industry. All of these colors can be found and experienced at the following website: www.yaelf.com/colour.shtml

- **Alice Blue:** baby blue
- **Alizarin Crimson:** bright sunny red
- **Antique White:** white with a beige tinge
- **Aquamarine:** greenish blue

- **Aquamarine medium:** darker greenish blue
- **Aureoline Yellow:** bright orangey leather
- **Azure:** light pastel turquoise
- **Banana:** greenish yellow
- **Beige:** gray tone with a tinge of brown
- **Bisque:** light tan
- **Black:** pure black
- **Blanched Almond:** yellowish tan
- **Blue:** rich royal blue
- **Blue Light:** medium dull blue
- **Blue Medium:** darker rich royal blue
- **Blue Violet:** medium mauve
- **Brown:** brown with lots of red
- **Brown Madder:** warm red
- **Brown Ochre:** medium brown
- **Burly Wood:** light warm beige
- **Burnt Sienna:** deep reddish brown
- **Burnt Umber:** deep reddish-brown
- **Brick:** light brown with a yellow tinge
- **Cadet:** blue with a green tinge
- **Cadmium Lemon:** bright warm yellow

- **Cadmium Orange:** neon orange
- **Cadmium Red Deep:** Christmas red
- **Cadmium Red Light:** neon red
- **Cadmium Yellow:** tangerine orange
- **Carrot:** medium orange
- **Cerulean:** blue with a turquoise tinge
- **Chartreuse:** bright neon green
- **Chocolate:** orangey-brownish beige
- **Chrome Oxide Green:** medium leafy green
- **Cinnabar Green:** leafy jungle green Cobalt: medium sapphire blue
- **Cobalt Violet Deep:** rich pinkish-purple
- **Cornflower Blue:** bright sapphire blue
- **Cobalt Green:** warm grass green
- **Cold Gray:** medium gray with a hint of green
- **Coral:** light orangey red
- **Coral Light:** light orangey pink
- **Corn Silk:** white with a yellow tinge
- **Cyan:** bright turquoise
- **Cyan White:** white with a turquoise tinge
- **Dark Orange:** bright medium-orange

- **Deep Ochre:** Cadbury's milk chocolate
- **Deep Pink:** shocking pink
- **Dim Gray:** medium gray
- **Dodger Blue:** bright medium blue
- **Eggshell:** contrary to popular belief, this is about a brown egg, not a white one
- **Emerald Green:** beautiful green gemstone
- **English Red:** red mixed with orange
- **Fire Brick:** warm dark red
- **Flesh:** bright pastel orange
- **Flesh Ochre:** life-vest orange
- **Flora White:** white with a very faint touch of rose
- **Forest Green:** lush medium green
- **Gainsboro:** more gray than white
- **Geranium Lake:** bright pure red
- **Ghost White:** so white it's almost translucent
- **Gold:** medium yellow
- **Gold Ochre:** light brown
- **Goldenrod:** light yellowish-brown
- **Goldenrod Dark:** light yellow-greenish brown
- **Goldenrod Light:** pastel green

- **Goldenrod Pale:** pastel green with a golden tinge
- **Green:** bright medium green
- **Green Dark:** Christmas tree green
- **Green Pale:** bright pastel green
- **Green Yellow:** bright pastel green with a yellow tinge
- **Greenish Umber:** bright neon red
- **Gray:** bright pure gray
- **Honey Dew:** white with a light-green tinge
- **Hot Pink:** bright candy pink
- **Indian Red:** one shade darker than Fire Brick
- **Indigo:** navy blue
- **Ivory:** off-white or white with a slight beige tinge
- **Ivory Black:** slightly diluted black
- **Khaki:** light yellowish-green
- **Khaki Dark:** medium yellowish-green
- **Lamp Black:** dark grass green
- **Lavender:** very light purple
- **Lavender Blush:** very light purple with a pink hue
- **Lawn Green:** *see* "Chartreuse"
- **Lemon Chiffon:** light yellow
- **Light Beige:** light yellowish pastel green

- **Light Goldenrod:** pastel green with a darker golden tinge
- **Light Gray:** silver
- **Light Salmon:** light orangey pink
- **Lime Green:** rich green jade
- **Linen:** white with a light touch of beige
- **Madder Lake Deep:** medium red
- **Magenta:** hippy pink
- **Manganese Blue:** sea green with blue hue
- **Maroon:** light purplish red
- **Mars Orange:** warm medium-brown
- **Mars Yellow:** warm medium-orange
- **Mauve:** pastel purple
- **Melon:** warm brownish-beige
- **Midnight Blue:** Sri Lanka sapphire blue
- **Mint:** light pastel green
- **Mint Cream:** very light pastel green
- **Misty Rose:** very light pastel rose
- **Moccasin:** orangey beige
- **Naples Yellow Deep:** orange with a golden tinge
- **Navajo White:** similar to Moccasin but a bit darker
- **Navy:** deep, dark cobalt

- **Old Lace:** off-white
- **Olive:** warm, full, lush green
- **Olive Drab:** warm medium olive green
- **Olive Green Dark:** darker medium olive green
- **Orange:** pure orange
- **Orange Red:** bright reddish-orange
- **Orchid:** soft light mauve
- **Orchid Dark:** dark mauve
- **Orchid Medium:** medium mauve
- **Papaya Whip:** mix of yellow and orange hue
- **Peach Puff:** pastel peach
- **Peacock:** medium blue with a slight green tinge
- **Permanent Green:** bright emerald green
- **Permanent Red Violet:** Alizarin Crimson with a drop of purple
- **Peru:** leather-brownish beige
- **Pink:** medium-warm pink
- **Pink Light:** one shade darker than Pink
- **Plum:** pastel mauve
- **Powder Blue:** baby turquoise
- **Purple:** bright lavender
- **Purple Medium:** medium lavender

- **Raspberry:** purplish lilac
- **Raw Sienna:** orangey brown
- **Raw Umber:** matt medium brown
- **Red:** Chinese New Year red
- **Rose Madder:** warm medium red
- **Rosy Brown:** light purplish-beige
- **Royal Blue:** darker bright sapphire blue
- **Saddle Brown:** warm medium-brown, dark
- **Salmon:** orangey red with some pink
- **Sandy Brown:** coral medium
- **Sap Green:** leaf from a papaya tree
- **Sea Green:** U.S.-dollar green
- **Sea Green Dark:** medium washed-out green
- **Sea Green Light:** beautiful blue with a tinge of green
- **Sea Green Medium:** light emerald green
- **Seashell:** white with the slightest touch of pink
- **Sepia:** old red wine
- **Sienna:** warm medium-brown
- **Sky Blue:** soft light blue
- **Sky Blue Deep:** medium-soft blue
- **Sky Blue Light:** intense medium blue

- **Slate Blue:** light purple
- **Slate Blue Dark:** rich purple
- **Slate Blue Light:** purple lilacs
- **Slate Blue Medium:** darker purple lilacs
- **Slate Gray:** medium gray with a tinge of dark blue
- **Slate Gray Dark:** medium gray with a tinge of dark green
- **Slate Gray Light:** medium steel gray
- **Snow:** warm white with a faint tinge of pink
- **Spring Green:** bright green
- **Spring Green Medium:** bright green with a blue hue
- **Steel Blue:** medium grayish-blue
- **Steel Blue Light:** metal grayish-blue
- **Tan:** medium beige
- **Terre Verte:** deep leafy green
- **Thistle:** pastel purple
- **Titanium White:** white with a slight yellow tinge
- **Tomato:** bright orange-red
- **Turquoise:** blue with soft green
- **Turquoise Blue:** green aquamarine
- **Turquoise Dark:** dominant blue with green tinge
- **Turquoise Medium:** lighter dominant blue with green tinge

- **Turquoise Pale:** pastel turquoise
- **Ultramarine:** electric navy blue
- **Ultramarine Violet:** beautiful amethyst
- **Vandyke Brown:** deep brownish-red
- **Venetian Red:** deep royal red
- **Violet:** matt mauve
- **Violet Dark:** medium purple
- **Violet Red:** dark pink
- **Violet Red Medium:** one tone darker pink than violet red
- **Violet Red Pale:** antique rose
- **Viridian Light:** bright green with a yellow tinge
- **Warm Gray:** medium gray with a tinge of olive green
- **Wheat:** light golden amber
- **White:** office-paper white
- **White Smoke:** white with a very soft gray tinge
- **Yellow:** bright neon yellow
- **Yellow Green:** medium yellowish-green
- **Yellow Light:** soft pastel yellow
- **Yellow Ochre:** light orangey leather
- **Zinc White:** white with a very soft tinge of pink

The Art of Retail Buying

APPENDIX 4

COMMON SHIPPING TERMS

Many companies do not have their own shipping department. Nevertheless, buyers need to be aware of shipping terms and conditions before they conduct direct imports. The following is a list of some of the commonly used terms that will assist you when placing orders abroad. We begin with the terms of sale, because this is where you can save or lose a lot of money.

TERMS OF SALE

These come into play when sellers have fulfilled their obligations so that the goods could, in a legal sense, be said to have been delivered to the buyer. They are shorthand expressions that set out the rights and obligations of each party when it comes to transporting the goods.

There are 13 Terms of Sale reflected in the International Chamber of Commerce Terms of Trade (INCOTERMS), as follows:

- **EXW (Ex Works) (...Named Place):** Indicates that the seller fulfills the obligation to deliver when he or she has made the goods available at his/her premises (that is, works, factory, warehouse, etc.) to the buyer. In particular, the seller is not responsible for loading the goods in the vehicle provided by the buyer or for clearing the goods for export, unless otherwise agreed. The buyer bears all costs and risks involved in taking the goods from the seller's premises to the desired destination. This term, thus, represents the minimum obligation for the seller.

- **FCA (Free Carrier) (... Named Place):** Indicates that the seller fulfills his or her obligation when he or she has handed over the goods, cleared for export, into the charge of the carrier named by the buyer at the named place or point. If no precise point is indicated by the buyer, the seller may choose, within the place or range stipulated, where the carrier should take the goods into their charge.

- **FAS (Free Alongside Ship) (...Named Port of Shipment):** Indicates that the seller fulfills his obligation to deliver when the goods have been placed alongside the vessel on the quay or in lighters at the named port of shipment. This means that the buyer has to bear all costs and risks of loss of, or damage to the goods from that moment.

- **FOB (Free On Board) (...Named Port of Shipment):** Indicates that the seller fulfills his or her obligation to deliver when the goods have passed over the ship's rail at the named port of shipment. This means that the buyer has to bear all costs and risks to loss of, or damage to the goods from that point. The FOB term requires the seller to clear the goods for export.

- **CFR (Cost and Freight) (...Named Port of Destination):** Here, the seller pays the costs and freight necessary to bring the goods to the named port of destination, but the risk of loss of, or damage to the goods, as well as any additional costs due to events occurring after the time the goods have been delivered on board the vessel, is transferred from the seller to the buyer when the goods pass the ship's rail in the port of shipment. The CFR term requires the seller to clear the goods for export.

- **CIF (Cost, Insurance and Freight) (...Named Place of Destination):** Under this term, the seller has the same obligations as under the CFR, but also has to procure marine insurance against the buyer's risk of loss or damage to the goods during the carriage. The seller contracts for insurance and pays the insurance premium. The CIF term requires the seller to clear the goods for export.

- **CPT (Carriage Paid To) (...Named Place of Destination):** Requires that the seller pays the freight for the carriage of the goods to the named destination. The risk of loss of, or damage to the goods, as well as any additional costs due to events occurring after the time the goods have been delivered to the carrier, is transferred from the seller to the buyer when the goods have been delivered into the custody of the carrier. If subsequent carriers are used for the carriage to the agreed destination, the risk passes when the goods have been delivered to the first carrier. The CPT term requires the seller to clear the goods for export.

- **CIP (Carriage and Insurance Paid To) (...Named Place of Destination):** Here, the seller has the same obligations as under CPT, but with the addition that the seller has to procure cargo insurance against the buyer's risk of loss of, or damage to the goods during the carriage. The seller contracts for insurance and pays the insurance premium. The buyer should note that under the CIP term, the seller is required to obtain insurance only on minimum coverage. The CIP term requires the seller to clear the goods for export.

- **DAF (Delivered At Frontier) (...Named Place):** Under this term, the sellers fulfill their obligation to deliver when the goods have been made available, cleared for export, at the named point and placed at the frontier, but before the customs border, of the adjoining country.

- **DDU (Delivered Duty Unpaid) (...Named Port of Destination):** Here, the seller fulfills his obligation to deliver when the goods have been made available at the named place in the country of importation. The seller has to bear the costs and risks involved in bringing the goods thereto (excluding duties, taxes and other official charges payable upon importation) as well as the costs and risks of carrying out customs formalities. The buyer has to pay any additional costs and bear any risks caused by failure to clear the goods in time.

- **DDP (Delivered Duty Paid) (...Named Port of Destination):** The seller fulfills his obligation to deliver when the goods have been made available at the named place in the country of importation. The seller has to bear the risks and costs, including duties, taxes and other charges of delivering the goods thereto, clear for importation. While the EXW term represents the minimum obligation for the seller, DDP represents the maximum.

- **DES (Delivered Ex Ship) (...Named Port of Destination):** The seller fulfills his/her obligation to deliver when the goods have been made available to the buyer on board the ship, uncleared for import at the named port of destination. The seller has to bear all the costs and risks involved in bringing the goods to the named port destination.

- **DEQ (Delivered Ex Quay, [Duty Paid]) (...Named Port of Destination):** Here, the term has been fulfilled when the goods have been made available to the buyer on the quay (wharf) at the named port of destination, cleared for importation. The seller has to bear all risks and costs including duties, taxes and other charges of delivering the goods thereto.

OTHER USEFUL TERMS

The terms set out below have been carefully selected from the myriad of terms encountered in the shipping business. For a more complete list, go to http//www.marad.dot.gov.

- **AAR:** Against All Risks (insurance clause).

- **Advising bank:** A bank operating in the seller's country that handles letters of credit on behalf of a foreign bank.

- **Agent (Agt.):** A person authorized to transact business for and in the name of another person or company. Types of agents comprise (1) brokers, (2) commission merchants, (3) resident buyers, (4) sales agents, (5) manufacturer's representatives.

- **Air waybill:** The forwarding agreement or carrying agreement between shipper and air carrier and issued only in non-negotiable form.

- **Acceptance:** A time draft (or bill of exchange) that the drawee (payer) has accepted and is unconditionally obligated to pay at maturity. Also any agreement to purchase goods under specified terms.

- **Advice of shipment:** A notice sent to a local or foreign buyer advising that shipment has gone forward and containing details of packing, routing, and so on. A copy of the invoice is often enclosed together with, if desired, a copy of the bill of lading.

- **Arrival notice:** A notification by the carrier of the ship's arrival to the consignee (the Notify Party).

- **Assignment:** A term commonly used in connection with a bill of lading. It involves the transfer of rights, title and interest in order to assign goods by endorsing the bill of lading.

- **Beneficiary:** Entity to whom money is payable, or for which a letter of credit is issued; the seller and the drawer of a draft.

- **Bill of Exchange:** Also commonly known as a "Draft", this is an unconditional order issued by a person or business which directs the recipient to pay a fixed sum of money to a third party at a fixed or negotiable future date. A bill of exchange must be in writing, signed and dated.

- **Bill of Lading (B/L):** A document that establishes the terms of a contract between a shipper and a transportation company. It serves as a document of title, a contract of carriage and a receipt for goods.

- **Blanket rate:** A rate applicable to or from a group of points; a special rate applicable to several different articles in a single shipment.

- **Bank guarantee:** Guarantee issued by a bank to a carrier to be used in lieu of lost or misplaced original negotiable bill of lading.

- **Base rate:** A tariff term referring to ocean rate less accessorial charges, or simply the base tariff rate. Ocean rates are charged by either weight or measurement of the shipment, whichever yields greater revenue to the carrier. Accessorial charges include stop-off in transit; pallet exchange/loss; detention of equipment; driver load/unload; week-end delivery; or temperature control.

- **C&F Terms of Sale, or INCOTERMS:** Term of sale meaning "cargo and freight" whereby the seller pays for cost of goods and freight charges up to destination port. Now obsolete but still heavily used (was replaced by "CFR" (see Appendix 3) in 1990).

- **CAF ("Currency Adjustment Factor"):** A charge, expressed as a percentage of a base rate, applied to compensate ocean carriers for currency fluctuations.

- **Cash against documents (CAD):** Method of payment for goods, in which documents transferring title are given to the buyer upon payment of cash to an intermediary acting for the seller, usually a commission house.

- **Cash in advance (CIA):** A method of payment for goods in which the buyer pays the seller in advance of the shipment of goods. Usually employed when the goods, such as specialized machinery, are built to order.

- **Certificate:** A document certifying that merchandise was in good condition immediately prior to its shipment.

- **CI ("Cost and Insurance"):** A price that includes the cost of the goods, the marine insurance and all transportation charges, except the ocean freight, to the named point of destination.

- **CIF ("Cost, Insurance, Freight") (Named Port):** Similar to C&F or CFR except seller also provides insurance to named destination.

- **CIF&C:** Price includes commission as well as CIF.

- **CIF&E:** Cost, Insurance, Freight and Exchange.

- **CIFCI:** Cost, Insurance, Freight, Collection and Interest.

- **Clean Bill of Lading:** A receipt for goods issued by a carrier, with an indication that the goods were received in "apparent good order and condition," without damage or other irregularities. If no notation or exception is made, the B/L is assumed to be "cleaned."

- **COD:** Collect (Cash) on Delivery.

- **Collection:** A draft drawn on the buyer, usually accompanied by documents, with complete instructions concerning processing for payment or acceptance.

- **Consignment:** (1) A stock of merchandise advanced to a dealer and located at his place of business, but with title remaining in the source of supply; (2) A shipment of goods to a consignee.

- **Consolidation:** Cargo containing the shipments of two or more shippers or suppliers. Container-load shipments may be consolidated for one or more consignees.

- **Consolidator:** A person or firm performing a consolidation service for others. The consolidator takes advantage of lower full carload (FCL) rates, and savings are passed on to shippers.

- **Contract:** A legally binding agreement between two or more persons/organizations to carry out reciprocal obligations or value.

- **Customs:** Government agency charged with enforcing the rules passed to protect the country's import and export revenues.

- **Customs entry:** All countries require that the importer make a declaration on incoming foreign goods. The importer then normally pays a duty on the imported merchandise. The importer's statement is compared against the carrier's vessel manifest to ensure that all foreign goods are properly declared.

- **Customs invoice:** A form requiring all data in a commercial invoice, along with a certificate of value and/or a certificate of origin.

- **Discrepancy letter of credit:** When documents presented do not conform to the requirements of the letter of credit (L/C), it is referred to as a "discrepancy." Banks will not process L/Cs which have discrepancies. They will refer the situation back to the buyer and/or seller, and await further instructions.

- **Documents against acceptance (D/A):** Instructions given by a shipper to a bank, indicating that documents transferring title to goods should be delivered to the buyer only upon the buyer's acceptance of the attached draft.

- **Commercial invoice:** Represents a complete record of the transaction between exporter and importer with regard to the goods sold. Also reports the content of the shipment, and serves as the basis for all other documents about the shipment.

- **Confirmed letter of credit:** A letter of credit, issued by a foreign bank, whose validity has been confirmed by a domestic bank. An exporter with a confirmed letter of credit is assured of payment even if the foreign buyer or the foreign bank defaults.

- **Consignee:** The person or company to whom commodities are shipped.

- **Consignee mark:** A symbol placed on packages for identification purposes; generally a triangle, square, circle, and so on, with letters and/or numbers and port of discharge.

- **Documents against payment (D/P):** An indication on a draft that the documents attached are to be released to the drawee only on payment.

- **Door-to-door:** Through-transportation of a container and its contents from consignor to consignee. Also known as "House to-house." Not necessarily a through rate.

- **Draft, Bank:** An order issued by a seller against a purchaser; directs payment, usually through an intermediary bank. Typical bank drafts are negotiable instruments, and are similar in many ways to checks on checking accounts in a bank.

- **ETA:** "Estimated time of arrival" or "Estimated time of availability." Depending on the pre-arranged terms and conditions, the ETA can state the estimated time of arrival at port, or at the receiver's warehouse.

- **Force Majeure:** A common clause in contracts, exempting the parties from fulfillment of their obligations as a result of conditions beyond their control, such as earthquakes, floods or war.

- **Import license:** A document required and issued by some national governments authorizing the importation of goods.

- **In transit:** In the course of transportation or passage.

- **Inspection certificate:** A certificate issued by an independent agent or firm, attesting to the quality and/or quantity of the merchandise being shipped. Such a certificate is usually required in a letter of credit for commodity shipments.

- **Invoice:** An itemized list of goods shipped to a buyer, stating quantities, prices, shipping charges, and so on.

- **Irrevocable letter of credit:** Letter of credit in which the specified payment is guaranteed by the bank if all terms and conditions are met by the drawee, and which cannot be revoked without joint agreement of both the buyer and the seller.

- **Landed cost:** The total cost of goods to a buyer, including the cost of transportation.

- **Landing certificate:** Certificate issued by consular officials of some importing countries at the point or place of export when the subject goods are exported under bond.

- **Letter of indemnity:** In order to obtain the clean bill of lading, the shipper signs a letter of indemnity to the carrier on the basis of which may be obtained the clean bill of lading, although the dock or mate's receipt showed that the shipment was damaged or in bad condition.

- **Licenses:** Some governments require certain commodities to be licensed prior to exportation or importation. Clauses attesting to compliance are often required on the B/L.

- **Ocean Bill of Lading (Ocean B/L):** A contract for transportation between a shipper and a carrier. It also evidences receipt of the cargo by the carrier. A bill of lading shows ownership of the cargo and, if made negotiable, can be bought, sold or traded while the goods are in transit.

- **Original Bill of Lading (OBL):** A document which requires proper signatures for consummating carriage of contract. Must be marked as "original" by the issuing carrier.

- **P&I:** An insurance term meaning "Protection and Indemnity."

- **Packing list:** Itemized list of commodities with marks/numbers, with no cost values indicated.

- **Payee:** A party named in an instrument as the beneficiary of the funds. Under letters of credit, the payee is either the drawer of the draft or a bank.

- **POD:** "Port of Discharge" or "Port of Destination"; "Proof of delivery": A document required from the carrier or driver for proper payment.

- **POL:** "Port of Loading."

- **Prepaid (Ppd.):** Freight charges paid by the consignor (shipper) prior to the release of the bills of lading by the carrier.

- **Pro forma:** A Latin term meaning "For the sake of form."

- **Pro forma invoice:** An invoice provided by a supplier prior to the shipment of merchandise, informing the buyer of the kinds and quantities of goods to be sent, their value, and specifications (weight, size, and so on).

- **Pro rata:** A Latin term meaning "In proportion."

- **Quarantine:** A restraint placed on an operation to protect the public against a health hazard. A ship may be quarantined so that it cannot leave a protected point. During the quarantine period, the "Q" flag is hoisted.

- **Quota:** The quantity of goods that may be imported without restriction during a set period of time.

- **Quotation:** An offer to sell goods at a stated price and under stated terms.

- **Rebate:** A form of discounting or refunding that has the net effect of lowering the tariff price. The granting of a freight rebate to the shipper is not uncommon, but the rebate can be either legal or illegal. For example, the commission of the freight forwarder is about 2–5% in ocean freight and about 10% in airfreight. It is legal for the airfreight forwarder to pay back to the shipper a portion of the commission it earns from the carrier. However, such a payback may be deemed illegal in ocean freight, which is governed by the Shipping Act of 1984, and operates on competitive worldwide fixed rates. See full Act at www.fmc.gov/about/ShippingAct.asp

- **Recourse:** A rights claim against the guarantors of a loan, or draft, or bill of exchange.

- **Remittance:** Funds sent by one person to another as payment.

- **Shipper:** The person or company supplying and/or owning the commodities shipped. Also called the "Consignor."

- **Shipper's instructions:** Shipper's communication(s) to its agent and/or directly to the international water-carrier. Instructions may be varied; for example, specific details/clauses to be printed on the B/L, directions for cargo pickup, and delivery.

- **Straight bill of lading:** A non-negotiable bill of lading which states a specific identity to whom the goods should be delivered.

- **Surcharge:** An extra/additional charge.

- **Surtax:** An extra/additional tax.

- **T&E "Transportation and Exportation":** United States customs form used to control cargo movement from port of entry to port of exit, meaning that the cargo is moving from one country, through the United States, to another country.

- **Tariff (Trf.):** A publication setting forth the charges, rates and rules of transportation companies.

- **Validation:** Authentication of B/L and when B/L becomes effective.

- **Variable cost:** Costs that vary directly with the level of activity within a short time. Examples include costs of moving cargo inland on trains or trucks, stevedoring in some ports, and short-term equipment leases.

- **Waybill (WB):** A document prepared by a transportation company at the point of a shipment; shows the point of the origin, destination, route, consignor, consignee, description of shipment, and amount charged for the transportation service. It is forwarded with the shipment or sent by mail to the agent at the transfer point or waybill destination. Unlike a bill of lading, a waybill is not a document of title.

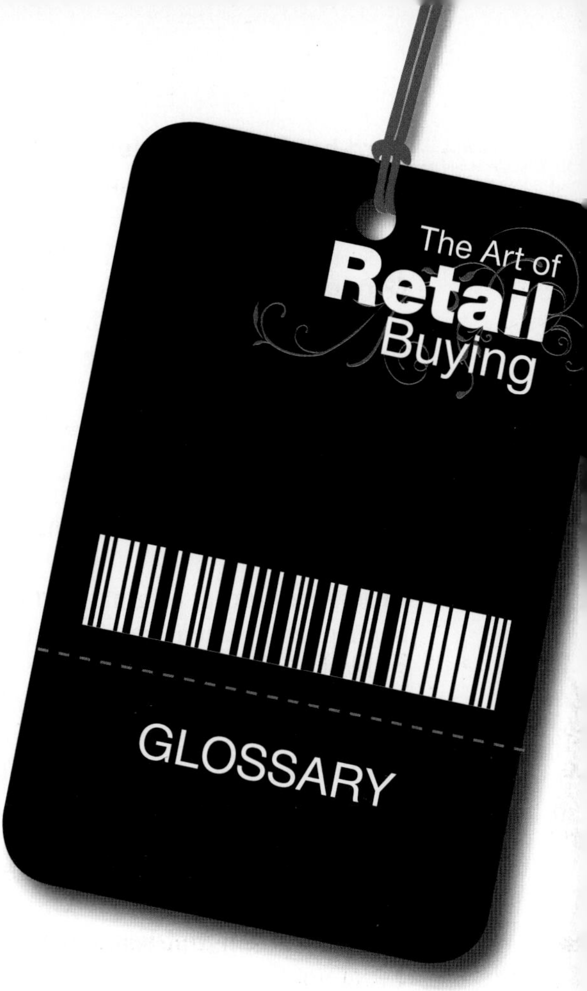

GLOSSARY OF USEFUL RETAIL TERMS

- **Average selling price (ASP):** The price at which a certain class of goods or services is typically sold.

- **BOM (Beginning of the month):** The levels of stocks at the end of a month are rolled over and expressed as beginning-month stocks.

- **Buying office:** Represents many retailers in the same line of business in a central wholesale market or country; provides information on market developments, guidance in purchasing, and actual placing of some orders for clients.

- **Card-holder discounts:** Discounts offered by some stores to customers holding the store's credit card, privilege card, or VIP club member card.

- **Concessionaire:** A dedicated sales area for a specific brand/ company product offer that is situated within a larger store. Usually found in department stores.

- **Conversion rate:** The ratio of customers who actually make purchases in a store to the total number of people who visit the store. Thus, if 200 people visit the store, and two people buy, the conversion rate is 1%.

- **Cruise:** A concept originating in the early 1980s in the northern hemisphere, when retailers found that traditional spring collections received in January-February were too lightweight and bright for those cold months. "Cruise" lines were new fashion silhouettes in nautical colors—red, white, navy—and medium-weight fabrics acceptable during freezing months. Others opted for true "cruise" lines—soft, lightweight fabrics in beige, off-white or soft pastels—for rich people travelling to warmer climates to escape the winter.

- **DMM:** Divisional merchandising manager.

- **Dogs:** A term used to describe un-sellable merchandise.

- **EAS (electronic article surveillance):** A loss-prevention technique that utilizes security tags and labels at building entrances, exits, and enclosed areas to activate an alarm when items protected with an active tag or label pass through the detection zone.

- **EDI (electronic data interchange) technology:** The exchange of information from one company to another using a computer network. Computerized exchanges of invoices, orders, and other business documents enable cost savings and improve efficiency.

- **EPO (electronic purchase order):** A system by which retailers transmit re-orders (via computer) direct to the vendors.

- **Factory outlets:** Retail stores managed by manufacturers to sell over-productions, faulty merchandise, or samples.
- **Gap analysis:** A business resource assessment tool that enables a company to compare its actual performance with its potential performance. (*see also* Strategic gap analysis)
- **Gross profit (GP) margin:** The difference between sales and the cost of goods. Can be expressed both in dollar terms and as a percentage of sales.
- **Index:** A numerical scale used to compare variables with one another or with a given reference number.
- **Jobbers:** People who buy clearance goods at very low prices.
- **Margin:** The amount of the final selling price that is profit; expressed as a percentage using the formula: %Margin = ($Retail – $Cost) ÷ $Retail.
- **Mark-down (MKD):** A reduction in price.
- **Mark-on/Mark-up:** The amount added to the cost of an item in order to establish an initial or original retail price. Can also be expressed as a percentage.
- **Mind map:** A diagram used to represent words, ideas, tasks or other items linked to, and arranged radically around, a central key word or idea. It is used to generate, visualize, structure, and classify ideas.
- **MM:** Merchandising manager.
- **Net profit:** Profit made after deduction of all expenses. Calculated using the formula: Net Profit = Sales – Cost of goods sold – Expenses.
- **OOS:** Out of stock.

- **Open to buy (OTB):** The dollar amount of merchandise that a buyer can order for a particular period based on the difference between planned purchases and stock already ordered.

- **Product-knowledge session (PKS):** Training session in which a buyer or manager explains the features and benefits of a product to the selling staff.

- **PO:** Purchase Order.

- **Point of sale (POS):** Terminals at which sales staff electronically read and record bar-codes on the items being bought by customers.

- **Product lifecycle:** The stages through which a product passes: introduction, growth, expansion, maturity, saturation and decline.

- **Retail formats:** Different types of retail store.

- **Return on investment (ROI):** A measure of the economic return on a project or investment. Measures the effectiveness of an investment by calculating the extent to which the original investment is covered by the net benefits.

- **Season-end sales:** Events staged by the retailer to sell off broken sizes, leftover ranges, slow-selling merchandise and bought-in discounted merchandise. The discounts given vary, but are usually between 30–50% and, at times, 70%.

- **Shrink(age):** Inventory recorded on a company's books but not on hand because of theft, loss or accounting error.

- **Stock-keeping unit (SKU) identification:** Data stored for inventory updates and timely replenishment of stock. "Parent SKU" describes and captures top-line information such as brand/vendor, style/class, and date of entry. A "child SKU" drills down further to record information on color, fabric and size.

- **Source tagging:** The application of EAS labels and tags on products or packaging during the manufacturing or packaging process.

- **Strategic gap analysis:** Forecasting technique in which the difference between the desired performance levels and the extrapolated results of the current performance levels is measured and examined. This measurement indicates what needs to be done, and what resources are required to achieve an organization's strategic goals.

- **Stock turn:** An business-efficiency measure of how many times the stocks sell against the average level of stocks held in inventory during a certain period. Also called "stock turnover rate."

- **SWOT Analysis:** Methodology for identifying an organization's strengths, weaknesses, opportunities and threats. Provides a good framework for reviewing the strategy, position and direction of a company, a business proposition, personal growth, and so on.

- **Universal product code (UPC):** A code commonly used in hypermarkets/supermarkets for tagging products; eliminates costly manual tagging.

- **Visual merchandising (VM):** A variety of methods used by shops and department stores to display their merchandise through the creation of special effects or decor within the store and in their window displays.

The Art of
Retail
Buying
INDEX

B

C

D

E

F

J

K

L

M

N

O

P

Q

R

S

T

U

V

W

X

Y

Z

GOOD GUT,
GREAT HEAL H